Social Work with Children and Families

by the same author

Divorcing Families
Children's Experiences of their Parent's Divorce
Ian Butler, Lesley Scanlan, Margaret Robinson, Gillian Douglas and Mervyn Murch
ISBN 978 1 84310 103 1

of related interest

The Survival Guide for Newly Qualified Child and Family Social Workers
Hitting the Ground Running
Helen Donnellan and Gordon Jack
ISBN 978 1 84310 989 1

The Child's World
The Comprehensive Guide to Assessing Children in Need
    2nd edition
Edited by Jan Horwath
ISBN 978 1 84310 568 8

Good Practice in Safeguarding Children
Working Effectively in Child Protection
Edited by Liz Hughes and Hilary Owen
ISBN 978 1 84310 945 7
Good Practice in Health, Social Care and Criminal Justice series

The Social Worker's Guide to Child and Adolescent Mental Health
Steven Walker
Foreword by Stephen Briggs
ISBN 978 1 84905 122 4

Making Sense of Child and Family Assessment
How to Interpret Children's Needs
Duncan Helm
Foreword by Brigid Daniel
ISBN 978 1 84310 923 5

A Practical Guide to Fostering Law
Fostering Regulations, Child Care Law and the Youth Justice System
Lynn Davis
ISBN 978 1 84905 092 0

Relationship-Based Social Work
Getting to the Heart of Practice
Edited by Gillian Ruch, Danielle Turney and Adrian Ward
ISBN 978 1 84905 003 6

Social Work with Children and Families

Getting into Practice

Third Edition

Ian Butler and Caroline Hickman

Jessica Kingsley *Publishers*
London and Philadelphia

Crown copyright material is reproduced with the permission of the
controller of HMSO and the Queen's Printer for Scotland.
Figure 1.1 is reproduced by permission of UNICEF

Previous editions published in 1997 and 2004 by Jessica Kingsley Publishers

This third edition published in 2011
by Jessica Kingsley Publishers
116 Pentonville Road
London N1 9JB, UK
and
400 Market Street, Suite 400
Philadelphia, PA 19106, USA

www.jkp.com

First edition copyright © Ian Butler and Gwenda Roberts 1997
Second edition copyright © Ian Butler and Gwenda Roberts 2004
Third edition copyright © Ian Butler and Caroline Hickman 2011

Library of Congress Cataloging in Publication Data
Butler, Ian, 1955-
 Social work with children and families : getting into practice
/ Ian Butler and Caroline Hickman. -- 3rd ed.
    p. cm.
 Includes bibliographical references and index.
 ISBN 978-1-84310-598-5 (alk. paper)
 1. Social work with children--Great Britain. 2. Family social work-
-Great Britain. I. Hickman, Caroline, 1961- II. Title.
 HV751.A6B87 2011
 362.76'530941--dc22

2011013556

British Library Cataloguing in Publication Data
A CIP catalogue record for this book is available from the British Library

ISBN 978 1 84310 598 5

Printed and bound in Great Britain

Dedication

From Ian: to my Dad and to brand new baby George. Wow!

From Caroline: to Flora, Amber, Toby, Bryony, Jackson and Jess.

Contents

List of Figures

List of Tables

Acknowledgements

This edition of 'Getting into Practice' has been prepared without Gwenda Roberts' direct involvement. The book however, still owes a great deal to her. It remains a joint effort in my view and like most *enfants terribles*, it wouldn't have made it this far without at least two 'parents' to look after it. The book also owes a great deal to the 'extended family' of those who helped Gwenda and I develop the material when we both taught at Cardiff University: Dolores Davey, Penny Lloyd, Richard Hibbs, Geoff Waites and the late Tony Bloore. Thanks are due also to the many students who took part in our experiments at Cardiff, the Open University, Keele University and latterly at Bath University.

If people remember anything from previous editions of this book, it is likely to be the cricket match at the start of the first chapter. (Those interested can catch up with 'the story so far' in the preface to the third edition immediately following.) This tiny anecdote seems to have struck a chord with many readers. So once again, I want to acknowledge all that I have learned from my children and from being their dad. When they read this (assuming they do!), they can at least see what it was I was *trying* to do...

Ian Butler

I'd like to acknowledge all the clients, students, colleagues and perfectly imperfect families and friends (two and four legged) for all the walks and talks that directly and indirectly have taught me about relationships.

Justine and Julian, Yvonne and Dave, Helen and Jay, Jacki and Ian, Pem and Ralph, Eileen, Pat, and particular thanks to Louise Brown and Darby Costello for their wise words. I'd finally like to thank the young carers from Off The Record project, Bath, who during their days spent at the University of Bath with social work students have made learning together a lot of fun.

Caroline Hickman

Preface to the Third Edition

The children who populated previous prefaces to this book are no longer children. The youngest has celebrated his 21st birthday and the law now recognizes all three of them as adults. From their father's perspective, this new-found status is a considerable source of surprise in that he still thinks of them (some of the time) as the 'tots, spots and grots' they once were. One (Mark) is working as a paediatrician in a busy London hospital; the middle one (Dan) is running his own social enterprise helping disengaged and disenfranchised young people in Cardiff and the third (Matt) is a year into his medical training in Leicester. They lead lives that are much more independent of their father's than they once were and it has been ever such a long time since any cricket was played in our garden.

Even if not children in a strictly legal sense, they will always be my children, of course and so my parenting days aren't over yet. I realize now that, as children grow older, the challenges and anxieties that they present to their parents may change but I am not sure how much they diminish. They still cause me sleepless nights, albeit for different reasons than they used to.

But I have been a fortunate parent and my children have been fortunate children. We worked hard to do what we wanted to do and we have had our ups and downs but we did not have to struggle against the overwhelming odds that face many families. For some parents, building and holding on to a family will be a much greater and a much more uneven struggle. Despite the best will in the world, the circumstances in which parenting takes place and in which children grow up, can have a decisive impact on both the experience and the outcomes of childhood.

Since the last edition of this book was published, we have seen several more substantial pieces of legislation brought forward in the name of children. We have seen several more iconic child death inquiries. We have seen many more newspaper headlines that alternately idealize, idolize, infantilize or vilify children and young people. Children and young people certainly have more if not necessarily any better 'protection' than in previous years; more are physically healthier; more are in prison; more are achieving better educational outcomes; more are taking their own lives. Apparently, the UK is the worst place among all the economically developed countries in the world to be a child and absolutely the worst in terms of family and peer relationships, behaviour and risks and subjective well-being (UNICEF 2007).

Since the last edition of this book, as well as my children growing up and as well as a whole new set of laws, guidelines and processes being developed, my father, George Butler, died and my eldest son and his wife, Vicky, have added the first member of the next generation to these prefaces (welcome baby George!). I wonder what my first grandchild's early years will be like, compared to mine or that of my sons or even that of my dad? The cycle continues it seems, both at the level of the unique individual, child and parent as well as at the level of policy and professional practice.

In preparing this edition, the familiar format has been retained although a considerable amount of updating has been attempted and some wholly new material has been included. Essentially, we have pushed the balance back towards the core skills of practice and away from the policy and legislative context. We have done this for several reasons. First, devolution in the UK has meant that there is no single UK policy or legislative framework in which social workers operate any more or for which students can easily be prepared within the confines of a single text. This book has proved to be of use in jurisdictions well beyond the shores of the UK too and, in an increasingly globalized profession, it seems unnecessarily limiting to assume too great a familiarity with the latest swing of the UK children's policy pendulum. We have not forgotten that the primary audience for this book will be students in the UK but we hope to encourage a critical perspective when we do make reference to legislation or to the broader policy framework. I sometimes have to remind my own students that had I been encouraged to follow the best practice model of those who taught me, we would still be sending orphaned or disadvantaged children to be looked after in the colonies!

The most important reason for returning to a focus on what is common to all practitioners in this field, namely the core skills of assessment, planning, child protection and relationship based social work, was our belief that social work students were beginning to place too much faith in the managerialist, bureaucratic tools and instruments that have come to characterize, if not dominate, direct practice with children and families over recent years. We believe these, in general terms, to be not only context specific but lacking the depth and breadth necessary to do the job of helping families address the problems and challenges that they face. At least, there is a danger that they will be used in a superficial, process driven way if the practitioner does not have access to the underpinning knowledge, core values and key skills of a fully developed model of professional practice.

Because of this and because there is so much for us still to do, our hope for this edition of 'Getting into Practice' is that it will help you prepare for the much needed contribution that you will make, both as a professional and as a person, to the apparently never ending, constantly changing, challenging, delightful and desperate task of bringing up our children.

Ian Butler

Preface to the Second Edition

The first chapter of this book begins with an account of a cricket match being played in the garden. By the time it came to write the preface to this, second edition, the batsman had finished his first year at secondary school. He has spiked his hair and wears a studded dog collar. His big brother is now a medical student. Neither has touched a cricket bat for years. Their middle brother (who was up in his bedroom playing his guitar when the other two were playing cricket) is the one who has turned out to be the serious sportsman in the family. How times change!

On the other hand, the England side has had another disappointing winter and their father is still at his desk, still writing and still thinking he would rather be outside in the sunshine. Some things never change. So, too, with the task in hand. In preparing a second edition of this book, we were struck by how much we had to do to bring the text up to date. Social work education has been transformed and entirely new regulatory structures have come into being. There is another Green Paper out for consultation that may usher in widespread changes in the local delivery of services to children. There is new legislation to consider, both general and specific. There have been new policy initiatives, new inquiries into child deaths, new regulations, new guidance, new jargon, new Jerusalems. But still, much remains the same. There are still a great many children and their families in the UK who are denied the opportunities in life that others are afforded. There are still far too many social workers who think that they can know and understand others without knowing or understanding themselves. There are too many people who think that there are easy solutions to complex problems (there are, of course, but they are almost always the wrong answers!).

In revising this book, we have updated and considerably expanded the 'hard knowledge' we include, reflecting changes in the law and incorporating evidence from research published in the period since the first edition of this book went to press. In particular, we have taken much fuller account of the policy context in which contemporary forms of practice are set. This means that we have included detailed reference to a number of central government initiatives (such as 'Quality Protects') and to the relevant 'standard forms' of practice that have developed over recent years (such as the Framework for Assessment of Children in Need). We do not do so uncritically and we make some reference to the controversies that surround the new orthodoxy of evidence-based practice and 'third way welfare'. We have also taken account of the new regulatory framework that surrounds contemporary practice and included sections on, for example, the National Care Standards Commission and various National Minimum Standards.

There is always more that one could add and so, in order to extend the scope of what can be included within the covers of a single book, we have added to each Unit a section providing access to resources available via the internet. We have however retained the form of the book (how to use this book is explained a little later) and we have not altered in our belief that it is through a process of 'study, reflection and application' that we can best 'get into practice'.

We would very much like to acknowledge the additional help we have received in preparing this edition of the book. In particular, we want to thank Graham Allan (Keele University) for his help in revising certain sections of Unit 2 and Alison Brammer (also of Keele University) for her meticulous review of those sections of the book that deal with the law. We are also enormously grateful to artist and therapist Elaine Holliday for the drawings that bring the text to life.

We would also like to note, with sadness, the death of a former colleague of ours, Tony Bloore, who was a leading light in the delivery of the lectures and seminars around which the original book was written. He was the most conscientious of social workers and one of the kindest.

Ian would also like to acknowledge the part played by the Calshot Bankers (The Daddy, Prince Marco, The Captain, Three-Piece, American Dave, Rocco and Stevo), not the best but certainly the coolest cycling team in the UK, for providing so many insights into how to live with personal problems!

Ian Butler and Gwenda Roberts

Introduction

Any teacher will tell you that it is often the simplest questions that require the most complicated answers. What kind of work do social workers and other professionals undertake with children and families? Where does such work take place? What do you need to know in order to begin work with young people and their carers? Even the terms of the questions defy easy definitions. What exactly do you mean by 'children'? What precisely is a 'family'? This book is offered in response to such deceptively simple enquiries.

It has its origins in a series of seminars for first- and second-year students following a basic social work qualifying course. The seminars were intended to introduce participants to the nature and range of child and family social work, to provide them with opportunities to apply their broader appreciation and knowledge of social work theory and practice to work in this area and to encourage them to reflect on what they brought to the helping process. The first part of this book is intended to fulfil the same ambitions. It is aimed at those who have recently begun or who are intending to work with children and families and who recognize the need to start from first principles. The second part of the book is aimed more directly at supporting the development of specialist knowledge and skills, or rather the application of generic skills in particular settings.

Of course, if we really could fully answer the questions that we began with, then this book would probably be a great deal longer than it is. It would also be the only one of its kind on the shelves. The fact that it is neither is proof enough that we do not make any exaggerated claims for it. What we aim to do in this book is to ask what are, in fact, fiendishly complex questions in such a way that the reader can provide the answers for him- or herself using all the means at his or her disposal, including his or her own experience and knowledge drawn from elsewhere. The structure of the book reflects this aim in that each Unit is predicated on the active involvement of the reader, who will ideally have the opportunity to compare his or her developing understanding with others in the same position. Although it is perfectly possible to use this book as a self-contained introduction to child and family social work, in neither situation could it be considered a passive read. In this way it is different to other textbooks in this area.

This book is different also in that it contains sufficient 'hard knowledge' to enable serious engagement with the key themes of social work practice with children and families but without pretensions to exhaustiveness. As such, we hope we have provided a framework through which knowledge derived elsewhere, possibly as part of a broader-based social work or specific child care training, can be extended and applied. We firmly believe that whatever interventive technologies or fashions currently exist, or are likely to emerge in future years, ultimately it is only people who change people. In the classroom, and in this book, our aim has been to encourage social workers to know themselves better: their prejudices, strengths and limitations and what they bring to the helping process. Practitioners must be able to reflect on what they do and be able to articulate and defend their motivations, theoretical perspectives and beliefs. We hope that the process of study, reflection and application – the pattern for each Unit in this book – will impress itself upon the reader, who will then be able to 'get into practice' with children and families in both senses of the term.

How to Use This Book

The material in each Unit is arranged under headings as follows:

 Course Text – this stands in lieu of the trainer or teacher. The 'Course Text' introduces and links the themes and issues that are the focus of each Unit.

 Exercises – at the core of each Unit are a number of exercises for you to complete. In the second part of the book, most of the exercises are based on an extended case study.

 Study Texts – these are intended to provide you with sufficient factual information and background knowledge to complete the exercises and extend your specialist knowledge of the field.

 Points to Consider – these are prompts to reflect more broadly on key issues that should occur to you as you complete the exercises.

 Notes and Self-Assessment – these, which come at the end of each Unit, will provide you with an opportunity to think back over all that you have read in the Unit and to locate what you have learned in a wider professional and personal context.

 Recommended Reading – here you are recommended two books that will help you to extend and develop your understanding of the material presented in the Unit. We have decided to recommend books rather than journal articles, simply on the grounds that many readers may not have easy access to the kind of libraries that will carry professional or academic journals. All of the books that we have recommended are in print and can be ordered from any local authority or university library.

 Trainer's Notes – these are suggestions of how to adapt or extend the exercise material contained in the Unit for use as a basis for working in groups and are intended for teachers.

PART I

Developing Basic Knowledge and Skills

Children and Childhood

OBJECTIVES

In this unit you will:

- Reflect on your own and others' experience of childhood.

- Examine how childhood is socially constructed.

- Extend your understanding of children's developmental needs.

- Examine your understanding of children's rights and their relationship to a child's needs.

COURSE TEXT: PLAYING CHILDREN

As these words are being written, there is a game of cricket in progress outside. The batsman is aged six and the bowler thirteen. The six-year-old is taking the game very seriously. In between balls, he is practising shots, examining the pitch and checking for any changes to the field settings. The thirteen-year-old is messing about, running up to bowl on 'wobbly legs' and broadcasting a much exaggerated, and very loud, commentary on the game. From his desk, their father is watching the game. He is caught between knowing that he has to finish this chapter and desperately wanting to go out and play. By staring out of the window, he manages to do neither and, out of frustration, shouts at the players to take their game elsewhere. Which one of these three could best be described as being a child or as behaving like one?

It seems entirely appropriate that we should begin this book with a question about children. We suspect that everyone would claim to know something already about the subject and it is a sound educational principle to ask questions only when one has a reasonable expectation of receiving an answer. It's obvious who the children are, isn't it? Possibly, but on what basis do we decide? Age doesn't seem to be the determining factor; the six-year-old is the one behaving in the most recognizably 'grown-up' way. Size isn't decisive either as the thirteen-year-old is just as tall as his dad and, as for knowledge and skills, all three are as good (or as bad) as each other when it comes to cricket. If we were to ask these three characters themselves how they might respond to being likened to children, the thirteen-year-old, despite his behaviour, is the one most likely to object and the forty-year-old, within reason, is the one most likely to be pleased at being mistaken for someone younger. The six-year-old wouldn't expect to be referred to as anything else. Perhaps the answer to our question is not quite so obvious after all.

Few of the everyday terms and 'common-sense' ideas encountered in social work with children and families, such as 'childhood', 'family' or 'parenthood', are as straightforward as they first appear. It is central to the purpose of this book to explore the meaning of such terms and to recognize how our understanding of them might affect our practice. If we were to look at childhood beyond this trivial example, across generations and geographical boundaries, then our sense of what the term means would become much less certain and clear-cut. What are the similarities and differences between these three lives and those of the thousands of young people who, in the thirteenth century, went off to fight in the Children's Crusade? Or with the daily lives of those children press-ganged into the eighteenth-century Navy or who, not much more than a century ago, pulled wagons of coal to the earth's surface just a few miles from where these words were written? What links the experiences of these children with the 40,000 others who will die today and every day from malnutrition or the 150 million more who live on in poor health across the world?

This Unit is about children or, more accurately, social work in relation to our understanding of children. The first exercise in this Unit and the Study Text that follows it are intended to sensitize you to the variability of childhood and encourage you to question some of the assumptions you and others may make about it.

EXERCISE 1.1: IMAGES OF CHILDHOOD

Assemble a selection of recent newspapers and general interest magazines. Look through them for pictures of children. All kinds of images (including advertisements) should be included. Once you have collected about twenty images, spread them out so that you can see all of them at once.

TASKS

1. 'Quickthink'[1] a few words that you associate with each image.

2. Write down for what specific purpose you think each image is being used.

3. Write down what each image reminds you of about your own childhood or those of children for whom you are personally or professionally responsible.

Then complete the following sentence with at least ten different answers:
   Childhood is...

POINTS TO CONSIDER

1. Does your collection of images suggest that childhood is experienced or represented differently depending on gender or race, for example? If so, how?

2. Would you say that there are any universal components to the experience of childhood? If so, what are they?

3. Overall, do the images suggest that children are highly valued in contemporary society? What qualities/attributes seem particularly valued or discounted?

4. Do you detect any differences between how you, as an adult, and the children in the images might describe what each image contains?

5. How much of what you understand by childhood is determined by your own experience of it do you think?

6. Would you like to be a child again? What is attractive/unattractive about the idea?

i STUDY TEXT 1.1: THE MYTHS OF CHILDHOOD

In broad terms, the history of childhood has been described as a gradual process whereby the 'distance in behaviour and whole psychological structure between children and adults increases in the course of the civilizing process' (Elias 1939, p.xiii). This particular view of the history of the separation of (Western) childhood from adulthood, developed in quite different ways by Aries (1960),

---

1   'Quickthinking' is a little word association. All you have to do is write down, without 'editing' as many words as you can think of that you associate with the particular stimulus or prompt.

de Mause (1976), Shorter (1976) and Stone (1977), and subsequently criticized, not least on historical grounds, by Pollock (1983) and MacFarlane (1986), now constitutes something of an orthodoxy (see, for example, Hayden and others 1999, James and James 2003). Aries' central thesis, to take perhaps the best-known example, was that, in early-medieval European society, childhood as a recognizable set of social roles and expectations did not exist and that the transition from the physical dependency of infancy to the social maturity of adulthood was unbroken. Young people quite literally occupied the same social, economic and psychological space as older people, playing, working and sharing relationships on much the same terms. According to Aries, 'childhood', as a distinct set of social roles and expectations, was 'discovered' in the fifteenth century, slowly diffusing throughout European society over the next three hundred years or so.

Whatever the historical accuracy of such accounts as Aries', their importance for our purposes lies in the contribution they made to the development of what has been called the 'theoretically plausible space called the social construction of childhood' (James and Prout 1997, p.27). Put simply, this idea, which stems from a tradition in sociology that is concerned with the meaning rather than the function of social events and processes, implies that very little of what we associate with children or the kind of childhood that they experience is universal, fixed or certain. In fact, childhood is built up, or 'constructed', in society and is occupied by young people in much the same way that adults occupy the various social roles available to them; for example, 'parent', 'worker', 'middle-aged'. (However, see Hockey and James 2003 for a detailed analysis of the part that differential power relations play in the process of 'construction'.) Hence, the meaning, social significance and experience of childhood will vary across time, even within generations and between cultures, as the society in which it is embedded changes and develops. (See Montgomery, Burr and Woodhead 2003 for a broad international perspective on the experience and nature of childhood and for some more detailed, specific cross-cultural analyses, see, for example, Kenney 2007 and Nieuwenhuys 2009).

An appreciation of childhood as a social artefact like many others allows social scientists to ask interesting questions about why it should take a particular form at any given time and what historical, social and cultural processes shape the social realities that young people have to face. It also allows questions to be asked about whose interests are best served by any particular construction of childhood, especially which generational interests are dominant. More important, understanding childhood as a social construction requires us, as adult professionals or simply as professional adults, to question our 'taken for granted' understanding of children and childhood and to recognize that our account is not the only one possible.

From a sociological point of view, how childhood is 'constructed' may say as much about us and the society we live in as it does about the real lives of the children we encounter. Indeed, opinions about childhood are as variable as the lived experiences of children. As well as recognizing that there are significant differences in what childhood *is* and how it is experienced, we also have to recognize that there are differences of opinion over what it *ought* to be too. Childhood, in this sense, is a *normative* category (one that seeks to establish a standard or 'norm') as well as a *descriptive* one. A great deal of the debate about children and young people in the media, for example, is often carried on in terms of the declining 'state of the nation's children' which is then used as a form of commentary on the declining state of the nation itself (see Pearson 1992).

At an individual level too, it is difficult to escape the personal, social and cultural assumptions that we bring to our understanding of childhood and our understanding of individual children. We may, for example, simply assume that because we were all children once, we already know all that we need to know about childhood ('been there, done that, got the t-shirt'). However, it can be a more subtle process. We would probably agree that there is a strong tradition of understanding childhood, at least in much of the Western world, as a kind of idealized age of innocence, almost as a state of grace; what Cook (2009) calls a sense of a 'sacred' childhood. This sacral form of childhood is characterized by freedom from 'adult' cares such as money, work, complicated relationships, exploitation and death. Cook argues that as this construction of childhood is relatively rare and increasingly threatened by commercialization, premature sexualization, the economic pressures on parents as well as by external dangers (from global warming to 'stranger danger', for example), so its 'emotional force is growing' (p.8). With each actual or perceived threat to this particular construction of childhood, our political, emotional and psychological attachment to it intensifies, especially if we are parents. Cook concludes (p.9) that keeping children as children *in this way* becomes an 'adult priority' that 'gives adults – parents or those aspiring to parenthood, especially, – a role, a duty as moral protector, a reason-to-be, and, yes, a certain form of power.'

In other words, any challenge to what is probably the dominant construction of childhood in the western world today, is understood as a direct threat to us as adults and one which we may resist as it threatens our own sense of who *we* are and the power we have as adults to 'define' children. The salience of Cook's observations is that they are based on his experience of teaching students about the social construction of childhood! Accepting that it is difficult to stand outside of our own personal histories and cultural context, it is important that as social workers, we are able at least to be aware of our assumptions, presumptions and 'constructions' and to be prepared to have them challenged, however uncomfortable this may feel.

A striking challenge to such idealized constructions of childhood as the one that Cook describes, comes from the demographic and biographical 'facts' of children's own lives. In 2007, UNICEF, an agency of the United Nations originally established to help countries improve the health and education of children, produced a 'comprehensive assessment of the lives and well-being of children and young people in 21 nations of the industrialised world'. The table below gives you an idea of those aspects of children and young people's lives that were used to produce an international index of well-being. You will note also that the United Kingdom ranked lowest in relation to 'family relationships' and 'behaviours and risks', second to lowest in relation to 'subjective well-being' and last overall.

Some of the strongest challenges to your personal construction of contemporary childhood may come directly from children and young people themselves, of course. It is important to recognize that it is not only adults who construct childhood or even determine the experience of being a child or young person. Children do too. There is a growing body of evidence (e.g. Butler and others 2003; Jensen and McKee 2003) that children have the potential to be (and actually are) much more significant authors of their own biographies, both literally and figuratively, than many adults might assume. How we conceive of the limits of children's capacities to be significant actors in their own lives is also a function of the way in which we construct childhood.

Many 'therapeutic' constructions of childhood reflect particular views of children that tend to focus on limitations rather than capacities. Some social workers, particularly those steeped in the developmental psychologies of Freud, Jung and Adler, for example, understand childhood almost exclusively as a state of *becoming*, not one of *being*. The primary value of childhood in such accounts lies in its use as a preparation for adulthood simultaneous with its capacity to ensure the stability of social and cultural norms. Childhood is understood merely as a transitional process driven by a fury of evolutionary, biological and hormonal imperatives until the advent of the staid, middle-aged individual of modest, moderate and settled needs. Some accounts of childhood acknowledge the influence of other children in the socialization process and focus on the peer group as a factor in the production and maintenance of (usually deviant) behaviour. Other accounts reflect the relative powerlessness of children to prevent their victimization by adults. But a common thread running through many such accounts of childhood is the way in which the experience of children is presented and largely understood in terms of their incapacities and *naïveté*

Table 1.1 An overview of child well-being in rich countries

Dimensions of child well-being	Average ranking position (for all 6 dimensions)	Dimension 1 Material well-being	Dimension 2 Health and safety	Dimension 3 Educational well-being	Dimension 4 Family and peer relationships	Dimension 5 Behaviours and risks	Dimension 6 Subjective well-being
Netherlands	4.2	10	2	6	3	3	1
Sweden	5.0	1	1	5	15	1	7
Denmark	7.2	4	4	8	9	6	12
Finland	7.5	3	3	4	17	7	11
Spain	8.0	12	6	15	8	5	2
Switzerland	8.3	5	9	14	4	12	6
Norway	8.7	2	8	11	10	13	8
Italy	10.0	14	5	20	1	10	10
Ireland	10.2	19	19	7	7	4	5
Belgium	10.7	7	16	1	5	19	16
Germany	11.2	13	11	10	13	11	9
Canada	11.8	6	13	2	18	17	15
Greece	11.8	15	18	16	11	8	3
Poland	12.3	21	15	3	14	2	19
Czech Republic	12.5	11	10	9	19	9	17
France	13.0	9	7	18	12	14	18
Portugal	13.7	16	14	21	2	15	14
Austria	13.8	8	20	19	16	16	4
Hungary	14.5	20	17	13	6	18	13
United States	18.0	17	21	12	20	20	-
United Kingdom	18.2	18	12	17	21	21	20

OECD countries with insufficient data to be included in the overview: Australia, Iceland, Japan, Luxembourg, Mexico, New Zealand, the Slovak Republic, South Korea, Turkey.

Source: UNICEF 2007, p.2.

rather than in terms of their strengths and experiences. Such deficit models of childhood can imply that childhood is less subtle, complex and meaningful than adulthood and consequently less interesting, valuable and important.

It is not our purpose to persuade you to any particular understanding or view of childhood. Our aim is to encourage you to reflect on what images of childhood you carry around with you and to question the attitudes, values and knowledge that inform your particular view. By being aware of your socio-cultural and personal construction(s) of childhood, we hope that you will be better able to avoid imposing your myths and meanings on the lives of the unique children and young people who you will meet in your work.

NEEDS AND RIGHTS

We can see how the contested nature of childhood has a direct bearing on social work practice by exploring the apparent opposition that is sometimes established between children's needs and children's rights. At a general level, the proponents of a rights-based model for practice might argue that an emphasis on children's particular needs tends to infantilize them well beyond the period of their infancy. It might also be the case that talk of 'needs' sometimes derives from a desire to impose adult constructions upon children's lives, such as when adults say that a child 'needs' a 'highly structured and controlling environment' when what they mean is that they want the child to be locked up; or when a child is said to 'need' 'clear boundaries and explicit means of discipline' when what is intended is that the child should be subjected to corporal punishment. One commentator has advised children that whenever 'they hear the word "need", [they should] reach for their solicitor' (Shaw 1989, p.2). On the other hand, an advocate of a needs-based approach might acknowledge that, while it is perfectly possible to use the rhetoric of rights to protect the integrity of individual children and to encourage them to play their full part in civil society, it is also the case that 'rights-speak' can look suspiciously like neglect when it leaves eight-year-olds 'free' to carry automatic weapons or to be exploited and sexually abused in brothels and back streets.

The social work task is located right at the centre of such apparent contradictions. How you resolve them in practice will depend on the particular image or construction of childhood that you bring to your work as much as on the particular theoretical frameworks that you bring from your knowledge of the social sciences or elsewhere. The following exercise is intended to sensitize you to your understanding of children's needs and rights and to explore further the particular model of childhood to which you currently subscribe.

EXERCISE 1.2: NEEDS AND RIGHTS

Using the grid (see Figure 1.1), write down what you consider to be the most important needs and rights of the individuals concerned.

	Needs	Rights
Person aged 0–5	1.	1.
	2.	2.
	3.	3.
	4.	4.
	5.	5.
Person aged 5–10	1.	1.
	2.	2.
	3.	3.
	4.	4.
	5.	5.
Person aged 10–18	1.	1.
	2.	2.
	3.	3.
	4.	4.
	5.	5.
Person aged over 18	1.	1.
	2.	2.
	3.	3.
	4.	4.
	5.	5.

Figure 1.1 Needs/rights grid

POINTS TO CONSIDER

1. How important is the age of the individual to any consideration of his or her needs or rights?

2. Would your account of needs or rights be different if the individuals were differentiated by race, gender or disability? If so, how?

3. Does an individual have a right to have all of his or her needs met?

4. How far does an individual have a need to be able to exercise his or her rights?

5. Compare the words that you have used to describe rights and those you have used to describe needs. What does the difference tell you about how you regard the two concepts?

6. What does your understanding of needs and rights tell you about your own construction of childhood? Where would you stand on a continuum that ran from maternalism/paternalism at one end to radical liberationist at the other?

NEEDS AND CHILD DEVELOPMENT

Discussion of children's needs tends to be associated with ideas about children's development. For example, a number of key policy documents and practice tools (discussed in more detail later in this book) such as the *Framework for the Assessment of Children in Need and their Families* (DH 2000 – see Units 3, 4 and 7) and *Working Together to Safeguard Children* (DCSF 2010f – see Units 9 and 10) make frequent reference to child development. The *Framework for the Assessment of Children in Need and their Families*, describes itself as 'rooted in child development' (DH 2000 § 1.36) and its preface elevates meeting 'developmental needs' to one of the 'primary aims of Government policy.' Child development is a concept embedded in legislation too; see for example the Children Act 1989, s. 17 and s. 31(9) (DH 1991a).

The widespread use of the term 'child development' should not be taken to imply that there is a relatively straightforward, well-defined and widely accepted understanding of what we mean by the term, however. In fact, the subject of child development is a broad and a dynamic one and is not without its controversies. There are several models and theories of development in common use, not all of which are entirely consistent with each other. Indeed, the broad areas in which development might be said to occur are not universally agreed, even within those key policy documents and practice tools that we referred to earlier. For example, the Children Act 1989 makes reference to physical, intellectual, emotional, social and behavioural development (s. 31(9)) to which *Working Together* adds the idea of 'moral development' (DCSF 2010f § 2.37). We might easily add further domains such as cultural identity or spiritual development.

It has been argued (e.g. Taylor 2004) that all models of child development make claims to 'universal truths' without sufficient recognition of cultural and societal differences. Despite the fact that the Children Act 1989 (s. 22(5)) clearly points to the importance of social workers taking account of the racial, religious, cultural and linguistic needs of children, translating this into practice may be more challenging. Robinson (2007) Jones (1991b) and Yeh and Huang (1996) all point to the risk of staged developmental theories failing to take into account the importance of ethnic identity in a child's development. Woodhead (1999) emphasizes that the 'vast majority of studies of early child development and education have been carried out in a very narrow socio-economic and cultural context, mainly in Europe and North America. Yet, Europe only constitutes 12 per cent of the world's population, North America a further 5 per cent' (Penn 1998, cited in Woodhead 1999, p.9).

Notwithstanding these difficulties and recognizing that child development is also too large a subject for a single chapter such as this, we do intend to introduce you to one specific formulation or 'mapping' of children's developmental needs as it is one that has particular currency in contemporary social work practice. It is the model of children's developmental needs that informs the inter-departmental *Framework for the Assessment of Children in Need and their Families* (Department of Health and others 2000). (You should note that 'in need' is being used here in a 'technical' sense, which is explained in Study Text 4.1. You can take the term at face value for our present purposes.) The *Framework* takes into account a much broader range of factors that workers will need actively to consider when undertaking assessments, and we will discuss these in more detail in Units 4 and 7. Our interest in the *Framework* at this point is in seeing how it describes the nature and scope of children's developmental needs, see Figure 1.2 below:

Health

Includes growth and development as well as physical and mental well-being. Genetic factors may also need to be considered. Involves receiving appropriate health care when ill, an adequate and nutritious diet, exercise, immunizations where appropriate and developmental checks, dental and optical care and, for older children, appropriate advice and information on issues that have an impact on health, including sex education and substance misuse.

Education

Covers all areas of a child's cognitive development, which begins from birth. Includes opportunities to play and interact with other children, to access books, to acquire a range of skills and interests and to experience success and achievement. Involves an adult interested in educational activities, progress and achievements, who takes account of the child's starting point and any special educational needs.

Emotional and Behavioural Development

Concerns the appropriateness of response demonstrated in feelings and actions by a child, initially to parents and caregivers and then, as the child grows older, to others beyond the family. Includes the nature and quality of early attachments, characteristics of temperament, adaptation to change, response to stress and degree of appropriate self-control.

Identity

Concerns the child's growing sense of self as a separate and valued person. Includes how a child views him- or herself and his or her abilities, feelings of belonging and acceptance by the family and wider society, and the strength of his or her positive sense of individuality.

Family and Social Relationships

Concerns the child's development of empathy and the capacity to place oneself in someone else's shoes. Includes a stable and affectionate relationship with parents or caregivers, good relationships with siblings, increasing importance of age-appropriate friendships with peers and other significant persons in the child's life and the response of family to these relationships.

Social Presentation

Concerns the child's growing understanding of the way in which appearance and behaviour are perceived by the outside world and the impression being created. Includes appropriateness of dress for age, gender, culture and religion; cleanliness and personal hygiene and availability of advice from parents or caregivers about presentation in different settings.

Self-Care Skills

Concerns the acquisition by the child of both practical and emotional competencies required for increasing independence. Includes early practical skills of dressing and feeding, opportunities to gain confidence and practical skills to undertake activities away from the family and independent living skills as older children. Includes encouragement to acquire social problem solving approaches. Special attention should be given to the impact of disability and other vulnerabilities on the development of self-care skills.

Figure 1.2 A child's developmental needs.
Source: Department of Health and others (2000), p.19 (Crown Copyright)

You will certainly need to refine and develop your understanding of children's needs and general development through further reading and direct observation of children (see Unit 7) but, as you do so, you should also consider some general points about the maturational process and the needs of children.

First, the speed of development, particularly of very young children, is one of the real wonders of the natural world. The proverbial cry of 'My, hasn't s/he grown!' from friends or relatives who have only occasional contact with a child has a real basis in fact. If you consider that in a little over four years most of those snuffling new-born bundles of sensation and smells are transformed into neat rows of school children making their first attempts to put their 'news' down on paper, then you would probably agree that the rate of change is breathtaking. In focusing on any child's needs, at any age, be aware of the amazing pace of change and do not 'trap' a child into a stage of development or a pattern of needs that he or she has long outgrown.

Always be mindful of the complexity of all human beings. There is infinite variety in the interaction of all human needs and no-one, at any age, should be reduced to only one or two dimensions of their personalities or attributes. It is never appropriate to focus all our effort on meeting the physical needs of a child if we fail to meet its social or emotional needs, to take an obvious example. Children, just like everyone else, have to be considered holistically and their needs should be understood as dynamic rather than fixed and enduring. One of the continuing and fascinating controversies to occupy social scientists still is the way in which extrinsic factors, such as economic disadvantage and/or parental inadequacies, interact with intrinsic factors, such as temperament or personal resilience; and how these impact on a child's development (see Daniel, Wassell and Gilligan 1999).

Finally, whatever our views on the determining influence of genetic inheritance or environmental influence (nature versus nurture), we would all probably agree that each human being is unique and individual. All babies do not look the same! Nor do all five-year-olds act or think in the same way or have identical needs, any more than all forty-year-olds do. There are consistencies, of course; but there are differences too and they are often the more important considerations.

As one might anticipate, just as understanding children's needs is a complex and contested subject, the same is true of children's rights, as the following Study Text illustrates.

i STUDY TEXT 1.2: CHILDREN'S RIGHTS

The enfranchisement of any subordinated group is always a slow and halting process and the contemporary debate on children's rights is of surprisingly recent origin. It wasn't until 1993 that Peter Newell was able to declare that children's rights had 'come of age' (Newell 1993, p.xi. See also Reynaert, Bouverne-de-Bie and Vandevelde 2009 for a critical review of the literature on the UN Convention on the Rights of the Child). The legitimacy of children's claims to rights, and indirectly the occasion of Newell's remarks, was the adoption by the United Nations General Assembly in November 1989 of the Convention on the Rights of the Child (UNCRC). You might usefully compare the list of rights that you have devised with those established by the Convention (see Figure 1.3).

As well as establishing some important general principles, the Convention establishes the following rights for children:

- The inherent right to life (Article 6)

- The right to have a name from birth and to be granted nationality (Article 7)

- The right to live with parents (unless incompatible with best interests), the right to maintain contact with parents if separated (Article 9)

- The right to leave any country and to enter their own in order to be reunited with parents or to maintain the child–parent relationship (Article 10)

- The right to express an opinion and to have that opinion taken into account in matters affecting the child (Article 12)

- The right to freedom of expression (Article 13)

- The right to freedom of thought, conscience and religion (Article 14)

- The right to freedom of association (Article 15)

- The right to protection from interference with privacy, family, home and correspondence (Article 16)

- The right of access to appropriate information that promotes social, spiritual and moral well-being (Article 17)

- The right to be protected from abuse and neglect (Article 19)

- The right to special protection for those children deprived of a family environment (Article 20)

- The right to special protection for refugee children (Article 22)

- The right of children with disabilities to special care, education and training (Article 23)

- The right to the highest level of health possible and to health and medical services (Article 24)

- The right to periodic review of placement for children placed by the State for reasons of care, protection or treatment (Article 25)

- The right of children to benefit from social security including social insurance (Article 26)

- The right to an adequate standard of living (Article 27)

- The right to education (Article 28)

- The right of children of minority communities and indigenous peoples to enjoy their own culture and to practice their own religion and language (Article 30)

- The right to leisure, play and participation in cultural and artistic activities (Article 31)

- The right to be protected from the exploitation of their labour (Article 32)

- The right to be protected from drug abuse (Article 33)

- The right to be protected from sexual exploitation (Article 34)

- The right to be protected from sale, trafficking and abduction (Article 35)

- The right to respect for human and civil rights in relation to the administration of justice (Article 40)

Figure 1.3 The UN Convention on the Rights of the Child

Although the UK government ratified the Convention in 1992, it does not have legal force in the UK. While the UK government must seek to observe its provisions and publish reports accordingly, the Convention cannot be relied upon in any legal proceedings in the courts of England and Wales, although it can be taken into account in the interpretation of domestic law. This is not the case in respect of another potentially important source of authority in establishing children's rights, the Human Rights Act 1998 (HRA). This Act, essentially the European Convention on Human Rights, which the UK signed in 1950, came into force in October 2000. Under the Act, courts can make a judgement in response to a case made by an individual that their rights under the Act have been infringed. Figure 1.4 sets out some of the rights established by the Act. The Act also requires public authorities (such as local authority social services departments) to uphold a person's rights, not just to avoid infringing them.

The following are the individual citizen's rights set down in Schedule 1 of the Act. In our view, all of them are relevant for children.

- Article 2 Everyone's right to life shall be protected by law

- Article 3 No-one shall be subjected to…inhuman or degrading treatment or punishment

- Article 4 No-one shall be held in slavery or servitude. No-one shall be required to perform forced or compulsory labour

- Article 5 Everyone has the right to liberty and security of person. No-one shall be deprived of his liberty save in the following cases…[among others] the detention of a minor by lawful order for the purposes of educational supervision or his lawful detention for the purposes of bringing him before the competent legal authority

- Article 6 In determination of his civil rights and obligations or of any criminal charge against him, everyone is entitled to a fair and public hearing within a reasonable time by an independent and impartial tribunal

- Article 7 No-one shall be held guilty of any criminal offence…which did not constitute a criminal offence…at the time it was committed

- Article 8 Everyone has the right to respect for his private and family life, his home and his correspondence

- Article 9 Everyone has the right to freedom of thought, conscience and religion

- Article 10 Everyone has the right to freedom of expression

- Article 11 Everyone has the right to freedom of peaceful assembly and to freedom of association with others

- Article 12 Men and women of marriageable age have the right to marry and to found a family, according to the national laws governing the exercise of this right

- Article 14 The enjoyment of the rights and freedoms set forth [here] shall be secured without discrimination on any grounds such as sex, race, colour, language, religion, political or other opinion, national or social origin, association with a national minority, property, birth or other status

Under Part II of the First Protocol of the Act, the following rights are also listed:

- Article 1 Every natural or legal person is entitled to the peaceful enjoyment of his possessions ...

- Article 2 No person shall be denied the right to education ... the State shall respect the rights of parents to ensure such education is in conformity with their own religious and philosophical convictions

Figure 1.4 The Human Rights Act 1998

It is possible, with only a little distortion (see Archard 1993, 2001; Fortin 1998; Van Bueren 1995 for more detailed accounts), to group those rights defined by the Convention and the Human Rights Act into four categories:

- Survival rights (e.g. Art. 6 of the Convention and Art. 2 of the HRA).

- Development rights (e.g. Art. 28 of the Convention and Art. 2 of Part II of The First Protocol of the HRA).

- Protection rights (e.g. Art. 34 of the Convention and Art. 5 of the HRA).

- Participation rights (e.g. Art. 13 of the Convention and Art. 14 of the HRA).

Specific formulations of the first three groups of rights – which we might describe together as 'nurturance rights' (see Rogers and Wrightsman 1978) – might command wide acceptance (although you should note that many countries have entered specific reservations concerning the Convention and do not accept all of its provisions). It is probably the case that many of the rights that you described in Exercise 1.2 were broadly of this type. In practice, such rights may, at worst, represent little more than good intentions and, at best, be no more than a reflection of current ideas of what constitutes children's developmental needs. For the most part, rights of this type, even where they are enforceable in law (e.g. the right to education), are defined and enforced by adults on the child's behalf. The fourth group of rights, participation rights, are of a different order in that they have 'self determination orientations' (Rogers and Wrightsman 1978) and so make a case not for 'welfare' but for 'liberty' (Franklin 1995). It is rights of this sort that pose the greatest challenge to the dominant deficit models of childhood that we described in Study Text 1.1 and which provide the liveliest debates in social work with children and their families.

There are a number of arguments and counter-arguments that are routinely made concerning the exercise of children's participation rights (see Lansdown 2002 for a more detailed discussion). For example:

- *Children are not sufficiently rational or intellectually capable to make competent choices.* In the case of infants this will be true but it does seem that children's capacity for rational thought is considerably greater than most adults are prepared to credit. We know of no research findings that suggest that the social world of children is less subtle, complex and nuanced than that of adults (see Butler and others 2003). Also, if reason and intellectual capacity rather than age are the criteria, then many adults should be denied their rights too.

- *Children lack sufficient experience on which to base their decisions, which can only develop with maturity.* This might be considered a self-fulfilling prophecy in the light of the previous argument and does seem to rest on a touching faith in the capacity of humans to learn from their mistakes. This argument usually rests on a confusion between 'the right to do something [and] doing the right thing' (Franklin 1995, p.11) and if the ill-judged consequences of the exercise of certain rights are sufficient to deny those rights then a similar argument should, logically, apply to many adults too.

- *Children are not self-sufficient and, as dependent individuals, do not qualify as full stakeholders in civil society.* On this basis, almost everyone might be denied their rights to some degree but certainly those who are ill, elderly or with a disability might be denied theirs. Another variation on this argument is the suggestion that children must accept responsibilities before they can exercise their rights but surely, one of the best ways of encouraging young people to be responsible citizens is to provide opportunities for them to have their citizenship taken seriously?

- *Children's rights can only be achieved at the expense of the inalienable rights of parents.* We explore the changing balance of power between parents and children in Unit 3, although this argument is usually only a thinly disguised attempt to protect the institution of the family from the inquisitorial attentions of the State. This, in turn, is sometimes only a thinly disguised argument for the dismantling of welfare provision of all sorts and contains echoes of the 'no such thing as society' point of view that makes all talk of civil rights redundant.

How far governments have been persuaded to observe the UN Convention on the Rights of the Child can be traced in the 'concluding observations' that the Committee on the UNCRC produces after its periodic reviews of signatories to the Convention (see Butler and Drakeford 2010 for a detailed, first hand account of the reporting process, including attendance at the Committee). The periodic reviews consider evidence provided by the government, selected non-governmental organizations (NGOs), children's commissioners or ombudsmen and young people themselves. At the 2008 periodic review of the UK, each of the devolved administrations of the UK (England, Scotland, Northern Ireland and Wales) produced separate reports; each very different from each other. Accordingly, a number of the Committee's observations reflected the very different stages reached in the four countries of the UK in implementing the UNCRC but the 'concluding observations' included some very sharp criticisms at the UK level (UNCRCC 2008).

The Committee took the view that the Westminster government needs to go further in incorporating the UNCRC into domestic law (n.b. in June 2010, the Welsh Assembly Government which adopted the UNCRC as the basis for all children's policy in 2001, began the process of making it a statutory duty on Welsh Ministers to have 'due regard' to the UNCRC in all policy and legal decisions). The Committee also made specific reference to the relatively poor co-ordination of the implementation of the Convention across the UK. It urged the UK government to do more to improve understanding and awareness of Convention rights by children and young people. It criticized the intolerance and inappropriate characterization of children, especially adolescents, by government and in the media (marking out for particular disapproval the various 'nanny' programmes which subjected children, in effect, to humiliating treatment). It was critical of ASBOs (Anti-Social Behaviour Orders) and urged the end of corporal punishment.

In a sense, the most recent set of concluding observations by the Committee of the UNCRC represents a further challenge to any complacency that we might feel in the UK about our attitudes to and provision for children and young people and it is an open invitation to re-evaluate the policy and professional context in which we work. The same would be true for a great many other English speaking nations – except the USA, which is not even a signatory to the Convention!

NEEDS VERSUS RIGHTS?

Underlying the debate at governmental level about how far children's policy should be predicated on needs and/or rights we see a glimpse of the central dynamic of childhood itself, the progress from dependency to autonomy; which, as we have indicated, is a matter of debate. In reality it is neither necessary nor helpful to think of 'needs' and 'rights' as opposites or as mutually exclusive concepts. Both 'needs-speak' and 'rights-speak' are useful correctives to one another. The biological dependency of infants, for example, calls forth a primal and beneficial concern for the nurture and protection of children. Similarly, in a society in which children are exploited and abused it is important that children possess a civil and legal status from which they can defend their interests.

The progress from dependency to autonomy is not the only dynamic along which childhood operates. It moves also between powerlessness and the possession of power, between innocence and experience and, for some, between a state of nature and a state of grace. The precise point at which you locate the circumstances and experiences of each child whom you encounter will be a function not just of the characteristics of the child him- or herself but of the image of childhood that you bring to the encounter. If you believe that children should be seen much more than heard, if you think that *Lord of the Flies* rather than *Swallows and Amazons* captures the true essence of childhood experience or if you believe that children are more Bonnie and Clyde than 'bonny and blithe' then you will, in all likelihood, find a plausible justification for your views in the conduct or circumstances of the child concerned.

It is axiomatic in social work practice generally that the attitudes and values that you bring to your work are critical to the process and outcome of any intervention. In working with children in particular, it is vital that you are aware of your particular construction of childhood and that you are able to explain and defend it when required.

To return to the central dynamic of dependency/autonomy, the next exercise will help you to determine your current position and how well you can articulate it.

EXERCISE 1.3: NEEDS AND RIGHTS IN ACTION

Read the text of Article 16 of the UN Convention on the Rights of the Child and think how you might apply its provisions in the situations described below. You should supply whatever additional material you need in order to determine your response.

No child shall be subjected to arbitrary or unlawful interference with his or her privacy, family, home or correspondence, nor to unlawful attacks on his or her honour or reputation. (Article 16 (part))

1. You are the responsible social worker and a young person asks you if he or she can make a private phone call to his or her father who is accused of abusing him or her.

2. You are visiting a children's home and the young person you are seeing tells you that another young person is in possession of stolen goods.

3. While on duty in your agency you overhear a conversation between two young people in which one tells the other that she thinks she is pregnant and is too scared to tell anyone else.

4. On a holiday you are planning for children known to your agency, you are asked to keep a covert watch on one young person's contact with another as it is believed that they are planning to commit a serious crime together.

5. The head teacher of a young person for whom you are responsible asks you for a copy of previous case conference minutes 'for the records'.

6. After a series of attacks on residents, your agency wants to install closed-circuit TV in a children's home. One of the cameras will unavoidably overlook the residents' recreational space.

7. You believe that a young person for whom you are responsible is injecting proscribed drugs. During a visit to the young person you have the opportunity to search his or her room without permission but with no risk of being observed.

8. A colleague has written a damning court report on a family based on what you know to be inaccurate information. A member of the family concerned asks you what the report says.

9. The parent of a teenager for whom you are responsible tells you that their son or daughter is enuretic and would you 'have a word' with them.

10. A child that you are working with is described as an abuser in a local newspaper. The opposite is in fact the case. A reporter asks you for your comments.

POINTS TO CONSIDER

1. Do children need privacy?

2. Are the limits on a child's right to privacy any different to those you would tolerate for yourself?

3. What, if any, needs have priority over a child's right to privacy?

4. Is your professional obligation to maintain confidentiality helped or hindered by a child's right to privacy?

5. In whose interests are you working when/if you decide to set limits on a child's right to privacy?

6. How would you integrate Article 16 into your own practice?

CONCLUSION

The history of the study of childhood is the history of *adults'* study of childhood and adults' accounts may be different from those of children themselves. The adult world, including the social work world, is littered with the never-consulted casualties of the social worker who 'knew best' or 'knew already'. Recognizing the 'otherness' of childhood, expecting and respecting difference, and accepting the limits of one's own experience and understanding are absolute prerequisites to working in the child's best interests.

The images of childhood that you bring to your work exert a powerful influence on the kind of social worker you are and the kind of work that you do. Since you will frequently find what you are looking for, we hope that you will make a strenuous and conscious effort to meet each child that you encounter as he or she really is and not as you remember, imagine or would like them to be.

NOTES AND SELF-ASSESSMENT

1. When does childhood begin and end? When did you stop being a child?

2. What does it mean to be treated like a child?

3. In what ways do you treat children differently to adults?

4. What potential for oppressive practice does your own construction of childhood have?

5. What do you think you have to learn from the children with whom you work?

6. How does your image of childhood help you to help children?

RECOMMENDED READING

James, A and James, A.L. (2008) *Key Concepts in Childhood Studies*. London: Sage.

Keenan, T. and Evans, S. (2009) *An Introduction to Child Development* (Second Edition). London: Sage.

TRAINER'S NOTES

Exercise 1.1: Images of Childhood

As well as newspapers and magazines, film and TV programmes are other sources of images for this exercise – although the very best source is the family photograph album. This exercise works equally well if participants are asked to provide written accounts of childhood from their own reading, especially their childhood reading. Similarly, any book of quotations will provide a list of concise and challenging accounts of childhood. Whatever the graphic or written stimulus, however, the liveliest discussion and the clearest reminiscences of childhood are produced by the purchase and consumption of the participant's favourite childhood sweets!

Exercise 1.2: Needs and Rights

This exercise can be started as a large group and with some quickthinking of both needs and rights. These needs and rights can then be attributed to various categories of individuals distinguished by age, gender, race, and so on, either in a large group or in smaller groups. Alternatively, a wide range of needs and rights can be written onto cards beforehand and, either as a large group or a series of smaller groups, they can be attributed to various categories. Discussion can be encouraged if there is a lack of consensus over any particular attribution.

Exercise 1.3: Needs and Rights in Action

A large group can be split into three smaller groups, one representing the child concerned, one the parent or carer of the child and the other the social worker. The several groups could then negotiate a consensus on the application of the right to privacy in each mini-scenario. This exercise works particularly well if tailored to the particular work or placement setting of group members. Participants can be encouraged to develop 'Practice Guidelines' for their particular work or practice learning context and to bring the views of colleagues back to the group for discussion.

UNIT 2

The Family

OBJECTIVES

In this Unit you will:

- Consider the variety of family forms and household structures to be found in contemporary Britain.

- Explore your personal construction of the family.

- Consider the complexity and subtlety of family life.

 **COURSE TEXT: MEET THE FAMILY**

Consider these two appreciations of the family:

- 'We must start by asking: how can we help families stick together. Of course, nurture, affection, discipline and security – the ingredients to a good start in life – can be provided within any family, whatever its shape or size. But the evidence shows that children are more likely to do well when both parents are there for them, together providing the love and the discipline.

  Now I don't believe government can make families work and stick together. But I do believe that the state can support families as they deal with all the different pressures they face. That's what our family-friendly reform plan is all about. Right at the heart of it is our commitment to …commitment.

  I think it is essential to say loudly and proudly that commitment is a core value of a responsible society and that's why we will recognize marriage, whether between a man and a woman, a woman and a woman or a man and another man, in the tax system. And yes, that is a commitment.'

- 'Family life, family values, decent normal family fun, family shopping, family leisure. The word is used these days as the word "Aryan" was used in Germany during the 1930s. Anything that isn't Family is "unfamily", and anything that is unfamily is unrepresentative of the joyful majority. Obedience, compulsion, tyranny and repression are family words as much as love, compassion and mutual trust. It rather depends on the family.'

The first quotation is from a speech made by the Rt. Hon. David Cameron as leader of the UK Conservative Party on January 11th 2010, a matter of months before his election as prime minister. The speech was entitled 'Building the Responsible Society: The importance of parenting and early years support' and was given at the launch of an inquiry 'investigating "character" and its importance in public and social life', undertaken by Demos (a 'think-tank focussed on power and politics'). The second quotation comes from actor and broadcaster Stephen Fry (1993), writing in his regular column for *The Listener*. Many of the issues that arise for social workers when thinking about the family are to be found in these two short extracts.

First, there is the recognition that the family as an idea, as well as a set of social roles and expectations, can mean very different things to different people. Second, it is clear that the family as a set of social realities is likely to vary. Third, the family can be an aspect of ideology and can be used to further particular socio-political ends. Finally, the experience of family life, as well as being widely variable, is also more equivocal and ambiguous than is immediately apparent. Like 'childhood', the 'family' is another of those central but elusive terms that are the common currency of social work but which are rarely tested either for their meaning or their value. Also, like childhood, the family is both a social and a personal construction rather than a fixed set of relationships or some aspect of a 'natural order' of things. 'Family', like childhood, is a normative as well as a descriptive category. Understanding your own construction of the family and being sensitive to the myriad other ways in which the term can be meaningful is an important part of understanding the families with whom you intend to work.

Before we explore our own ideas of what constitutes a family, we should, perhaps, take some account of what household structures and family forms exist in the UK today and how these are changing. The next exercise is intended to alert you to some of the assumptions that you might hold concerning family formation and household structure. You are not expected to know the right answers! You will find these in the Study Text that follows Exercise 2.1. The point of the exercise is for you to find out what assumptions you make about contemporary family forms and household structures.

EXERCISE 2.1: FAMILY FORTUNES

Make the best estimate that you can in answer to each of the following questions and note any pattern that emerges in the way that you have either under- or over-estimated the statistically correct answer:

1. Are more people living alone today than 30 years ago?

2. Is the average size of households today greater or smaller than 30 years ago?

3. Which are the two most common forms of household in Great Britain today?

4. What proportion of households have children under the age of 16 living in them?

5. What proportion of households consists of lone-parent families?

6. What percentage of the population lives in a family with children under the age of 16?

7. What percentage of children live in families with two parents?

8. Is the proportion of children in the population rising or falling?

9. What is the average age at which women give birth to their first baby?

10. What proportion of children are born outside marriage?

11. What proportion of births outside marriage are registered in the names of both parents in the UK?

12. Are more or fewer people marrying?

13. Is the divorce rate rising or falling?

14. What proportion of divorcing couples had at least one child under the age of 16 at the time of their divorce?

15. What proportion of these were aged under 11?

POINTS TO CONSIDER

1. On what sources of knowledge/information did you base your answers to these questions?

2. What are the usual sources of information about household structure and family formation to which the general public have easiest access?

3. Do you regard any of the rates or proportions that you have noted as actually *too* high or *too* low? Which one(s) and why?

4. Which, if any, of the rates or proportions that you have identified do you regard as problematic? Should anything be done about the state of affairs described?

5. How far can statistics help you to decide what is a 'typical' family? What is the difference between a 'typical' family and a 'normal' one?

i STUDY TEXT 2.1: THE FACTS OF FAMILY LIFE

This Study Text provides a digest of statistics drawn from government sources that illustrate the demographic realities of household structure and family form in the UK. It is highly selective and is intended to illustrate patterns of continuity as well as change, although it does focus particularly on emerging demographic trends and phenomena. For the purposes of data collection, the official definition of a household is a 'single person living alone or a group of people who live and eat together, whether related or not' and the definition of a family is 'a married or cohabiting couple with or without children, or a lone parent with one or more children' (ONS 2009, p.14).

HOUSEHOLDS

Generally speaking, the number of households in the UK continues to increase but household size is reducing. The total number of households in the UK has grown from 16.3 million in 1961 to 25.2 million in 2009, an increase of 55 per cent. In 2009, 29 per cent of all households were one-person households, a proportion that has increased from 14 per cent in 1961. The average household size has decreased over the same period from 3.1 persons in 1961 to 2.4 in 2008 (ONS 2010a, Table 2.1).

The proportion of households with children living in them is falling. The two most common types of households in the UK are single-person households and couples without children (each amounting to 29% of all households). The next most common is the couple with one or more dependent children (21%). Lone-parent households (with dependent children) make up 7 per cent of households. Accordingly, only 28 per cent of all households in the UK have dependent children living in them. This has fallen from 40 per cent in 1961 (ONS 2010a, Table 2.2).

FAMILIES

More people are living alone. Since 1971, the proportion of the population living alone had doubled to 12 per cent by 2008. As a proportion of the population of Great Britain, almost half of us in 2009 lived in a household with dependent children (48%), down from 55 per cent in 1961 (ONS 2010a, Table 2.3).

Of the 13 million dependent children in the UK in 2008, 64 per cent of children lived with married parents; 13 per cent with cohabiting couples; 22 per cent with lone mothers and 2 per cent with lone fathers. While it is the case that most children live with two parents (77%), this proportion has declined from 92 per cent in 1972 (ONS 2009: Table 2.5 and p.16). You should remember however, that this 'snapshot' figure does not reflect the fact that children may live in a variety of family and household structures during the course of their childhood.

There is a marked effect of ethnicity on family composition. Asian or Asian British and Chinese children were far more likely to be living with married parents (86% and 74% respectively) compared to Black or Black British children (39%). The proportion of children living with lone parents reflects this pattern with 56 per cent of Black or Black British children living with lone parents, compared to 23 per cent of White children and 14 per cent of Asian or Asian British children (ONS 2010a, Table 2.8 and p.18 ff.).

CHILDREN

The number of children and young people aged under 16 has fallen from 14.3 million in 1971 to 11.5 million in 2008. Young people aged under 16 now represent around 19 per cent of the population of the UK and this is projected to fall further to reach 18 per cent by 2031 (ONS 2010a, Fig. 1.3).

There are marked differences in the age structure of the population according to ethnic origin. In the Bangladeshi community, for example, 36 per cent of the population are aged under 16 with 33 per cent of the Black African population similarly aged under 16 compared to 18 per cent and 7 per cent of the White British and White Irish population respectively (ONS 2010a, Table 1.4).

FAMILY-BUILDING

Despite the fact that women are having their children later, the number of births in the UK is on an upward trend. The number of births in the UK has increased for each of the previous seven years to 2008 and is now at its highest rate since 1972. The average age at which women are giving birth for the first time has risen from 23.8 in 1972 to 27.5 in 2007 (ONS 2010a, Fig. 2.16).

Throughout Europe, the proportion of children born outside marriage is increasing. In the UK this proportion has increased to 45 per cent of all births – over four times more than in 1975 (ONS 2010a, Fig. 2.18 and ff.). Age of the mother is a significant factor with 94 per cent of births to women aged under 20 and 72 per cent of births to mothers aged between 20 and 24 being outside marriage. However, whereas in 1971, over half of births outside marriage were registered solely in the mother's name, in 2008, 65 per cent were registered by parents living at the same address and only 14 per cent were registered solely.

MARRIAGE AND DIVORCE

The number of marriages in England and Wales fell for the third consecutive year to 2007, reflecting a general downward trend since the early 1970s (ONS 2010a, Fig. 2.11). In 2008, the marriage rate in England and Wales was the lowest since such rates were first calculated in 1862, at 21.8 per 1000 unmarried men and 19.6 for women (ONS 2010b, Fig. 1). Nonetheless, in 2007 (ONS 2010a, Fig. 2.9), the majority of adults in England and Wales were living as a couple. Although varying by age group, the most common form of partnership was marriage, with 55 per cent of those aged over 30 being married.

The number of divorces in England and Wales fell to 121,779 in 2008 compared to 128,232 in 2007. This is the fifth consecutive year in which the number of divorces has fallen. Similarly, the divorce rate (measured as the proportion of people per 1000 of the married population) also fell to 11.2 per cent, compared to 11.8 per cent in 2007. Half of couples divorcing in 2008 had at least one dependent child under 16, a total of 106,763 children; 63 per cent of whom were aged under 11 (ONS 2010c).

COURSE TEXT: WHAT'S IN A NAME?

The demographic variability of family form and the degree to which patterns of change and continuity are evident in family formation and dissolution across time and between cultures, even within one set of national boundaries, ensure that any definition of the 'family' is likely to be partial, in both senses of the word. One commentator has noted that:

> … if not only family form, family activity, family functioning but also the emotional interior of the family is highly variable, then it is questionable whether the term 'family' should be dispensed with… 'family' would appear to refer neither to a specific empirical type nor to a theoretical type… (Harris 1984, p.246)

The almost infinite range of relationships, domestic arrangements, social circumstances and personal networks to which the term 'family' has been applied means that it can be used in the service of almost any political ideology or by any moral entrepreneur. For example, the vilification of absent fathers and lone mothers in some parts of the popular press over recent years has been a recurrent strand to a variety of socio-moral crusades. The following examples from across the spectrum of the printed media are not untypical:

Machetes by the door, drugs on the table – and mothers paid by the state to have babies with men they barely know. What HAVE we done to the British family?

(Headline: *Daily Mail*, 21 September 2009)

My problem with teenage mothers

On my way to the office I pass a block of flats with a wing of 'affordable housing'. The door has an entry code system that is often broken; if it isn't, I frequently see it being forced. In the unlikely event that it is working, several people, usually men, are pacing the pavement on their mobiles, asking to be let in. Those coming and going are mostly young women, some look like very young women, and all of them are pushing prams.

I won't pussyfoot around here. This annoys me. And not in a very altruistic way. I can dress it up as a liberal's concern for the children being brought up in such circumstances – without a live-in father and in an inner-city flat. But that's only a fraction of it. I'm annoyed because I know (or think I know) that my taxes are making life more agreeable for these girls than, deep down, I think it ought to be.

(*The Independent*, 2 October 2009)

I'm a full-time mum… Benefits ARE my wages

SHE sits surrounded by top-of-the-range flat-screen tellies, laptop computers, games consoles and two high-tech gaming chairs.

But single mum Pam Bainbridge hasn't earned a penny to pay for her luxury life – the bill has been footed by TAXPAYERS.

Mother-of-three Pam, 33, hasn't worked for 13 years and is proud she has managed to save from her benefits to pay for new bikes, a £1,600 Golf car and Sky TV throughout the house.

(*The Sun*, 16 February 2010)

Unwanted men, we need you to curb the welfare Amazons

It is hugely unfair to make responsible people who are struggling to support their own families struggle harder still to support women who won't work. Family life is in a fine mess in this country. Looking after your own children has become a luxury that few women can afford, married or single, unless they abandon responsibility for themselves and go on benefits.

(*The Sunday Times*, 7 March 2010)

It is not our intention to debate such responses to the changing form and nature of the family or to characterize particular ideological orientations towards it (but visit www.gingerbread.org.uk for a balancing view to the opinions reflected in the extracts from newspapers above). Our point is that, just as we saw in relation to defining children and childhood, as well as a wide variety of social 'facts' that need to be accommodated in our understanding of the term, there are a wide range of deeply held beliefs about the family that we need to take into account also if we are to work effectively with them. The next exercise is intended to sensitize you further to some of the attitudes you have towards the family.

EXERCISE 2.2: IS THIS A FAMILY?

Decide which of these households is a family and why. You may find the following criteria useful in determining family status:

- the degree of emotional commitment
- the degree of commitment to the future of the arrangements
- the degree of emotional interdependence
- the degree to which social and domestic life is interwoven
- the degree of financial interdependence
- the intimacy of the relationship(s)
- the duration of relationship(s)
- the exclusivity of relationship(s).

Note any other criteria that occur to you as you complete the exercise.

1. John and Jane are both students in their early twenties. They have shared a flat for nearly three years and divide all the household bills between them. They have bought some furniture and household items together. They eat together, spend a lot of time in each other's company, and frequently go out with each other socially. Over the last few months, they have slept together but both have had intimate relationships with others at the same time. When they leave college, John plans to return to his home area. Jane is thinking of travelling abroad for a year or two.

2. Betty and George have been married for eight years. They hardly speak to one another except to argue or to 'sort out' practical matters to do with the children, Jo aged four and Chris aged six. Betty has a long-standing relationship with another man. Both pay their wages into separate accounts, although each pays half of the household bills. Betty does most of the necessary child care during the week and George takes over at weekends.

3. Surinder is a lone parent. She cares for her daughter, Shama, aged ten. Shama's father does not support the family financially. He is married and has three other children of his own. He regularly brings the children to play with Shama and will sometimes baby-sit so that Surinder can go out by herself. Surinder receives a lot of practical help from her mother, with whom Shama spends a great deal of time. During long school holidays, Shama's grandmother moves into Surinder's house so that Surinder can carry on going to work.

4. Jason and Justin have lived together for nearly twelve years. They jointly own their own home, its contents and a car, and have left everything to each other in their wills. Theirs has been a monogamous relationship and they are deeply committed to each other. They have separate careers but spend all their free time together. They have a number of shared interests and hobbies.

5. Jean and Eric, both divorced, have lived together for three months. Eric's children, Sara aged 17 and Paul aged 15, together with Sara's baby, Amanda, and Jean's children, Thomas, James and Edward (all under five), live with Jean and Eric. Sara's boyfriend sleeps in the house most nights. The children, because of their ages, have little to do with one another. Jean 'will not get involved' with the care of Amanda and Eric disapproves of Sara's boyfriend. Bills are paid by whoever has the means at the time and are a cause of friction between Jean and Eric. The tenancy of the house is in Jean's name. The current arrangements were undertaken on a 'trial basis', the terms of which are not clear.

6. Glyn and Rita have been married for 18 years. They have no children. Rita has never worked outside the home. Glyn has a good job that more than covers their regular out-goings. They own their own home, run a car and have regular holidays abroad. Glyn and Rita describe themselves as 'soul mates' although they do not spend as much time in each other's company as they used to do.

POINTS TO CONSIDER

1. Which criteria did you regard as the most useful in determining whether these households could be called a family?

2. Are there any criteria that you would regard as critical in determining whether any particular household could be called a family?

3. On the basis of the choices you have made, how would you now define what you mean by the term 'family'?

4. How much does your definition of the 'family' originate in your own experience of family life do you think?

5. Which of the households described in Exercise 2.2 comes closest to your ideal of family life?

6. Which of the households described in Exercise 2.2 is the most likely to come to the attention of social workers and why?

COURSE TEXT: FAMILY INTERESTS

Expectations of what constitutes a family are not to be found only in the minds of social workers or the mouths of politicians or journalists. Every fast-food restaurant, railway carriage and holiday operator in Britain seems to proceed on the assumption that we eat, sleep and move around in groups or multiples of four! Just as we need to differentiate between, and respond to, families on the basis of how they are actually constituted (rather than on how we imagine they are or think they should be), so too do we need to differentiate between the interests and experiences of different family members.

Family life can be experienced in a wide variety of ways, even within the same family. For example, the division of domestic labour and child care might have implications for how mothers and fathers understand and play out their familial roles and 'life scripts' (see Berne 1964). In fact, the gendered division of labour remains remarkably persistent. While to a significant degree a function of the employment status of both partners, data from the Millennium Cohort Study (MCS), suggests that families with (young) children have actually become *less* egalitarian in their division of child care since the 1990s (Calderwood and others 2005). Although the MCS data relates at this point in its progress specifically to families with younger children, its findings are broadly consistent with other longitudinal studies. Again, significantly determined by the employment status of the parents, domestic chores (such as cleaning; laundry/ironing and cooking) would still appear to be carried out predominantly by women, although where both partners are working, the balance does approach a more even distribution.

Some of the reasons for the persistence of the gendered division of labour can be accounted for in socio-economic and structural terms (see Hakim 2004 or Scott, Dex and Joshi 2009 for a broad discussion of the key issues) and from the resilience of some very traditional views on 'the proper place of a woman'. Such 'old-fashioned' attitudes to domestic work are often sustained by some pretty 'old fashioned' sexism too. The roots of sexism extend well beyond the scope of this book, although its consequences for practice in this field are important. Sexism has been defined as 'the belief in the inherent superiority of one sex over another and thereby the right to dominance' (Lorde 1984, p.115) and as part of a 'cultural value system which perceives men as more valuable than women' (Burden and Gottlieb 1987, p.2).

As such, sexism disadvantages women more than men, although Phillipson (1992) and others have drawn attention to how sexism discriminates against both men and women in families by preventing each of them from achieving their full potential. Sexist stereotyping can not only condemn a woman for not appearing caring enough but also prevent a man from showing the caring part of his nature. It would be very remiss of us, for example, to exclude from our selection of data from the MCS, those data that describe the active engagement of men in the care of their young children. In fact, 53 per cent of fathers living with their 9–10 month old fed their baby at least once a day, 57 per cent changed a nappy every day and 60 per cent looked after the baby on their own at least a few times a week (Calderwood and others 2005, p.184). (See Featherstone 2003 for a fuller discussion on changing fatherhood in the context to changes in family forms and in relation to welfare policy in the UK, and Featherstone and others 2010 for a fuller discussion of the changing role of fatherhood in the context of child and family policy more broadly).

It may be that attitudes and beliefs more than demographic 'facts' guide our assumptions about family life to a greater degree than we might care to admit. The following exercise should help you to be clear about some of your attitudes to family life.

EXERCISE 2.3: A DAY IN THE LIFE

Consider the following descriptions of a day in the life of the Smith family, provided by Doreen and John Smith, then compare their accounts against the criteria you developed for the purposes of Exercise 2.2. You may wish to add to that list these additional measures:

- the degree of personal autonomy that each has

- the nature and extent of social networks to which each has access

- the relative social status that each might have in the eyes of others

- the degree of control over their time and labour that each has.

The Smiths have been married for 15 years. They have four children, three of whom are still living at home. John Smith is 37 and works at a local factory. Doreen is 31 and works part-time. They live on a large housing estate in a home they are buying through a housing association.

John: I get up every morning at six and take a cup of tea to Doreen. If she's been at work the previous night, I'll leave her to lie in till I leave for work at quarter to seven and I'll wake the two youngest for school. I don't usually bother with breakfast. I drive to work, which takes me about an hour through the traffic. I've been doing this for years but I still hate the journey. It's all stop, start, stop, start. I have to be at work by 8 a.m. I don't enjoy my job but I don't hate it either, like some of the lads at work do. It can be a laugh sometimes and I have got some good mates at work. We usually get out for half an hour at lunchtime and have a bit of a kick-around with a ball or read the paper. I finish at 4.30. You might not think so but it's hard work and by knocking-off time, I've had enough. Then I have to drive home, have a wash and I'm ready for something to eat. Doreen either makes me something if she's in or she leaves me something in the microwave. If she's working that's me sorted. I can't go out and I watch the box. Work, TV, bed, work. The kids more or less look after themselves until bedtime and, if Doreen's not in, I pack them off for the night. Whenever I do get the chance to get out, I do. I think that is not much to ask in return for the years I've put in at work. I need something to take my mind off the bills, the job, the journey. My marriage is like everybody else's, more habit than anything, but I have done my best for them and I won't let them down.

Doreen: If it needs doing in our house, I have to do it. John's out all day and would be every evening if he could be. I do get a cup of tea in the mornings but I've yet to come in to a hot meal. I work three mornings a week on the tills at the local supermarket and three nights a week stacking shelves at a big chemists. I have to fit everything around my work, including the kids. They're very good but they don't get much of a look in, even at weekends. I'm not interested in going out in the evenings. I'm usually too tired to care! I work because we need the money. Every penny I earn is spent before I get it. I'm not interested in what goes for entertainment around here – clubs, pubs, bingo – plus the fact that I haven't really got anyone I could go out with. I don't know many of the people on the estate. The housework doesn't do itself in this house and I don't think I could tell you what 'free time' means. I like to listen to the radio when I'm ironing. I worry about the kids and what they'll do for a living when the time comes. As for me, I have no choice but to carry on carrying on. I do sometimes think of just walking away from it all and, when the kids have gone, I might. If there was ever any love in our marriage, it's gone now. I need more than this.

POINTS TO CONSIDER

1. On the information that you have before you, who do you think derives most benefit from family life, John or Doreen?

2. How fairly do you think the household chores are distributed between John and Doreen?

3. Who contributes most to the 'maintenance work' that keeps this family going?

4. Would you regard this as a 'successful' family? Why/not?

5. With which aspects of John and Doreen's attitudes and behaviours would you most like to take issue? Why?

6. Do you think this family offers an appropriate environment for bringing up children? Why/not?

ALL IN THE FAMILY?

The research literature on how families 'work' for adults, especially in their parenting roles, is fairly extensive (see Featherstone and others 2010). It is almost as extensive as the lifestyle books, TV programmes and magazine articles on how to improve your family life that appear to be so popular these days; although neither are as extensive as the polemical accounts in newspapers and on the web that claim to know what families are *supposed* to be like and how they *should* work. There are far fewer accounts of family life provided by children and young people, other than in fiction. There is a substantial body of evidence on how children's needs and/or rights might best be met through the experience of family life and we will consider later how, for some children, social workers have to play a significant role in helping young people manage transitions both within and between families (see Unit 8). However, understanding the subtleties and complexities of family life, from a child's point of view, is fundamental to your task as social workers. With this in mind, the following Study Text, based on research undertaken by one of us, sets out to describe how ordinary families (not those known to social workers or who have been identified as facing particular problems) go about the everyday business of managing family life.

The original study was designed 'to investigate, with children, how they negotiate their involvement in family functioning, rule making and day-to-day decision making' (Butler, Robinson and Scanlan 2005) and it took its lead from a line of sociological investigation into what has been called the 'democratisation of the private sphere' (Giddens 1992, p.184) whereby intimate relationships (including family relationships) may be changing from being essentially hierarchical in nature to becoming more egalitarian in nature. The Study Text briefly summarizes that part of the research project based on lengthy interviews with 48 young people aged 8 to 11, drawn from 4 schools in Wales and the West Country. As well as reminding you of the importance of children and young people as significant authors of their own biographies (see Unit 1), demonstrating how complex family life really is, the Study Text will also prepare you for reflecting on the nature of parenting, which is the subject of the next Unit.

i STUDY TEXT 2.2: CHILDREN AND DECISION MAKING

Most families do not take decisions ('one off' choices over how something should be done) or make rules ('standing decisions' or general principles about how family business is managed) through formal means such as 'family meetings'. Instead, decision-making is altogether more subtle, complex and dynamic.

Complexity is a key concept here; it refers to the way that families operate like other complex systems, where 'we must understand not only the behaviour of the parts but how they act together to form the behaviour of the whole' (Bar-Yam 2003, p.1). This means understanding that families make decisions on the basis of the shared stock of common knowledge that grows up over time about 'the way we do things'. Families produce micro-cultures of their own that might be very well understood by family members but very difficult to describe to anyone else.

Generally speaking, even in respect of children aged 8–11, these subtle, interactive and complex processes tended towards the participatory (or democratic) but parents are usually regarded as having ultimate authority. Children can however be a decisive influence, even in major family decisions, including where to go on holiday or even where to live:

L: One night when I came home crying my mother said to my father, 'We have to move house'. And they involved me and my sister and us two said, 'Yes'.

Int.:   Did your mum and dad ask you where you'd like to move to?

L: Yea, well they said, 'Do you wanna move from here because we know you haven't got many friends?' And we both said yes. And then they asked us if we'd like to move over to Llanderyn and we both said yes and we moved then.

Int.:   How did mum and dad decide the house that they were going to buy?

L: Well what happened was we drove around after school all the streets looking to see if there were any houses up for sale. Then we went to number 71 'cos they were moving, and we liked that house. And we all said that we liked it and then we bought it off them and then we moved in.

Int.:   What do you think would have happened if you and your sister [aged 7] had said no, that you didn't really like the house and your mum and dad had really liked it?

L: They would have went [sic] and had another look for other houses.

(Lee, aged 10)

Where there was no consensus, parents usually had the final say. Children tended to trust their parents to make 'good' decisions, provided that the decision reached was one that was based on their parents' greater competence, knowledge and experience and not simply predicated on their status as parents. Authority had to be rational to be accepted and decisions based on 'because I say so' were not generally regarded as good decisions by children.

In fact, and not surprisingly in the light of how child care tasks still seem to be ordered in families (see above), mothers were usually regarded as the ultimate and final source of domestic authority, especially where the decision involved the children only or the 'at home' life of the family. When it came to matters that involved the social/public life of the family or where he was directly involved, authority usually shifted towards the father.

Where negotiation with parents is required over decisions that the child is not happy to accept, children do not usually rely on direct methods. Decisions by parents that seemed arbitrary or based on a general view of the child's behaviour during the day rather than on the specific merits of the case, were usually 'negotiated' in a similar way to how the original decisions was made. That is to say that children would adopt strategies of being 'good' or, alternatively, strategies of 'hassling and moaning', up to a point:

M: 'Cos if I just keep asking the same question, after a while she just goes, 'Ok'.

Int.:   So you just keep on and on asking?

M: Yea. Every five minutes. Every time I remember it I just ask. But if my mum's giving me something like, oh, we're going to town to buy some new stuff, I don't really mention it 'cos I know she's gonna say, 'Right, that's it, you're not having anything'. I just ask her every… if I really want it then, like, I'll just leave it and I tidy up stuff and after a while she says, 'Alright, then'.

Int.:   When you say you tidy up stuff you mean you try to be good, you try to be helpful?

M: Yea.

Int.:   What difference do you think that makes?

M: I'm being good but I know that if I keep doing it only when I want something, then I should do it all the time anyway.

(Mandy, aged 10)

The point here is that such subtle forms of negotiation rely on an intimate knowledge of the adults involved and their likely reactions.

Where children are prepared to go furthest in risking confrontation with their parents, something they usually try to avoid, is in relation to 'self-actualization' or 'doing your own thing', especially in relation to appearance, friends and social activities:

Int.:   What happens if mum wants you to have something you don't like?

J: I just say 'No, I don't wanna wear it' and I won't wear it. Yea, because it's like my body that I'm covering, and I should feel comfortable in the clothes I wear, and it should be my decision.

(Jenny, aged 11)

Hence, it is where children and young people are beginning to express themselves and their own sense of identity that they seek the highest degree of participation in the business of the family. Nowhere was this more apparent than in relation to bedrooms and having 'your own space' within the family:

For ten-year-old Mandy, the eldest of four sisters, her bedroom was the place where she could make the rules:

M: Yea, but if it's a bit messy, my mum always tidies my bedroom up for me. I don't mind. But I like to tidy it myself sometimes 'cos I have some stuff that I don't want her looking at and stuff, so I like tidying it myself.

Int.:   Is it important that you've got your own space?

M: Yea, space.

Int.:   Why is that important?

M: I dunno. I just have stuff I don't wanna tell them sometimes.

Int.:   Do you make rules about things that they're not allowed to do?

M: Yea. But my dad always, like, teases me and comes in and has a look anyway. And I push him out the way 'cos I wanna keep it to myself.

Int.:   What are the rules you have for your parents?

M: They're not allowed in. I'm having a lock on my bedroom soon 'cos my mother keeps saying to my dad I can have a lock if he keeps coming in.

Int.: Does your mum stay out?

M: Yea.

Int.: What's the rule?

M: They knock on my door usually.

Int.: Then they have to ask if they can come in?

M: Yea. Or sometimes I say, 'Alright, come in in a minute' and put away what I want or something.

Int.: And is it important that you can make your own rules about that?

M: Yea, because it's my bedroom and it's my stuff, ain't it?

Int.: Do they listen to your decisions?

M: My mum does but I don't think my dad always listens.

Int.: And what do you think about that?

M: I don't like it because it's my stuff and sometimes he teases me a lot. He keeps laughing and calling me stuff, like. He's only joking, but sometimes I don't like him seeing stuff.

Children see themselves developing more competence to make more autonomous decisions as they grow up:

Int.: Do you think things will change in terms of how things are decided and how independent you are over the next three years or so?

O: Yea.

Int.: Is it changing already?

O: Kind of yes. I talk more with them and I think they understand a bit more.

Int.: Do you think they listen to you more?

O: Yes.

Int.: Why?

O: Because you're older and people kind of listen to you more. I don't know why really because they should all listen.

Int.:   You don't think it should necessarily be because of your age?

O: No, if you're too young, like five or six, it would be harder for them to understand, but I think they should still talk about it. Every person is equal really, different ages, but they should try and talk when they're five or six but it would be hard for them sometimes. They should talk a bit and ask loads and loads of questions and if they don't understand they should ask. They should ask questions because that makes you know more, but if they had loads and loads of questions that wouldn't be so good.

(Oliver, aged 11)

For both parents and children, the precedent set by older brothers and sisters was important in determining what was the right time for children to be able to decide what. Consistency of approach within the family was much more important to children than comparisons with children in other families.

A recurring concern for children in our study was that decisions in families should be 'fair'. It was in the language of 'fairness' that children expressed sophisticated moral judgements on the quality of specific decisions and family rules and it was using the language of fairness that children most clearly articulated their preference for participatory decision making.

Laura, aged 11, expressed the view shared by a number of children that being asked one's views was imperative even if it had no bearing on the outcome of a decision – in this case about where her family went on holiday:

Int.:   Would you like to be asked where you'd like to go on holiday?

L: Yea, because, umm, I like going on holiday wherever, but I would like to have a say where I would like to go, even though we won't go there. I'd like to actually say 'Well, I'd like to go to Tenerife' or 'I'd like to go to Majorca'. And even if we don't go, I don't mind then, but I would like to say.

Int.:   What's more important, that you're asked or that you get your own way?

L: I'd like to be asked for my views.

It should be noted that as far as children were concerned, fairness has much more to do with being treated equitably than being treated identically, especially in relation to older or younger brothers and sisters and that fairness is a function of the *process* of decision making, not the *outcome*. It should be recognized that 'fairness' is one of the few moral levers in the hands of children, given the power differentials that are acknowledged to operate in most families and fairness is therefore definitely not a trivial concept as far as children are concerned. While accepting the limits to fairness (regarding some matters as wholly private between their parents, for example), most children regarded this as a defining characteristic of the way in which their family went about its daily life. Conflict was much more likely where parents acted unfairly (i.e. did not act in a participatory way) or failed to see the importance of fairness to the child.

If you as children and adults (and in some cases as parents) think for a moment of the complexity, interdependence, tacit knowledge, shared history, subtle forms of negotiation precedent and tradition that operate in your own family, you will begin to understand just how difficult it can be to understand the interior lives of other families.

As social workers, there are other implications arising from this Study Text that you will need to consider. In particular it should serve as a reminder that you must make determined effort to

- understand and respect the complexity of family processes, family histories and the particular ways that families have of going about their everyday business

- understand and respect the diversity of family micro-cultures and to resist the impetus to categorize or to abstract behaviours and relationships from their context

- respect the authority of parents, the confidence that many children have in their parents and the capacity of children to engage meaningfully and purposefully in determining the conduct of family life

- respect children's inclination towards participatory forms of engagement in family life and be sensitive to children who are in the process of developing their capacity for autonomy and independence

- respect and respond to children's claims to fairness and equitable treatment.

CONCLUSION

Both as an idea and as a particular set of personal and social relationships, the family is a major organizing principle in our lives. But, just as much as our lives are infinite variations on a single theme, so too are our ideas and experiences of the 'family'. The family is all of the things that this Unit has described and much more besides. In this richness and variety lies the family's capacity to respond and adapt to the changing social context in which it continues to evolve. The death of the family has been much exaggerated. Because of its richness, variety and adaptability, the family satisfies many individual and societal needs. The only thing that the family is not is a fixed set of expectations and common experiences. It isn't even a demographic fact! As a social worker you will encounter the family in all its many, varied and complex forms. You should celebrate its diversity rather than condemn its deviations from what you may have experienced, were expecting or might prefer to find.

 **NOTES AND SELF-ASSESSMENT**

1. Where do you set the limits on whom you count as 'family'?

2. Do you think that others might define your family differently? Who and why?

3. Are your relationships with members of your family fundamentally different to your relationships with other people?

4. Is your family a 'typical' family? Why/not?

5. What does the phrase 'to start a family' mean to you? Have you or do you intend to do so? Why/not?

6. What does the phrase 'family values' mean to you?

RECOMMENDED READING

Butler, I., Robinson, M. and Scanlan, L. (2005) *Children and Decision Making.* London: National Children's Bureau for the Joseph Rowntree Foundation.

Calderwood, L., Kiernan, K., Joshi, H., Smith, K. and Ward, K. (2005) 'Parenthood and parenting'. In S. Dex and H. Joshi (eds) *Children of the 21st Century: From Birth to Nine Months.* Bristol: The Policy Press.

TRAINER'S NOTES

Exercise 2.1: Family Fortunes

In a group setting, the questions can be put in the form of a quiz, following the pattern of any one of a number of TV game shows. Plotting individual answers on a chalkboard or flip chart can provide a graphic account of the range of answers that will be provided. Reviewing the results in this way (as though they were obtained by some kind of survey) is useful in encouraging a debate on the sources of people's (mis)perceptions without participants having to defend their own position or particular guesstimate. All of the answers are in the Study Text so we will not reproduce them here!

Exercise 2.2: Is this a Family?

A larger group can be broken down into smaller groups and answers compared in the usual way. A much more challenging (but safe) discussion can be engendered by having pairs take the position of the various putative families and argue their case with the larger group for their being accorded 'family' status. Some 'families' have an 'easier' case to argue so the larger group may need to be encouraged to range more widely in their reasons for denying such status; for example, by considering communal forms of child care, such as kibbutzim, as more appropriate to true family life. At the end of the 'debate' the whole group should consider what difference it would make to the 'families' concerned whether they were accorded family status or not. Practical consequences, such as entitlement to state support, should be considered as well as more personal considerations, such as one's sense of identity and the degree of social in/exclusion that follows from recognition as a family.

Exercise 2.3: A Day in the Life

A similar approach to that used in Exercise 2.2 can be adopted here with group members 'taking sides' in a debate. However, it is important that the group should focus on the inter-relatedness of the conditions that impinge upon both John and Doreen and how adjustments in one area imply consequences in others.

UNIT 3

Parenting

OBJECTIVES

In this Unit you will:

- Explore the nature of parenting and examine the core skills and tasks of parenting.

- Explore what is understood by the term 'good enough parenting'.

- Develop an understanding of parenting ability, parenting styles and parental capacity.

📖 COURSE TEXT: PARENTING

In Unit 1, we explored the needs and rights of children and concluded that children both have needs to be met *and* have rights to be respected. They certainly have a need and a right to have someone around to look after them – someone to care for them during the period when they are unable to care entirely for themselves. In this Unit we will focus on parenting and develop our understanding of what is involved in the everyday business of parenting. We will explore what is meant by 'good enough parenting', consider a variety of parenting styles and look briefly at parenting in the context of the additional challenges that can be associated with parental drug and alcohol abuse, mental health problems and domestic violence.

Just whom we are referring to when we talk about 'parents' is not necessarily obvious these days. At one time, the term might have been reserved for biological parents or, at a push, adoptive parents. Now, we will include in the same breath step-parents, grandparents, step-grandparents, green parents, gay and lesbian parents, yummy mummies and slummy mummies! What parents are busy doing seems to be expanding too. The topics on 'Mumsnet' (a hugely popular and influential on-line 'knowledge and know-how' sharing website in the UK) range from advice on breastfeeding, recipes, political news, the best nappies, living with teenagers, internet safety, travel, finance, product news and choosing a name.

The following Study Text illustrates how elusive any fixed sense of what we mean by parenting can be, and begins with a consideration of what motivates people to become parents in the first place.

i STUDY TEXT 3.1: DEFINING PARENTING

It is not always clear what it is that motivates people to become parents. You may wish to speculate on why your parents had you. The sort of reasons which are usually advanced include:

- personal fulfilment
- to please a partner or a parent
- for immortality
- failed contraception
- to secure housing
- to complete a family
- to have someone to love you
- to have someone to love.

It is important to realize that parenting can be begun for largely selfish reasons but, even if people choose to have children with the noblest of intentions, parenting is something in which parents also have a stake. Parenting is not something 'given' to children disinterestedly. The frustration of parental expectation can, in itself, sometimes be the cause of breakdown in adult relationships. Walker and others (2010) in their research on the relationship support needs of couples, found that in couples with children, significant proportions cited tensions in their relationships that were directly related to the transition to parenthood. The kinds of tensions included:

- when and if to start a family or have more children
- unexpected and difficult pregnancies
- miscarriages and postnatal depression
- changing roles and responsibilities

- coping with child care

- financial pressures resulting from having children

- caring for children with special needs

- resentment about the changes in routine that disrupted the couple relationship and the time spent caring for a new baby

- juggling work and child care.

Clearly, adults have a variety of personal investments and challenges to meet in their roles as parents and as partners in their couple relationships. We make this point to remind ourselves that parenting needs to be understood more broadly than as a simple set of responses to the needs and rights of the child.

We should note however that parents in the UK today demonstrate a remarkable commitment to their children in terms of the sacrifices that they are prepared to make. According to the National Survey of Parents and Children (Gilby and others 2008, p.16), 61 per cent of parents agreed (18% strongly) that once you have children your own needs should take a lower priority. However, there was also an acknowledgement that there is a limit to how much a parent can do for their children (59% agreeing, 8% strongly).

Parenting would appear to be a negotiated process; and not just between parents and their children. We have seen how childhood can be socially constructed (Unit 1) and it is useful to consider parenting in a similar way and as equally problematic. What passes for appropriate parenting varies over time, and according to social structure, just as fascinatingly as does childhood. Before the Industrial Revolution in Britain, for example, parenting was more evenly shared among the wider family, along with much economic activity. Later, when paid labour was organized outside the home, women increasingly became the primary caregivers (see Course Text: 'Family Interests' in Unit 2).

A good illustration of how ideas about parenting can change even over a relatively short time can be found in a comparison of the advice given in parent manuals and baby-care books. In 1946, for example, mothers were advised that:

Babies and children are all the better for a little 'wholesome neglect'. From the beginning an infant should be trained to spend most of his time lying alone... Do not point things out to him. (Frankenburg 1946, p.171)

Little more than a generation later, parents were instructed:

After love the next most important thing that you can give your child is stimulation. A small child is like a sponge soaking up practically every new idea and experience he or she comes in contact with. So, to be good parents, start introducing your child to the outside world. (Stoppard 1983, p.12)

The basis on which parenting advice has been offered has clearly seen some sharp paradigm shifts, reflecting changes in both scientific understanding and broader socio-cultural changes, not least those in relation to the place of women in society. To take just one more example, attitudes and responses to postnatal depression have altered from a position where it was effectively ignored to being 'medicalized' in the 1940s and 50s. It was later 'socialized' (see Brown and Harris 1978) when poverty and social exclusion were recognized as key factors and subsequently 'personalized' as relational and interactional effects were better understood.

It remains very tempting to forget the socially constructed nature of parenting and understand it only in the context of our own situated experience and our personal construction of family life. However, there is a danger in judging parents according to only one, often very restricted, standard or set of experiences. As with childhood, the nature of parenting varies across cultures, as well as over time. Indeed, Rashid (1996, p.75) has argued for a degree of 'cultural humility' when it comes to thinking about parenting. This is not to argue for a crude cultural relativism, such that all forms of parenting are equally acceptable. In Quinton's (1994) review of 'cultural and community influences' on development, while he makes the case that different developmental outcomes or features need to be located in their appropriate cultural context if their meaning is to be fully understood, he goes on to note that:

> it seems clear that many features of parent–child relationships have similar outcomes in widely different cultural settings and that within-culture variation on these features can be as great, if not greater, than cross cultural variations. (p.178)

Evidence of these cultural differences is to be found in the small things of family life. The *National Survey of Parents and Children* (BRMB and others 2008, p.15), for example, found that compared to parents with other faiths and those not associated with any faith, Muslim parents in the UK placed particular emphasis on family occasions (mealtimes, family time and days out). This focus did not diminish to the same degree as the children got older as it does in other faith and non-faith communities. By the same token, we might note that Muslim (and Black parents) were twice as likely as parents in general to worry about what they will do when their children leave home, further demonstrating possibly that some parents place a much stronger emphasis on shared family life than others (*ibid.*, p.40).

We will look in more detail in Study Text 3.3 at parenting in the face of particular challenges (such as domestic violence or parental substance misuse) but we should note at this point that parenting for some people is just so much harder than it is for others and consequently undertaken with varying degrees of reward and frustration. According to the *Parental Opinion Survey 2009* (TNS-BMRB 2009, p.17), nearly all parents (99%) agreed that they found being a parent 'rewarding' most or some of the time. However, non-resident parents were least likely to find parenting rewarding most of the time (73%). Other parents who were less likely to find parenting rewarding most of the time included parents on lower incomes and parents of children with special educational needs. Families with older children (18–19), families with children with special educational needs and larger families were those where parents expressed higher degrees of frustration (TNS-BMRB 2009, p.18).

One useful way of thinking of parenting that does not imply a particular household structure, class or cultural origin but which still provides for the care of children is to deconstruct it into its constituent parts and imagine it as a job like any other. That is the function of the next exercise.

EXERCISE 3.1: THE JOB OF PARENTING

TASKS

1. Using Figure 3.1, devise a job description for a parent.

2. Design a simple advertisement for the job.

3. Design a selection process so that the right person gets the job.

POINTS TO CONSIDER

1. Is this a 'post' that is best job-shared? If so, how?

2. What working environment would best suit this job?

3. What prospects of career development are attached to this post?

4. What training is most appropriate for this job?

5. Are the rewards commensurate with the duties?

6. Is it a job that you would ever consider taking on? Why/not?

JOB DESCRIPTION and PERSON SPECIFICATION
Post: Parent
Hours: ....p.w.   Salary: £ ....p.a.   Annual leave entitlement:
Responsible to:
Responsible for:
Main areas of activity:
Qualifications required:
Previous experience required:
Personal qualities required:

Figure 3.1 Parenting job description

📖 COURSE TEXT: PARENTING SKILLS

While it might be amusing to think of parenting in the way that you might think of paid employment, the comparison is an instructive one. In terms of the commitment of time and effort, parenting would stand comparison with almost any job, of course. But thinking of it in this way might also have prompted you to consider how, like many other jobs performed in the home, it is undervalued, exhausting and highly skilled. Just how skilled a role it is, we shall explore in the following exercise.

EXERCISE 3.2: CORE SKILLS OF PARENTING

TASKS

1. Make a list of skills needed to parent a child of 0–10 years.

2. Make a list of skills needed to parent a child of 10–18 years.

3. Compare both lists and underline similarities and note the differences.

4. Identify the core skills of parenting.

Make sure that you concentrate on skills, not on qualities – that is, patience may be needed, but it is a quality. The skill lies in how a parent actually copes with the behaviour of the child that requires patience; for example, by the use of non-verbal skills, listening skills, or the ability to switch off!

POINTS TO CONSIDER

How well does your list of parenting skills fit your map of children's needs, constructed in Exercise 1.2?

1. Which parenting skills (if any) come 'naturally'?

2. If not by nature, where or how do you think people acquire the appropriate skills for parenting?

3. Is it likely that any one individual or couple will possess *all* of the skills that you have identified as being appropriate to the tasks of parenting?

4. Is it possible to teach particular parenting skills?

5. If it were, what skills would be required by the person providing the training?

COURSE TEXT: GOOD ENOUGH PARENTING

We have hinted already that parenting cannot be fully understood simply as a set of motivations and particular skills. We have indicated that there are other, contextual factors to be taken into account, such as cultural, economic and community influences. Seeing parenting as a set of narrowly defined skills or behaviours also fails to recognize how little we know from research about how to relate particular aspects of parenting to particular outcomes or to weigh parenting 'strengths' against parenting 'weaknesses'. Moreover, there are some dimensions of parenting, such as emotional warmth, that are more difficult to describe or measure in the way that one might measure or describe specific manual skills (such as changing a nappy or preparing a meal). Parenting is certainly a dynamic and an interactive process and will frequently be mediated by the child him- or herself. Parenting will also vary according to much more mundane considerations such as the number of children in the family and a child's position in his or her family. (Un)fortunately, there are no simple check-lists, skills inventories, or sets of core competencies available by which you can come fully to understand parenting.

Yet, examining parenting and making judgements on its adequacy in relation to particular children is a core social work activity. It is the second of the critical dimensions of the *Framework for the Assessment of Children in Need and their Families* (Department of Health and others 2000) that we introduced to you in Unit 1. The *Framework* describes six key dimensions against which parenting might be assessed (see Figure 3.2).

Basic Care

Providing for the child's physical needs, and appropriate medical and dental care. Includes provision of food, liquid, warmth, shelter, clean and appropriate clothing and adequate personal hygiene.

Ensuring Safety

Ensuring the child is adequately protected from harm or danger. Includes protection from significant harm or danger, and from contact with unsafe adults/other children and from self-harm. Recognition of hazards and danger both in the home and elsewhere.

Emotional Warmth

Ensuring the child's emotional needs are met and giving the child a sense of being specially valued. Includes ensuring the child's requirements for secure, stable and affectionate relationships with significant adults, with appropriate sensitivity and responsiveness to the child's needs. Appropriate physical contact, comfort and cuddling sufficient to demonstrate warm regard, praise and encouragement.

Stimulation

Promoting child's learning and intellectual development through encouragement and cognitive stimulation and promoting social opportunities. Includes facilitating the child's cognitive development and potential through interaction, communication, talking and responding to the child's language and questions, encouraging and joining the child's play, and promoting educational opportunities. Enabling the child to experience success and ensuring school attendance or equivalent opportunity. Facilitating child to meet challenges of life.

Guidance and Boundaries

Enabling the child to regulate his or her own emotions and behaviour. The key parental tasks are demonstrating and modelling appropriate behaviour and control of emotions and interactions with others; and guidance, which involves setting boundaries, so that the child is able to develop an internal model of moral values and conscience, and social behaviour appropriate for the society within which he or she will grow up. The aim is to enable the child to grow into an autonomous adult, holding his or her own values, and able to demonstrate appropriate behaviour with others rather than having to be dependent on rules outside him- or herself. This includes not over-protecting children from exploratory and learning experiences. Includes social problem solving, anger management, consideration for others and effective discipline and shaping of behaviour.

Stability

Providing a sufficiently stable family environment to enable the above dimensions of parenting to operate reasonably consistently. Includes responding in a similar manner to the same behaviours, providing consistency of emotional warmth over time. In addition, ensuring children keep in contact with important family members and others.

Figure 3.2 Dimensions of parenting capacity.
Source: Department of Health and others (2000), p.21 (Crown Copyright).

The empirical support for this particular 'map' of parenting is set out by Jones (2001) and builds on research which suggests that conflict between parents, inadequate parental monitoring and lack of positive parental involvement are very likely to be associated with behavioural and/or emotional problems in children.

i STUDY TEXT 3.2: GOOD ENOUGH PARENTING

According to many contemporary definitions of parenting, including that on which the *Framework for the Assessment of Children in Need and their Families* (Department of Health and others 2000) is based, parents not only provide physical care but they show affection, stimulate, discipline and reward their children. They also socialize them and give them room to become independent. The hours are long and the pay can be very poor indeed. And so far we have only considered the more generic components of parenting. Some parents may need to take into account other considerations; a Black parent, for instance, will need to teach his or her child to counteract racism (Madge 2001) or the parent of a child with disabilities may need to deal with daily discrimination and denial of opportunities (Beresford 1994; Meyer 1995). Some parents with disabilities themselves or with other support needs will be taking care of their children but will also have to manage their own feelings about their child caring for them in turn (Dearden and Becker 2004).

Thus while parenting might be 'mapped' in this way, we must recognize also that certain structural conditions may prevent a parent from developing, maintaining or exercising his or her parenting capacity. Poor housing, unemployment and poverty add to the stress of child rearing and may limit a person's ability to parent adequately. Such considerations form the third set of factors included in the *Framework for the Assessment of Children in Need and their Families* (Department of Health and others 2000). (See Figure 3.3.)

Family History and Functioning

A child's inheritance includes both genetic and psychosocial factors. Family functioning is influenced by who is living in the household and how they are related to the child; significant changes in family/household composition; history of childhood experiences of parents; chronology of significant life events and their meaning to family members; nature of family functioning, including sibling relationships, and its impact on the child; parental strengths and difficulties, including those of an absent parent; the relationship between separated parents.

Wider Family

Who are considered to be members of the wider family by the child and the parents? This includes related and non-related persons and absent wider family. What is their role and importance to the child and parents and in precisely what way?

Housing

Does the accommodation have basic amenities and facilities appropriate to the age and development of the child and other resident members? This includes the interior and exterior of the accommodation and immediate surroundings. Basic amenities include water, heating, sanitation, cooking facilities, sleeping arrangements and cleanliness, hygiene and safety and their impact on the child's upbringing.

Employment

Who is working in the household, what is their pattern of work and are there any changes? What impact does this have on the child? How is work or absence of work viewed by family members? How does it affect their relationship with the child? Includes children's experience of work and its impact on them.

Income

Income available over a sustained period of time. Sufficiency of income to meet the family's needs. The way resources available to the family are used. Are there financial difficulties which affect the child?

Family's Social Integration

Exploration of the wider context of the local neighbourhood and community and its impact on the child and parents. Includes the degree of the family's integration or isolation, their peer groups, friendship and social networks and the importance attached to them.

Community Resources

Describes all facilities and services in a neighbourhood, including universal services of primary health care, day care and schools. Includes availability, accessibility and standard of resources and impact on the family.

Figure 3.3 Family and environmental factors.
Source: Department of Health and others (2000), p.23 (Crown Copyright).

We will consider how all of the various components of the *Framework* knit together in Unit 4. For our present purposes, it is important simply to note how most parents, at some time, will be too worried about making the money stretch to the end of the week to remember to praise and encourage their children, or will be too tired, too busy or preoccupied with their own needs, perhaps dealing with mental health difficulties or relationship problems. There are some obvious and some unexpected delights in being a parent but it can be a difficult job, not least because it seems to demand so much commitment and emotional investment. It should not be surprising that parenting cannot always be maintained at the highest level or that it sometimes breaks down altogether. So, if perfect parenting is unachievable, what might constitute 'good enough' parenting?

D.W. Winnicott coined the phrase 'good enough parenting' in his 1965 book, *The Maturational Process and the Facilitative Environment* and his construct of 'good enough parenting' has been widely adapted and used. Winnicott represented 'good enough' parenting as where parents provide what he described as a 'facilitating environment' that permitted each child to have her or his needs met and potential developed. It meant parents adapting their behaviour and lifestyle as far as possible for the child's well-being rather than their own, and for parents to put their child's needs first in all major family plans and decisions (see reference to Gilby and others 2008, above). Although this account of good enough parenting might be considered to represent a counsel of perfection, the term clearly implies that there is no such thing as simple, undiluted good parenting. It implies that no parent can meet her or his child's needs all of the time and that it will be important to find a balance between parents' own needs, their circumstances and those of their children.

'Good enough' parenting could also suggest that parenting is situational, that several different forms of parenting can be good and that there is no single universal model across class and cultures. Jones (2001, p.265) has suggested that the idea of 'parenting' is not especially helpful unless 'it is set within a broader ecology of the child's world'. Thus, our understanding of parenting must extend to include not just the specific motivations, skills and behaviours of parents towards their children; it must include also a consideration of the 'influences of family relationships on parenting, extended family networks and the influence of neighbourhoods on the capacity of parents to care for their children' (Jones 2001, p.265) as well as broader cultural influences.

However when Winnicott talked about 'good enough' parenting he was also recognizing the complex emotions that are a natural part of parenting. He listed a range of emotions a 'good enough' mother may feel in relation to her child. He included the more positive emotions of joy and warmth but he also made specific mention of feelings of exhaustion, feeling drained, criticized and controlled. He argued that some ambivalence was inevitably attached to the parenting role, that such feelings are quite normal and to be expected in all parents at one time or another. The 'good enough' parents would manage or contain these ambivalent feelings rather than either blame or withdraw from their child.

Winnicott certainly contemplated the making of mistakes in parenting! In fact it is these mistakes or failing to be a perfect parent that were at the heart of his idea of 'good enough parenting'. He suggested that 'perfect' mothers who were completely tuned into their babies' every need and who never made a mistake, were also preventing their babies from developing, or certainly inhibiting their development. The 'good enough mother' leaves a gap between the baby's demands and her response. By increasing this gap slightly over time she is preparing and supporting her baby to adapt to external realities, and to develop trust that the parent–child relationship will be repaired after a break, while also developing resilience and independence on the part of the child.

Clearly, however, the term 'good enough' also implies that the parenting still needs to be good. If a child is abused or rejected, the parenting is clearly not 'good enough'. So how do you, as social workers, come to recognize and be able to articulate where your threshold of tolerance of 'good enough' parenting stands? In part, your judgement will arise from your understanding of the needs and rights of children and from a realistic assessment of what is involved in parenting. Part of your judgement, however, will be based on your own untested assumptions, attitudes and values. The next exercise is intended to provide you with the opportunity of examining the foundations of your own judgements of 'good enough' parenting.

EXERCISE 3.3: GOOD ENOUGH PARENTING

TASKS

For each of the following five scenarios, rank the parenting on a scale from 1 to 5 (1 = good enough; 5 = totally unacceptable).

Identify very clearly on what basis you have reached your decision.

1. Jim and Sue have three children under five. They have just won first prize in the national lottery and decide to put their three children up for adoption, buy a boat and sail around the world. It is something that they both dreamed of doing before they had children. All three children are adopted by a childless couple who could never have had their own children.

Good enough		*1*	*2*	*3*	*4*	*5*	*Totally unacceptable*

2. Liz is a single parent living in a damp twelfth-storey flat. She has two children: Sarah, aged nine and Tom, aged five. Tom is still in nappies; even Sarah still wets the bed at night. She is rarely in school or seen out playing. Liz says that she needs to keep Sarah at home to help look after Tom and to mind the flat, especially if Liz has to go out to the shops, as she is scared that the flat would be broken into again if left unoccupied. Sarah is Liz's only company, according to Liz. She has suffered several attacks on the house.

Good enough		1	2	3	4	5		Totally unacceptable

3. Mary had Jason, now aged two, when she was 17 years old. Alan, Jason's father, is 22 and lives with Mary and Jason. Mary says that Alan is too strict with Jason and won't let her pick him up if he cries at night or even play with him when Alan is around. Mary says that this is partly Jason's own fault as he is very demanding and does wear her out. 'He has never been a good baby, like other people's.' She has been to the doctor to get something to make Jason sleep at night. 'Things were Ok between Alan and me before Jason was born.'

Good enough		1	2	3	4	5		Totally unacceptable

4. Pete and Steph are solicitors with busy, high profile practices. Pete is often abroad for long periods. Steph works long hours. Sophie, the youngest child, aged four, is collected daily from play school and spends the afternoon at her child minder's house. In the evenings, Mrs Evans, a qualified nanny, puts Sophie to bed and reads her a story. Pete and Steph's other two children are at boarding school. During the holidays Pete and Steph take the children on exotic holidays. At the weekend, the children, if at home, go to the cottage that the family have in Norfolk, usually with Mrs Evans.

Good enough		1	2	3	4	5		Totally unacceptable

5. Sian has been in prison three times for shoplifting since the birth of her children. Bill, her husband, takes off for long periods 'working away'. The three children of her marriage, aged three, five and seven, have all been fostered on several occasions, separately and together. Bill's idea of helping at home is to smack the children if they are naughty. He says this is a hard world and the children have got to learn to stand on their own two feet and the sooner the better. Sian refuses to do all the cooking and washing. 'Why should I?' she says, 'Bill doesn't do anything'. There are lots of arguments between Sian and Bill. The children often have to fend for themselves.

Good enough		1	2	3	4	5		Totally unacceptable

If you find it difficult to come to a decision, you may wish to examine each scenario more closely by means of the 'Parenting profile' grid (see Figure 3.4) and consider how each example of parenting meets the different needs of a child and then calculate an average score for the purposes of comparison.

Needs of child	Good enough			Totally unacceptable	
	1	2	3	4	5
Health					
Education					
Emotional and behavioural development					
Identity					
Family and social relationships					
Social presentation					
Self-care skills					

Figure 3.4 Parenting profile

POINTS TO CONSIDER

1. Do parents have to be 'good enough' in all areas or is it sufficient to be only 'good enough' in most?

2. Does being 'good enough' in one area compensate for not being 'good enough' in others?

3. How might a child's view of 'good enough' parenting differ from that of an adult?

4. Is the lack of 'permitting circumstances' sufficient to excuse not 'good enough' parenting?

5. Is your parenting or that which you received as a child 'good enough'? Why/not?

6. Is the term 'good enough' a meaningful tool for a social worker to use when coming to a decision about the care of a child?

COURSE TEXT: A BALANCING ACT?

Several of the scenarios in Exercise 3.3 reinforced the point that we have been making that a critical aspect of 'good enough' parenting is the balance struck between the needs and rights of the child and those of the parent. You probably found it fairly easy in the first scenario to recognize that the balance was far from right. In Scenario 4 the decision is a little less straightforward. If the two carers had less glamorous occupations and their economic circumstances were a little less comfortable, the balance might be said to have shifted. In Scenario 2 the situation is altogether more complicated. As well as asking you to think about 'good enough' parenting, scenarios 2, 3 and 5 also introduce the idea of parenting capacity, considered in more detail below.

The next Study Text will build on our discussion on good enough parenting by looking at parenting when the balancing act is even more difficult to achieve as parents themselves face up to particular challenges of their own that extend beyond the demands of parenting itself.

i STUDY TEXT 3.3: PARENTING CAPACITY

Before we can begin to understand more about parenting capacity, we wish first to consider the broader question of parenting style. We have already suggested that it would be impossible to produce an exact and incontrovertible categorization of something as elusive, complex, interpretive and negotiated as parenting. However, developmental psychologists, and others, as part of their study of how parenting impacts on the development of the child, have described a number of parenting taxonomies. One of the best known is that developed by Diana Baumrind in the 1960s (Baumrind 1967). Based on her observations, she identified four key dimensions of parenting:

- disciplinary strategies

- warmth and nurturance

- communication styles

- expectations of maturity and control.

Baumrind concluded that parents operate one of three different parenting styles, depending on the particular configuration of each of these key dimensions:

- *Authoritarian parenting* – 'because I say so' parenting where children are directed in their conduct and behaviour, without explanations as to why. Such parents usually have high expectations of their children but can be unresponsive to their children's particular needs.

- *Authoritative parenting* – although this is parenting with clear rules, there is much more scope for negotiation. Parents will explain and answer questions. Baumrind notes that these parents monitor and impart clear standards for their children's conduct. They are assertive, but not intrusive and restrictive. Their disciplinary methods are supportive, rather than punitive. They want their children to be assertive as well as socially responsible, and self-regulated as well as co-operative (Baumrind 1991, p.62).

- *Permissive parenting* – 'free range' parenting. Permissive parents, according to Baumrind, are more responsive than they are demanding. They are nontraditional and lenient, do not require mature behavior, allow considerable self-regulation, and avoid confrontation. (*ibid.*)

Later work by Maccoby and Martin (1983c) has added a fourth parenting style to Baumrind's original list:

- *Uninvolved parenting* – 'Whatever…' parenting where parents are uninvolved, make few demands of their children and are generally unresponsive.

Other categories of parent have been described in less scientific terms, sometimes in the popular press. One example would be 'helicopter parents'. These are parents who hover over everything that their child does and who verge on the obsessive about their child's education and sporting or cultural accomplishments. They may involve their children in endless clubs and activities, leaving the children with little or no time for self-directed play or the development of their own interests and so for the development of self-confidence and independence.

A recent, UK based survey found that parents themselves identified three 'basic philosophies' that underlay their approach to parenting (BMRB and others 2008, p.23).

- Parent is *facilitating/guiding* the young person towards adulthood. Sees themselves as consciously 'role modelling' for the young person; understands a need to build skills and to move them towards increased independence at an appropriate age.

- Parent is *shielding/safeguarding* the young person from the world. Exerts a strong level of control over their young people and sees their role as delaying the impact of the outside world on their child until they are 'old enough'.

- Parent is *provider* of basic resource for the 'continuing evolution' of the young person. For these parents, the family amounts to little more than a resource for food and shelter, either because the young person rejects a more positive connection or because the parent has limited interest in the parenting role and experience.

Although not quite describing parenting styles in the way that Baumrind does, the very different way in which parents themselves talk about their parenting does demonstrate how difficult it can be to link parenting practice to actual outcomes for children. Difficulties in establishing consistent and consensual definitions of the components of the parenting process, alongside the perennial difficulties in describing outcomes for children can make a simple association very difficult to establish. Developments in neuropsychology may prove a fruitful avenue for further exploration (see Gerhardt 2004 for example) and there are good examples of studies that do provide robust evidence of direct associations between parenting and problem behaviours in children (see for example, Aunola and Nurmi (2005) for an unexpected association between high levels of maternal affection, linked with high levels of 'psychological control' and young children experiencing problems as they progressed from kindergarten to primary school). Perhaps unsurprisingly, following Baumrind's taxonomy, the children of authoritative parents turn out to be the happiest, most capable and successful (Maccoby 1992) and those whose parents are uninvolved do least well, especially in relation to self-esteem and social competence.

What is clear though is that any abstracted construction of parenting style has to be set in the context of the lived experience of parents. Parents will often be facing their own difficulties and problems that will then impact on their capacity to provide care to and parent their children. Racism, homophobia, separation, divorce, substance misuse, domestic violence, mental health difficulties, financial problems, difficulties in relationship with one or more of their children, caring responsibility for older parents, physical illness or disability, redundancy, coping with memories of their own childhood abuse which can sometimes be triggered as their own children develop can all add significant stress to what is already a very demanding 'job'. Within the confines of just one Study Text, we cannot hope to provide an account of each of these possible additional stressors. Accordingly, we have focussed on just three in order simply to sensitize you to some of the factors that set limits on many parents' capacity to parent.

DOMESTIC VIOLENCE/ABUSE

Walby and Allen (2004) found that women who are parents are nearly twice as likely to experience domestic abuse as women without children, and that in cases of severe domestic violence the perpetrator is most likely to be male. In the first major UK study of its kind, Mullender and others (2002) demonstrated very clearly just how aware children are of the violence men perpetrate against women, the importance of listening to what children have to say about their experiences of witnessing domestic abuse, and the complexity of the feelings many need to work through in order to come to terms with it. Domestic abuse often leaves children feeling anxious and confused. Sometimes children feel they are to blame for it. Sometimes they are encouraged by abusive adults to partake in it. Sometimes they feel guilty because their mothers have endured victimization so they can continue living with their fathers. Often children are frightened, distressed, and overcome with feelings of loss with respect to relationships, property and pets that have either been destroyed by violence, or have to be abandoned when refuge is sought (Stalford, Baker and Beveridge 2003).

In many cases, however, the damage done by domestic abuse is far from irreversible; children's resilience to its harmful effects may be strengthened when they are given the time, space and support they need to make sense of it (Mullender 2004). Service provision in this area, however, is at best patchy, particularly so in the case of boys who have lived with domestic abuse (Stanley and others 2009; Worrall, Boylan and Roberts 2008). Few, if any, refuges for women allow mothers to bring boys over the age of 12 into safe accommodation with them. The under-acknowledged consequence of this is that boys whose mothers have little choice but to move into refuges have either to live with abusive fathers or stepfathers, be brought up by other relatives or older siblings, or to move into institutional care. Such arrangements can compound the effects of witnessing violence with a sense of abandonment and anger that some abusive men manipulate in order to turn children against their mothers.

MENTAL HEALTH

Generally, any mental health difficulty has the potential (which is to say that it is far from inevitable!) to impact negatively on someone's ability to make and sustain relationships, to be consistent and predictable in relationships and to provide care for others. The implications for the capacity to parent are self-evident; Brandon and others (2008) drew attention to the association between mental health problems in parents and the high level of risk of harm for children in an overview of special case reviews; Somers (2007) has identified that a higher incidence of mental health difficulties was identified in children whose parents were diagnosed with schizophrenia, and Skarsater (2006) emphasized the need for improved treatment of parental depression to reduce symptoms that impair parenting.

Usually parental mental health difficulties will vary over time and parenting capacity will also vary, partly dependent also on other variables such as support available from mental health services, family and friends. Parents with mental health problems may lack confidence in their parenting ability and be more confused about their child's needs. Hospital admissions can be disruptive and frightening for both parents and children as well as very disruptive to family life.

One of the additional complexities that social workers face in assessing parental capacity alongside mental health difficulties is that they may not be easily identified as the stigma attached to mental ill-health may lead parents to hide the reality of their problems. Sheppard and Kelly (2001), for example, examined social work interventions with mothers who were depressed and found that often the depression was unrecognized. In some cases parents may avoid seeking help for their mental health difficulties to the detriment of their own mental health needs for fear that this may lead to hospital admission and separation from their children.

SUBSTANCE MISUSE

Stanley and others (2009, p.336) make the point that 'it is not inevitable that parenting capacity will be adversely affected by having a drug or alcohol problem but it certainly makes the task of parenting more difficult'. The substance misuse itself of course causes difficulties, but Stanley and others also point to the complex range of associated social, legal and financial pressures that follow such use. Neglect has been recognized as a relatively common form of mistreatment by parents who misuse substances (see Alison 2000 and Forrester and Harwin 2008). If the relationship between the substance user and the substance itself tends to become the primary relationship in that person's life, with often increased attention being given to securing a supply of the substance in question, then the increased neglect of others, either adult partners or children may be more likely (Kroll 2004).

Kearney, Levin and Rosen (2000) estimate that overall more than one third of families referred to children and families social services teams are also dealing with mental heath difficulties and drug and alcohol problems, often they found the percentage is much higher. Corbett (2005), and Kroll and Taylor (2003) point to the secrecy, stigma and denial that characterizes such issues in families which then raises complex practice issues for social workers. They also draw clear links between risk, vulnerability, resilience and protective factors when considering parental substance misuse.

However, we would not wish to leave you with the impression that it is only in such challenging circumstances that parenting can be hard. It can be tough for anyone, at any time as the following exercise suggests.

EXERCISE 3.4: WHAT KIND OF PARENT ARE YOU/ MIGHT YOU BE?

Imagine yourself as the parent or responsible adult in each of the following scenarios and describe your likely response.

1. Your 3-year-old, 8-year-old and 13-year-old all ask you for sweets at the supermarket checkout.

2. Your 13-year-old phones you from school asking to stay at an (unknown to you) friend's house that night.

3. Your 15-year-old asks for help with their homework on Sunday night, having avoided it all weekend.

4. To which of the Baumrind/Maccoby and Martin parenting styles (described above) do your responses most closely correspond?

5. Now repeat steps 1 and 2 but this time imagine yourself to be short of money, under pressure at work and tired.

POINTS TO CONSIDER

1. Consider which of the responses you have described would best meet the 'needs and rights' of the children concerned (look back at the list that you prepared (and hopefully revised) in Exercise 1.2).

2. Which of the responses that you described are 'good enough'?

3. Which of the primary skills of parenting are most called for in each situation?

4. How confident are you that your parenting would be 'good enough' all the time?

CONCLUSION

There can be little doubt that parenting is a demanding and highly skilled occupation. We have concentrated rather more on the 'performance' aspect of the role in order to broaden your appreciation of just what is involved in the 'flesh and snot' realities of parenting. We have also extended the discussion to examine some pressures on parental capacity and how parents' own needs can sometimes impact on outcomes for their children. We hope that you will appreciate more sensitively the myriad opportunities there are for parenting to go awry. It is important to remember this if you are to recognize that

…parents are entitled to help and consideration in their own right. Just as some young people are more vulnerable than others, so are some mothers and fathers. Their parenting capacity may be limited temporarily or permanently by poverty, racism, poor housing or unemployment or by personal or marital problems, sensory or physical disability, mental illness or past life experiences. Lack of parenting skills or inability to provide adequate care should not be equated with lack of affection or irresponsibility.

(Department of Health 1990, p.8)

Parenting is a bit like juggling. It looks really easy when you see others doing it and, in fact, it's not all that hard to develop a basic level of skill. But getting the hang of it means making mistakes, picking up where you left off and persevering. Now imagine what juggling is like when someone throws you an extra ball. And then another. Then another. Parenting can seem a bit like that too.

NOTES AND SELF-ASSESSMENT

1. Is parenting a full-time occupation?

2. Does everyone have a right to be a parent if they choose?

3. What obligations do parents have towards their children and vice versa?

4. How would you assess the parenting that you give/have received and how does this experience affect the judgements you might make of others' parenting?

5. Are the criteria that you would apply in order to judge parenting in your own family the same as those that you would use for the families with which you will work?

6. How good a parent would/do you make?

RECOMMENDED READING

Ghate, D. and Hazel, N. (2002) *Parenting in Poor Environments: Stress, Support and Coping*. London: Jessica Kingsley Publishers.

Kroll, B. and Taylor, A. (2003) *Parental Substance Misuse and Child Welfare*. London: Jessica Kingsley Publishers.

👥 TRAINER'S NOTES

Exercise 3.1: The Job of Parenting

Group discussion, after comparisons of job descriptions, can focus on whether, on the basis of the advertisement, anyone present would apply for the job. This should allow a focus on the benefits as well as the disadvantages of being a parent; for example the child's first words, the first nativity play or special religious occasion. Role-playing 'interviews' for the job allows participants to review the kind of reasons that people give for wanting children and can give rise to a discussion on when people 'should' have children and on who 'should not'. A lively discussion is the surest way of encouraging participants to reflect seriously on their understanding and preconceptions about parenting.

Exercise 3.2: Core Skills of Parenting

Divide participants into two groups: one to consider the skills needed to parent a child of 0–10 and the other to parent a child of 10–18 years. Make sure both groups can see each other's 'results' and go through them quickly, underlining similarities and debating differences. Then ask both groups to identify some core skills and to consider whether these are universal for every culture, country, religion, era in history, and so on.

Exercise 3.3: Good Enough Parenting

Ask participants to work in pairs to rank the parenting on a scale of 1–5, identifying very clearly on what basis they have reached their decisions. Feed back by recording the range of scores for each scenario. This usually makes the point that the assessment of parenting, based on the same facts, will vary substantially from person to person (social worker to social worker).

You may wish to go a stage further and explore in more detail some of the reasons on which people based the scores they gave. This can be done in open discussion or by asking groups to reconcile widely varying scores and not to let them out until they agree!

Using the same five scenarios you could make changes to the parents sexuality, gender and disability to see what impact these changes have on student's perception of the same situation. For example in scenario 2 you could make Liz into Laurence for some groups and see if there is different perception in the group of 'good enough parenting' when the scenario depicts a single father. Similarly in scenario 4 you could make Pete and Steph into Pete and Steven.

Exercise 3.4: Parental Capacity

This exercise can easily be turned into an entertaining (but instructive) role-play in which participants (over)act the various responses they might make to each scenario. Those not directly involved in the performance should be asked to make a judgement of what each performance *looks* like – they too can be asked to take roles as they do this (such as an impatient person in the queue; an experienced grandparent or parent; a parent whose parenting style is *not* the one being performed, etc.). Those performing should be asked to comment on what it feels like to be a certain 'kind' of parent and to be a parent under stress and to respond to the comments of observers.

UNIT 4

Supporting

OBJECTIVES

In this Unit you will:

- Examine the statutory basis on which support services to children and families are provided.

- Explore the range of support services available to children in need.

- Consider the particular support needs of young carers.

📖 COURSE TEXT: SUPPORTING CHILDREN AND FAMILIES

Unit 3 concluded with an appreciation of the demands of parenting. Parenting is a dynamic process however and as a child grows, the skills required to parent effectively will continue to develop and adapt. Children and parents mature and their personalities, expectations and needs alter with the passage of time. There are any number of points, especially in the changing context of child-rearing practice and family formation, where relationships can come under pressure. Circumstances can be such that effective parenting is made even more exacting for some. It is hardly surprising therefore that most, if not all, parents and children need help with the business of growing up and getting on with each other at some time or other. Social work with children and families is substantially about the provision of such help.

It is important to recognize just how recently the question has arisen of how, or even if, there should be formalized and systematic services to help support families through the processes of parenting. The first half of the 20th century bore the indelible mark of deeply humiliating and publicly shaming Poor Law provision. Writing about the state of the law in 1947, S. Clement Brown (p.iii) reminds her readers how the legacy of the preceding age found a strong echo in her own time:

> Some of our laws still express the view that our duty to the homeless child ends when we have fed and clothed him and trained him in habits of soberness and industry. The duty of the local authority in respect of destitute children, beyond giving them 'relief', is still only to set [them] to work or put [them] out as apprentices.

In truth, the specific welfare of children was not much more than a minor note in the monumental social policy shifts that took place after the Second World War (see Butler and Drakeford 2003, p.56) although this period did produce the first major piece of legislation for forty years that bore on the welfare of children, the Children Act 1948.

The principle on which the Children's Departments that the Act established were to carry out their duties represented a significant break with previous legislation in that s. 12 of the Act required local authorities to carry out their responsibilities to a child 'so as to further his best interests and to afford him opportunity for the proper development of his character and abilities'. The second part of s. 12 required local authorities, in providing for children in their care, to 'make use of facilities and services available to children in the care of their parents'. It has been argued that any commitment of the 1948 Act to family preservation and to preventive work was more implied than expressed (see Butler and Drakeford 2011; James 1998) but the rise in short-term case-work that followed the implementation of the Act increasingly forced the staff of the new Children's Departments into face-to-face work with families and encouraged an interest in preventative and family support work that was to find expression in the 1963 Children and Young Persons' Act.

The 1963 Act, while primarily concerned with delinquency and the juvenile court system, began by granting local authorities specific powers to engage in preventive work (s. 1):

> It shall be the duty of every local authority to make available such advice, guidance and assistance as may promote the welfare of children by diminishing the need to receive children into care or keep them in care...

At the end of a decade which saw increasing economic pressure brought to bear on the universalism of the Welfare State, it was to be the 1969 Children and Young Persons' Act that would represent the final flowering of a family-orientated, preventative treatment ideology that had begun in the Children's Departments of the 1950s. However, the 1969 Act was never fully implemented as the political tide turned in favour of a more conservative approach to welfare provision (see Butler and Drakeford 2003; Hendrick 1994). To a degree, this was reflected in the Children Act 1975, which reflected some of the concerns that had arisen following the first major child care scandal of the post-war period, the death of Maria Colwell. Among other provisions, the Act made it easier for local authorities to assume parental rights and more difficult for parents to remove their children from the care of the local authority (see Holman 1975, 1988; Jordan 1981; Thoburn 1999). The 1970s also saw the beginnings of a decisive shift away from prevention and towards the detection of child abuse (see Butler and Drakeford 2011; Parton 1985, 1997).

By the 1980s both professionals and policy makers were becoming increasingly concerned, largely through the emergence of a body of research that called into question the quality of the care provided by local authorities, that an imbalance (Department of Health and Social Security 1985) had developed between the professional resources devoted to the 'blue light' child protection services and services aimed more at prevention and family support (see Department of Health 1995a; Tunstill and Aldgate 2000, pp.1–6). Moreover, a series of well-publicized 'scandals' relating to the deaths of children, many known to social workers, contributed to a general sense that social work services to children and families were of poor quality and limited effectiveness (see Reder, Duncan and Gray 1993 and Butler and Drakeford 2003). In describing the period from the death of Colwell through to the late 1980s, Corby (2006) notes that 'the public image of child care social work shifted from that of reasonably respected and necessary occupation to one that was seen to be of low status, staffed by incompetent practitioners who were deemed to be out of touch with the realities of life' (p.163).

The Children Act 1989, introduced in the aftermath of the Cleveland Affair (Cleveland Report 1988), sought to address this widely held concern by re-invigorating and recasting the role of local authorities in the provision of personal social services to children and families. According to Aldgate and Tunstill (1995, p.6), the 1989 Act 'represents a fusing of the concepts of prevention and family support' (see also Packman and Jordan 1991). Early guidance stressed that the Act would enable families to 'look to social services for support and assistance. If they do this they should receive a positive response which reduces any fears they may have of stigma or loss of parental responsibility' (Department of Health 1991c, para. 2.14). As such, the Act implied not only a degree of flexibility in how support services might be delivered but also a different relationship between the providers of services and their users.

Support provisions of the 1989 Act have been reinforced by the Children Act 2004, which was introduced following the Laming report (Secretary of State for Health and others 2003) of the inquiry into the death of Victoria Climbié in 2000. The Act introduced some structural changes into the delivery of social services to support children and their families, such as the introduction of Children's Trusts

(England only) to provide integrated services and Local Safeguarding Children Boards to provide greater accountability (see Study Text 9.2).

Even from this very brief review of the recent political and administrative history of support services to families, you will see that this is an area in which marked changes in the direction of policy are not infrequent. Notwithstanding this general observation, it could reasonably be argued that the 1989 Children Act has provided a remarkably stable statutory basis (see Unit 10) for the delivery of services to children and families in England and Wales. However, the socio-political context and consequent policy priorities for providing family support continue to change (see Unit 7). We will remain with the Act for a moment however in order to describe the formal basis for social work practice to support children and families. We begin with an account of the terms used in the Act to identify who might be eligible to receive services.

i STUDY TEXT 4.1: CHILDREN IN NEED

Part III of the Children Act 1989 establishes the local authority's duty to provide an appropriate 'range and level of services' for certain children with the aim of 'safeguarding and promoting' their welfare and, so far as is consistent with that aim, to do so by promoting 'the upbringing of such children by their families' (s. 17 (1)). The children concerned are those that the Act describes as 'children in need'.

The definition of a child 'in need' is to be found at s. 17 (10). A child is in need if:

(a) he is unlikely to achieve or maintain, or to have the opportunity of achieving or maintaining a reasonable standard of health or development without the provisions for him of services by a local authority under this Part;

(b) his health or development is likely to be significantly impaired or further impaired, without the provision for him of such services; or

(c) he is disabled.

'Development' means physical, intellectual, emotional, social or behavioural development and 'health' means physical or mental health (s. 17 (11)). A child is 'disabled' if he or she is 'blind, deaf or dumb or suffers from mental disorder of any kind or is substantially and permanently handicapped by illness, injury or congenital deformity'. This definition of disabled is the same as that contained in the National Assistance Act 1948 and so a person with disabilities qualifies for services both before and after the age of 18. Services may also be available under other legislation, including the Chronically Sick and Disabled Persons Act 1970. The Children Act 1989 makes allowances for services to be provided for a child's family or any member of the child's family as well as to the child itself, if these are provided 'with a view to safeguarding or promoting the child's welfare' (s. 17 (3)). 'Family' is defined widely to include 'any person with parental responsibility for the child and any person with whom he has been living' (s. 17 (10)). This definition of need is deliberately wide in order to reinforce the Act's commitment to provide services across a broad range. Local authorities cannot exclude any category nor can the definition of 'need' be restricted only to those children at risk of significant harm.

Direct services for children in need will not only be provided by local authorities, however. The local authority is required to 'facilitate the provision by others' of support services (s. 17 (5)). So, even if you are employed in the voluntary or independent sector, your work may derive from the provisions of Part III of the Act. New sections, (17A and 17B) were added to the 1989 Act by the Health and Social Care Act 2001 and the Carers and Disabled Children Act 2000 respectively. Section 17A enables regulations to be made for payments to parents in place of the direct provision of services for children in need. The recipient of the direct payment may use it to buy the required care services from a supplier other than the local authority. Section 17B enables regulations to be made for the issue of vouchers to enable the purchase of short breaks, usually for disabled children. It should be noted that although too fine a point to be pursued here, the regulations issued for England and Wales are different and reflect a quite different approach to the care planning process and to the provision of services to people with disabilities (see, for example, *Community Care, Services for Carers and Children's Services (Direct Payments) (England) Regulations 2009* (SI 2009/1887) and *Community Care, Services for Carers and Children's Services (Wales) Regulations 2004* (S.I. 2004/1748). (Please see the References section for specific website access).

The local authority is required to 'take reasonable steps to identify the extent to which there are children in need within their area' (Sch. 2, para. 1(1)) and to publish information about the services that they provide, or which are provided by voluntary or other organizations, in such a way as those who might benefit from them are informed (Sch. 2, para. 1(2)). The duty to publish information is reinforced by the Human Rights Act 1998 (HRA). Article 10 ('freedom of expression') has been interpreted as to include the right to receive information. If adequate information about services were not available, a person who might benefit from the service would be able to challenge the local authority under the HRA. The local authority is also required to open and maintain a register of children with disabilities in their area (Sch. 2, para.2(1)). There is no duty on the individual to register. As well as in relation to children in need, the Act also confers some other duties upon local authorities to provide support services. The authority is required, through the provision of services under Part III of the Act, 'to prevent children within their area suffering ill-treatment or neglect' (Sch. 2, para. 4). It is also required to take 'reasonable steps' to reduce the need for care proceedings and criminal proceedings against children, to encourage children within their area not to commit offences and to avoid the need to place children in secure accommodation (Sch. 2, para. 7).

In order to determine whether a particular child is a child 'in need', the Act acknowledges that some form of assessment will be required (Sch. 2, para. 3). Such an assessment may be carried out as part of a wider assessment of special needs. We have already introduced you (in Study Texts 1.2 and 3.2) to the *Framework for the Assessment of Children in Need and their Families* (Department of Health and others 2000), which is now the preferred means of carrying out such assessments. The three dimensions (the child's developmental needs, parenting capacity, family and environmental factors) are often presented as three sides of a triangle with the child and the statutory duty upon local authorities to 'safeguard and promote' his or her welfare at the centre (see Figure 4.1).

Figure 4.1 The Children in Need Assessment Framework

We will look in more detail in Unit 7 how the *Framework* is to be used in practice. For now, it is important to see with Rose (2001, p.40), that the *Framework* 'provides a conceptual map which will help professionals in their work with children and families.'

We hope that we have already indicated to you what a useful 'conceptual map' the *Framework* is but, as we have also suggested at several points in this book already, we should not expect it to do more than *help* us in our work. The *Framework*, like the Children Act itself, provides the context in which social workers must exercise their professional skill and judgement. Neither the *Framework* nor the Act can be substituted for such skill or judgement. Social work cannot be done simply by ticking boxes on a form or by reading from the pages of the statute book, as we discuss further in Unit 7. The following exercise will help us to make the point for our current purposes.

EXERCISE 4.1: IN NEED?

For each of these mini case studies, decide whether the child concerned is a child in need as defined by the Children Act 1989 and write down as precisely as you can how the child satisfies the criteria established in Part III of the Act.

1. Sharon is 15 and pregnant. She intends to look after her baby herself, with the help of her mother. Sharon currently shares a bedroom with her sister, aged 11. Her two brothers and her parents occupy the other bedrooms in her semi-detached house. Her mother seems reconciled to the facts of Sharon's situation but her father is angry and upset and refusing to speak to Sharon. Tension between family members is rising and there are frequent arguments between various members of the family.

2. John, aged four, lives with his mum and older brother, Ian, in a council maisonette on a very large estate on the outskirts of a major city. Mum survives on social security benefits but she is in debt (for about £500, used to buy a cooker) to a moneylender. John has few clothes and no winter coat. Food is not very nutritious but he never goes hungry. There are only a few toys in the home and the local playground has been vandalized.

3. Mark, aged 14, has been involved with others in petty theft in and around his home area. He has not yet come to police attention officially but his family are concerned that this will only be a matter of time. Mark's parents are teachers and live in one of the better parts of town. Neither Mark nor his family are happy with the slowly deteriorating state of family relationships that is occurring as a consequence of rows over Mark's behaviour. Relationships have always been good up to now. When Mark's father heard that his son had been truanting from school he telephoned the social worker saying that he had had enough and that something had to be done.

4. Robbie is aged 12. He is a keen supporter of the local football club and likes to dress in imitation of his heroes. Recently the club changed their first-team kit and Robbie now wants to buy a replica shirt and a suitable (and expensive) pair of trainers. He says that he has been excluded by his friends at school because he is dressed so badly and that he will soon have no friends left if he cannot keep up with them.

5. Sanjit is the lone parent of Ayse, aged three, who has severe learning difficulties and some mobility difficulties. Ayse can do very little for herself and requires almost constant attention. Sanjit is finding the physical demands on her exhausting. Ayse's father was killed in a traffic accident and she and her mother have no other friends or family in the area. Sanjit works in the local launderette part-time where she can take Ayse but she often feels lonely and at the end of her tether.

6. Mr Smith is having an affair with the wife of a family friend. He has been out of work for several years, despite numerous offers of work. Mrs Smith knows all about Mr Smith's affair and makes no secret of her contempt for her husband. Despite the fact that the family are in severe financial difficulties, both Mr and Mrs Smith have extravagant tastes and substantial credit card debts. The Smiths' son, Jamie, is aged eight. He is a very timid boy who has recently started to wet the bed at night. His bed is already ruined and Mrs Smith has asked you to help.

POINTS TO CONSIDER

1. What factors did you take into account when determining whether the development of the child concerned was at issue?

2. What factors did you take into account when determining whether the health of the child concerned was at issue?

3. How did you decide what was a 'reasonable standard' of health or development?

4. What factors did you take into account in deciding what 'significantly impaired' might mean in each case?

5. In your decision making, did you accord more importance to the particular characteristics of the children concerned or to the circumstances in which they found themselves?

6. Was the degree of responsibility or culpability of the parents an issue in deciding whether each child was a child in need?

📖 COURSE TEXT: A RANGE OF NEEDS AND SERVICES

Each of the mini case studies used in Exercise 4.1 is based on a real example from our own practice. We chose them because we regard them as broadly typical of the range of 'children in need' (except no. 4!). We would be able to get a better sense of just how typical they are if we were to set them in the context of reliable statistical data on all 'children in need'. In fact, this is not quite as straightforward as you might imagine. Statistical data have been made available through four 'children in need' surveys undertaken, using local authority administrative data, in England (and one in Wales, on a voluntary basis, in 2009[2]). The first survey, *Children in Need in England: First Results of a Survey of Activity and Expenditure as Reported by Local Authority Social Services' Children and Family Teams for a Survey Week in February 2000* (Department of Health/Office for National Statistics 2000) was followed by similar surveys in September/October 2001; February 2003 and February 2005.

Following the 2005 survey, the census was discontinued and no further data at national level were published for over four years. In the interim, a new framework for the collection of 'children in need' data has been in development (based on the financial year rather than the 'snapshot' approach taken by its predecessor) and two subsequent 'experimental statistical releases' were published in November 2009 (DCSF 2009b) and September 2010 (DfE 2010). The data reported in these two bulletins are much more limited in scope than in previous statistical releases, reflecting the state of development of the new data collection framework. Both the 2009 and the 2010 releases were based on incomplete data and, in the case of some local authorities, data of doubtful quality. Comparisons between pre-2005 data and post-2009 data are not possible.

One might acknowledge that definitional problems had, for some time, made research 'methodologically intimidating to researchers and politically intimidating to funders' (Tunstill 1996, p.154) (see also Tunstill and Aldgate 2000, pp.13–17) but one might still wonder why reliably providing a coherent and comprehensive census of this particular population should have eluded the UK's various means and mechanisms of 'social accounting' (an important part of which is the centralized collection of 'official statistics') for so long. It may be a reflection of the priority this group of children has had for policy makers, practitioners and legislators. In order to be officially counted, a given population has to count for something. As we indicated at the start of this Unit, this was not always the case and it should not be assumed that it will continue to be so.

---

2   A further CIN Census for Wales was commenced in March 2010.

Figure 4.2 gives an indication of the numbers of 'children in need' reported in 2010. Figure 4.3 provides some detail of the circumstances of children in need, based on the much more extensive data reported in the 2005 survey.

- There were 382,300 children in need at 31 March 2010, which was a rate of 339 per 10,000 children.

- The rate of children in need per 10,000 children in an area varied from 154.5 children in need per 10,000 children in Wokingham to 895.1 in Haringey.

- There were a total of 697,900 'episodes' of need throughout the year. (An individual child might be the subject of more than one 'episode' of need.)

- There were 607,500 referrals to children's social care services in the year ending 31 March 2010.

Figure 4.2 Children in need 2010.
Source: DfE 2010, Tables 1–4

In February 2005:

- There were just under 386,000 children in need known to local authorities in England as requiring some form of social work help or intervention.

- Eighty-one per cent of these children (313,300) were supported in their families or were living independently; 19 per cent (72,600) were looked after children.

- Of those children in need supported by their families or living independently, 30 per cent were receiving services because of abuse or neglect; 14 per cent because of family dysfunction; 12 per cent because of acute family stress and 12 per cent because of disability.

- Of those children in need who were being looked after, 55 per cent were receiving services because of abuse or neglect; 10 per cent because of family dysfunction; 6 per cent because of acute family stress and 13 per cent because of disability.

- Twenty-eight per cent of children in need supported by their families were aged under 5 and 37 per cent were aged between 11 and 18.

- Seventeen per cent of children in need who were looked after were aged under 5 and 57 per cent were aged between 11 and 18.

- Seven per cent of young people in need supported by their families were aged over 18 compared to 1 per cent of those looked after.

- Seventy-four per cent of children in need are of 'white' ethnic origin; 6 per cent are of 'mixed' ethnic origin; 4 per cent are of 'Asian' origin and 7 per cent are of 'black' origin.

- The average cost of services to a child in need looked after was £1425 per week; the average cost of services to a child supported by their parents or living independently was £1085.

Figure 4.3 Children in need 2005.
Source: ONS/DfES 2006, Tables 1, 5, 7, 8, 9 and 23

It is important to understand that the way in which we are using the term 'in need' in this Unit is in the technical sense introduced by the Children Act 1989 and explained in Study Text 4.1, above. Of course, other definitions of children and their needs are possible, not least using poverty indices (see Forester 2007). For example, in 2008/09 there were 2.8 million children living in households in the UK with an income below 60 of the median net disposable income (before housing costs) and 3.9 million (after housing costs) (DWP 2010). Some considerable progress has been made in reducing child poverty over recent years (but see MacInnes, Kenway and Parekh 2009: Brewer and others 2009) yet some obvious disparities remain. For example, comparing the children living in households at the top of the income scale with those living at the bottom,[3] 96 per cent of the better off children have outdoor space/ facilities to play safely compared to 78 per cent of the least well off; 92 per cent have at least one week's holiday away from home with their family compared to 34 per cent; 86 per cent have a hobby or leisure activity compared to 66 per cent and 82 per cent have friends round for tea or a snack once a fortnight compared to 57 per cent (DWP 2010: Table 7). It may be that the economic recession of 2009/10 and the political and economic responses that are made to it may add to these disparities, and not only in the UK.

The sheer scale of the population of children in need, however defined, may well have made an impression upon you and it would be unwise to generalize

---

3   Strictly, those in the top and bottom quintiles by net equivalized disposable household income, before housing costs. See DWP, 2010: Table 7.

too readily about the causes and correlates of the number of such children in the UK in the second decade of the twenty-first century (but see Bradshaw and Holmes 2010). A clearer feel for the lived experience of these children is to be found in Aldgate and Statham's review (Aldgate and Statham 2001) of 24 research studies commissioned by the Department of Health to examine the early working of the Children Act 1989. They conclude that (2001, p.32):

- Many families of children in need are struggling to bring up their children in conditions of material and emotional adversity.

- Poor health and poverty are dominant themes in the studies for the majority of families.

- Domestic violence and drugs and alcohol misuse are present in families with more severe problems.

- There are differences in the level and scope of problems – families whose children are subject to care proceedings have more entrenched and long-standing multiple problems.

- Families of children in need can be grouped in three ways: those who need help with specific issues, acutely distressed families and families with multiple and long-standing problems.

- Families move from one category to another as problems improve or deteriorate.

The daily struggle against what Beveridge once described as the 'five giants' of want, disease, squalor, ignorance and idleness, continues for many children still. Yet, what is equally clear is that much of the daily experience of the children who are our concern is lived out of the public gaze. There are few newspaper headlines reporting the reduced life chances and frustrated potential of the children in need we have described (unless, that is, they are subjects of abuse). You may wish to reflect further on why it is that these children do not raise the interest of journalists or the indignation of the general public more than they appear to do. As social workers, the Children Act 1989 at least provides you with some of the means to do something to meet the needs of some of our most vulnerable fellow citizens.

Study Text 4.2 sets out how the Act requires or permits certain forms of support service and provides a brief commentary on their relative effectiveness.

i STUDY TEXT 4.2: SERVICES FOR CHILDREN IN NEED

The Children Act 1989 (the Act) requires local authorities to make available the following services for children in need:

- advice, guidance and counselling
- occupational, social, cultural or recreational activities
- day care or supervised activity
- home help
- travel assistance
- assistance to enable the child to have a holiday
- maintenance of the family home
- financial assistance
- accommodation.

The local authority must provide or facilitate the provision by others of *advice, guidance* and *counselling* as well as *occupational, social, cultural or recreational activities* for all children in need living with their families (Sch. 2, para. 8). Such services may also be provided for other children not in need. Often such services will be available via family centres, which the local authority is required to provide under the Act (Sch. 2, para. 9). Day care, which includes day nurseries, playgroups, toy libraries, out-of-school clubs and holiday play schemes, must be provided for all children in need aged five or under (if not in school) and may be provided for other children too (s. 18). The local authority has no power or duty under the Act to make provision for home help, travel assistance or holidays other than for children in need (Sch. 2, para. 8). Where a child in need is living away from home (but is not being looked after by a local authority), the local authority must take steps, if necessary, to promote the child's welfare, to enable the child to live with its family and/or to promote contact between the child and its family (Sch. 2, para. 10).

In exceptional circumstances, not defined by the Act, the local authority may offer assistance in cash. Any service offered, excluding advice, guidance, or counselling, may be subject to a charge to the service user (s. 29 (1)).

The local authority *may* provide accommodation to children in need and their families (by virtue of an amendment introduced by the Adoption and Children Act 2002) and must provide accommodation for a child in need who requires accommodation if:

- there is no-one with parental responsibility for the child (s. 20 (1)(a))
- the child is lost or abandoned (s. 20 (1)(b))
- the person caring for the child is prevented from providing the child with suitable accommodation, for whatever reason and whether permanently or not (s. 20 (1)(c))
- the child is over 16 and the local authority considers that the child's welfare is likely to be seriously prejudiced if accommodation is not provided (s. 20 (3)).

It should be noted that when a child is accommodated under the provisions of Part III of the Act, the pre-existing distribution of parental responsibility is unaltered. The local authority does not acquire any parental responsibility for the child, although it does acquire certain duties and obligations to safeguard and promote the child's welfare (s. 22).

The legal basis under which accommodation is provided – either under s. 17 or under s. 20 can be crucial as was shown in the case of R(M) v Barnet London Borough Council [2008] EWHC 2354. A girl claimed that accommodation was provided for her under s. 20 rather than s. 17. If successful in her claim, leaving care services would have been available to her on reaching 18. The court decided that the accommodation could not have been provided under s. 20 as her parents were willing to accommodate her (and therefore not 'prevented' from doing so as in the wording of s. 20) but the authority accommodated her because of her unreasonable refusal to return home. As a result any accommodation required after the age of 18 had to be sought under homelessness legislation and not through the leaving care services of the relevant local authority.

WHAT WORKS?

As far as the overall delivery of services to children in need is concerned, the research evidence (see SSIA 2007) would suggest that the more successful services are those that are:

- accessible to children, young people and their families
- acceptable and non-stigmatizing, ideally located alongside universal, more open-access type services
- enabling and empowering
- closely linked to adult services

- integrated with existing services and networks
- sustainable, with support available for as long as is needed.

In general terms, parenting is likely to have the greatest influence on outcomes for younger children and a great many interventions on behalf of children in need are aimed at improving parenting or the parent–child relationship. Successful programmes include targeted health/home visiting; family centres offering multi-function family support; targeted parenting education programmes; targeted services for young parents and their children and specific interventions aimed at children's emotional and behavioural challenges (see Moran, Ghate and van der Merwe 2004 for a comprehensive account of 'what works' in parenting support).

There is no single 'magic bullet' as far as parenting support services are concerned however. On the other hand, there is evidence to suggest that some approaches work better than others and we would argue for a strong presumption in favour of evidence based interventions in the range of services for children in need. Apart from the obvious point that evidence based interventions are more likely to work (as they have already been proven to work elsewhere), such approaches can be more transparent about their aims and objectives and are therefore easier to explain and easier to evaluate. They are arguably more ethical too in that 'hoping for the best' rather than knowing what the best might be does not seem to us to be a strong basis on which to engage with children and families who are already facing particular challenges. (We return to the question of 'evidence' and evidence based practice in Unit 8.)

As far as older children and young people are concerned, specialist teams offering crisis support have proven efficacy; as does family group conferencing and specialist drug and alcohol abuse services. We would make the point again however, that there can be no 'one size fits all' approach to support services for young people (see SSIA 2007 for a review of the literature on 'what works' in supporting older young people in need).

Engaging the right form of family support will depend on the quality of the assessment that is made not only of the child, young person and their family but also of the various services on offer. We will consider assessment of need in much more detail in Unit 7.

WHOSE NEEDS?

Deciding whether a child qualifies as a 'child in need' as defined by the Children Act 1989 is clearly a complex, interpretive task, calling for the exercise of sound professional judgement. The same is true in relation to engaging children and families in the right type and level of support service. In order to provide you with a more precise illustration of how subtle and complex a process providing support to a child in need can be, we end this Unit by focussing our attention on a particular group of young people whom you might regard as self-evidently having additional support needs; those young people undertaking supporting roles themselves: young carers.

We certainly do not want to imply that every young carer is a 'child in need' (see Dearden and Aldridge 2010). Rather, we would wish you to recognize that social workers 'need to draw the fine line between helping and intruding' and to realize that 'everyone trying to help you at once' may not be so helpful after all – especially if you happen to be coping well at the time' (Morgan 2006, p.18). However, providing help where and when it is needed, and in a manner that is accessible and acceptable to the recipient is the key to providing effective support in any set of family circumstances.

i STUDY TEXT 4.3: YOUNG CARERS

Most families exchange caring and support roles back and forth between the generations over the life-course and as external circumstances demand. Whereas your parents may have cared for you as a child, they may now be caring for your children while you are studying or you may be caring for your parents. Indeed, it is important to remember that being a 'carer', young or otherwise, is a central part of most people's life history.

Just as the nature and direction of the caring relationship may change, so too might the type and amount of support required vary over time. 'Peaks and troughs' in the need for support are not uncommon. Additional help might be needed in a crisis, such as a sudden deterioration in an individual's health, for example. Key to providing effective support will be an active appreciation of the fluid nature of being a carer, at any age.

Not least because the carer role is clearly a dynamic one, defining what we mean by a 'young carer' is not straightforward. One of the more comprehensive definitions of the term has been provided by Becker (2000, p.378). Young carers are:

> …children and young persons under 18 who provide or intend to provide care, assistance or support to another family member. They carry out, often on a regular basis, significant or substantial caring tasks and assume a level of responsibility that would usually be associated with an adult. The person receiving care is often a parent but can be a sibling, grandparent or other

relative who is disabled, has some chronic illness, mental health problem or other condition connected with a need for care, support or supervision.

While much of Becker's definition could apply to a carer of any age, it does recognize that the young person is taking on responsibilities and tasks that would not usually be expected of him or her at that age and there is an implicit acknowledgement that young carers may indeed have additional support needs of their own that arise from their being children and young people rather than adults. We return to this point below.

Because of such definitional difficulties however, estimating just how many young carers there are is also not straightforward. Census data would suggest that there might be as many as 175,000 young people in the UK aged between 8 and 17 involved in providing care to members of their family on a regular basis (Dearden and Becker 2004; ONS 2001). The amount of care provided varies with most young carers (83%) providing less than 20 hours care per week but with 8 per cent providing over 50 hours per week. Census data rely on self-identification and so these figures are of limited usefulness. Some young people may not identify themselves as carers at all, of course. In their eyes, they are just 'helping' their family (Warren 2008, p.9) 'doing what anyone else would in the same position'. Frank (2002) has also noted that when asked, children themselves often describe their situation in terms of feelings and tasks rather than attempt a definition of themselves as a 'young carer'.

The routes by which young people travel to become carers are also very varied. Some children and young people will have been assuming the role of carer from a young age. For others, stepping into the role may follow a crisis or significant change in family circumstances. Some young people will share their caring role with adult family members; others may be the sole carer. Some will have taken on the role as carer voluntarily; others may feel as though they had been 'elected' or coerced by the family and to have had very little choice, not least because the support services available for the adults concerned were simply inadequate (Wates 2002).

Because of the wide variety of family histories and circumstances as well as the range of caring responsibilities and tasks undertaken by young people, it is clear that this is far from an homogenous group. Indeed, like all children, including children in need, each young carer is unique. For this very obvious reason, it is vitally important to understand how the young person and their family themselves define the various caring roles and the distribution of caring responsibilities between family members. It is only in this way that you will begin to understand what exactly a young carer's support needs are. Without such openness and professional humility, it would be all too easy not to recognize that young carers have distinctive support needs at all. As Morgan (2006, p.12) reports:

> Some [young carers] said that they had met social workers who mainly thought about how their parents were looking after their children, not about how to support one or more of the children as young carers. These sometimes seemed to want to take the child into care rather than support them being a young carer; 'first option is to take you into care, not help or solve problems'.

Some of the support needs of young carers arise out of the tasks that they themselves undertake. Many of these are similar to those undertaken by adult carers and include domestic work, nursing care, personal care such as washing and toileting, mental health monitoring, management of medication and supervision. Young carers may also take on child care responsibilities for other children in the family; act as translator, manage the family's finances or act as a 'messenger' between the family and outside world (see Aldridge 2008; Warren 2008). There can be additional emotional support asked of young carers too (Morgan 2006, p.7):

> 'Sometimes you feel you need to keep the person you are caring for company even if there are no jobs to do.'

> 'Mum spends a lot of time alone, so it doesn't seem right not to keep her company.'

While there is some research evidence to indicate that caring contains positive and rewarding aspects (such as feeling closer to each other as a family – see Aldridge and Becker 2003; Dearden and Becker 2000), there is evidence too to suggest that being a young carer brings its own challenges (see, for example Aldridge and Becker 1993; Frank 1995). Young carers report that they worry about getting ill and exhausted, making mistakes with medication, having problems lifting someone heavy, being bullied by their peers, and suffering their own emotional and psychological stress. There is evidence to suggest too that young carers' educational achievement may be detrimentally affected; their opportunities for recreation and leisure may be less and their scope for socializing may be reduced (see Warren 2008).

Hence, meeting the support needs of young carers will mean meeting their needs both as carers *and* as young people. You should remember that many young people will simply neither have the personal experience to draw on, the range of social supports that most adults have nor the capacity to act as independently as most adults. They don't drive and they don't have independent financial means, for example. As well as practical support, including providing information on where to go for help in an emergency, information and advice on aids and adaptations to make the caring task more manageable and information on particular illnesses and disabilities, young carers may also need help in securing the benefits and support to which the person for whom they are caring is entitled. They may also need emotional support in their own right. This may take the form of a complete break from caring for a period. It may also simply imply an opportunity for the young person to 'get it out of their system' or it may need a much longer-term supportive and nurturing relationship. They may also need support to just go about the ordinary business of being a young person – time to socialize, network, play (at any age) and to grow up in their own way.

In our experience, to adequately support a young carer, social workers will need to:

- adopt a flexible and adaptive approach to offering support, remembering that some problems (like a broken washing machine or help with transport) simply need a practical response (like a washing machine repair or a bus pass!)

- make sure that whatever needs the person being cared for might have are also being addressed by the appropriate adult services

- understand the young carer's position from the young carer's own perspective; you may have no experience of their experience

- understand and help to overcome the challenges presented to the young person by their caring responsibilities impacting on their lives as children and young people, especially in such critical areas as friendships, social networks and their own aspirations for the future

- understand and respect the limits of the care that a young person is able to give (this is just as likely to be more than you expect, as it is to be less)

- build up the family's support networks, where this is possible, including mobilising support from the wider family, friends and neighbours (where this is acceptable to the family)

- help the family to put in place an 'emergency' plan.

As with most individuals and families in need of support, young carers need the kind of help that they need, when they need it and how they want to receive it. This will mean that you will have to listen, learn and be creative, practical and reliable in your response.

While it is a term that is so widely used as to have almost lost all meaning, we would suggest that a partnership approach to working with young carers and their families is likely to be the most productive. Indeed, we would suggest this to be true for almost all forms of family support. Atherton and Dowling (1989) offer a statement of values that inform partnership practice which, while challenging, still seems to us to be a sound basis for providing family support:

- Partners trust each other. So they can be open and honest in how they behave to each other. They try to understand rather than to judge.

- Partners respect each other. There is complimentarity rather than equality where the special skills and knowledge of the worker are made accessible to the client in the way that has been negotiated with the client.

- Partners are working towards the same broad objectives.

- Partners share power. Nobody has a monopoly on it and nobody takes over. That power may never be equal but it should be possible for the balance of power to shift by negotiation and agreement.

- Empowerment of the client can be assisted by ensuring that the views of each partner carry weight and are respected and by sharing information.

- Partners share in decision making.

- Partners can call each other to account and have rights. Partnership practice does take the issue of accountability seriously and provides for any partner to call for explanations and challenge what work is going on.

The next exercise will help you put this approach into practice.

EXERCISE 4.2: BEING SUPPORTIVE?

Read the case study below and answer the questions that follow, drawing on your understanding of the Children Act 1989 and the three basic dimensions of the *Framework for the Assessment of Children in Need and their Families* (see Figure 4.1) as well as your understanding of the range of support services available to children in need.

Shari is 12 years old. She lives with her mother, Anna and her brother James who is 8. Anna, a lone parent, has suffered from depression for 16 years, which became worse after she had a difficult labour and birth with James. There are no family near by and because of Anna's depression and social withdrawal the family have few friends.

Anna is under the care of the community mental heath team and has visits from a community psychiatric nurse every two months to monitor her mental health. Shari is always present at these visits, as Anna will not allow anyone into the house unless Shari is present. Anna rarely leaves the house, which means that Shari has to do the family shopping and to take and collect James from school. Shari also monitors her mother's medication, reminding her to take it, otherwise Anna forgets.

Shari has been struggling since she changed school and no longer attends the same school as James. She sometimes falls asleep in class, or misses classes. Other children call her 'smelly' and 'stupid' and she is noticeably thinner than other girls her age.

1. How might Shari describe her support needs?

2. How might Anna describe both her needs and those of Shari?

3. How would you describe Shari's needs both as a young person and as a carer?

4. Would you describe Shari as a 'child in need' as defined by the Children Act 1989?

5. What support services might be most helpful to Shari, her brother and her mother?

POINTS TO CONSIDER

1. What is it about this situation that causes you most concern? Are these concerns likely to be shared by either the children or their mother?

2. Do you think that your view of the children's support needs would be shared by other professionals? If not, why might this be the case?

3. How helpful did you find the definitions of 'need' offered in s. 17 of the Children Act 1989 in reaching your answer to question 4 (above)?

4. How could you help Shari by helping her mother?

5. How could you help Anna by helping Shari?

CONCLUSION

In considering how families might best be supported through the difficulties that they encounter, we have suggested that the value and usefulness of that support and its appropriateness and acceptability are in some measure dependent on the terms on which it is offered. We have suggested that approaches which recognize the capacity of individuals to be witness to their own experience have a potential for establishing the kind of relationship best suited to helping families deal with their problems. This requires a thorough appreciation of what personal qualities and professional style social workers bring to the helping relationship. It has been known for a long time that the characteristics of social workers that service users most value are:

> honesty, naturalness and reliability along with an ability to listen. [Service users] appreciated being kept informed, having their feelings understood, having the stress of parenthood accepted and getting practical help as well as moral support. (Department of Health and Social Security 1985, p.20)

> Social workers are experienced as helpful if they really listen and take pains to understand the difficulties from the family's point of view. They are also valued if they are practical as well as sympathetic and supportive and do more than just listen. Honesty and directness are important qualities that parents are well able to appreciate – even if some messages are hard and unpalatable... (Department of Health 1991b, p.47)

> Honesty and reliability were particularly valued. Clearly presented information about what was happening and the options available were both very important. (Department of Health 1995, p.46)

> Parents value recognition of the circumstances that inhibit parental responsibility. Respect for different parenting styles is important... The power differential between parents and workers should be openly acknowledged. Parents respond well to being treated with dignity. (Aldgate and Statham 2001, p.73)

This is not a counsel of perfection. It is what is needed to do the job, assuming that the job is one of helping families resolve their difficulties.

NOTES AND SELF-ASSESSMENT

1. Why provide support services to children and families?

2. To whom do you regard yourself accountable in the exercise of your professional duties?

3. Do you trust the users of social work services?

4. In your working relationships with families, do you prefer to lead or to follow?

5. How well do you take guidance?

6. Is your practice characterized by 'honesty, naturalness and reliability along with an ability to listen'?

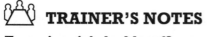 **RECOMMENDED READING**

Dolan, P., Canavan, J. and Pinkerton, J. (2006) *Family Support as Reflective Practice.* London: Jessica Kingsley Publishers.

Frank, J. and Mclarnon, J. (2008) *Key Principles of Practice for Young Carers and their Families.* London: The Children's Society.

TRAINER'S NOTES
Exercise 4.1: In Need?

In order to provide more 'context' for this exercise, it can be undertaken as a kind of 'balloon debate'. A scenario could be imagined in which resources are particularly scarce and only one case will receive any services at all. Each case study is represented by one or more members of the group, who have to argue the merits of their case and persuade other group members that their case should be the one to receive services (in a balloon debate proper, the participants have to imagine that they are in a hot air balloon that is slowly descending as it loses air. In order to stay aloft, participants have to jettison, in turn, one member of the balloon's company until only one person remains.).

The exercise can be extended further as a 'dreams and nightmares' exercise. Half of the group is asked to imagine the worst possible way in which a support service response for each of these families could be delivered. For example, day care could be provided in a vandalized building with untrained staff with convictions for child abuse, etc. The second half of the group has to imagine the perfect way in which such services could be delivered. Day care could be provided for free in a well-equipped building by caring staff who are all well qualified, etc. Then views are contrasted and a sense of what is practical and desirable established, as well as a possible action plan as to how the particular service could be developed.

Exercise 4.2: Being Supportive?

This exercise can be extended by asking the group to devise an 'emergency' plan in the event of a sudden crisis (such as Shari becoming too exhausted to help or Anna having to receive in-patient help for her mental health problems). The plan has to 'work' for every member of the family.

It can also be used as a basis for a group research activity whereby half of the participants are required to find out as much as they can about depression and what is available locally by way of community mental health support and then to present it to the whole group in a form that would be accessible to a 12-year-old. The other half of the group has to undertake a similar exercise but its focus is on identifying what resources are available to extend Shari's social network, to provide her with leisure and social activities and what specific resources are available to carers in the area. (This is actually a relatively straightforward task if the group has ready access to the internet.)

The point is not to provide a definitive account either of depression, community mental health services or of other support services in a given area but to reinforce the point about helping the young person be an effective carer as well as a young person.

Looking After

OBJECTIVES

In this Unit you will:

- Learn about attachment and separation.
- Develop your understanding of inclusive, corporate parenting.
- Reflect on what is best practice with looked after children.

COURSE TEXT: LOOKED AFTER CHILDREN

We noted in Study Text 4.2 that the provision of accommodation was included in the range of services made available to children in need by the Children Act 1989. We shall go on to learn (Unit 10) about the process through which a child is received into the formal care of the local authority by virtue of an order made in court. Both groups of children, those provided with accommodation on a voluntary basis under Part III of the Act and those placed in the care of the local authority at the direction of the court, are described by the Act as 'looked after children' (s. 22(1))[4] and it is 'looking after' in this specific sense of the term that is the focus of this Unit.

Any episode of being looked after away from home begins with an experience of separation. This may be a painful process that makes enormous demands on the emotional and personal resources of everyone involved, including the social worker, and it is an experience that can remain with someone long afterwards, despite appearances to the contrary. While this may appear as no more than a

---

4 Strictly, a 'looked after child' is one who is subject to a care order or interim care order under s. 31 and 38 of the CA 1989; a child placed (or authorized to be placed) with prospective adopters under s. 18(3) of the Adoption and Children Act 2002; a child accommodated under s. 20 of the CA 1989; a child who is subject to a court order with a residence requirement (e.g. secure remand to local authority accommodation), as per s. 21 of the CA 1989.

statement of the obvious, it has, on occasions, been forgotten in practice, as we can confirm from our own experience. The following is an accurate reconstruction of an episode that clearly demonstrates how painful the experience of separation can be (and how good intentions are simply not enough).

It concerns a young person, Steven, aged 15 at the time. He had been in care for 3 years, exactly. He had been removed from his mother's care as she had chronic problems with drug and alcohol abuse and her chaotic lifestyle had made it impossible for her to provide adequate parenting for Steven and his younger brother (see Study Text 3.3). She had disappeared shortly after the care proceedings and had died a few months later in traumatic circumstances. Steve's foster carers had laid on a party for him to celebrate the anniversary of his coming to live with them. Steve's relationship with his carers was excellent. They were clearly very fond of him and he was very much part of the family. The conversation between us, which took place the day after the party, went like this:

Me: How was the party?

Steve: It was good.

Me: Everyone is really pleased at how well you are doing. It's nice to be able to celebrate all that you have achieved.

Steve: You might be celebrating. I am 'celebrating' three years since my mum kicked me out.

Me: Sorry. That was insensitive of me. I should have thought.

Steve: It's three years since I saw my mother and months since I saw my brother properly and they gave me a cake!

Steve began to cry, something he very, very rarely did. He seemed inconsolable.

Steve: Stop trying to make me feel better. The more you lot show that you care about me, the more I think that my mum didn't care enough and I can't deal with that.

Try not to misunderstand Steve's reaction. Steve really was doing very well (he later went on to university and has some fantastic friends and is still very much part of his foster family). He was generally happy and he was very appreciative of everything his foster carers had done for him. He is a resourceful, kind and optimistic person. It is simply one of life's great ironies that we are rarely able to separate ourselves from our experiences of separation and our sense of personal loss. Steve recognized all of the positives in his life and understood, at least intellectually, what had happened to him and why. And notwithstanding all of this, his interrupted and now severed relationship with his mother was a critical part of who he was and how he thought about himself. It still is and it probably would be so for most of us.

The following Study Text provides a brief account of attachment theory as a prelude to an exercise that is intended to sensitize you further to the emotional and broader psychological impact of enforced or traumatic separation.

i STUDY TEXT 5.1: ATTACHMENT, SEPARATION AND THE LOOKED AFTER CHILD

ATTACHMENT

Attachment theory, 'a theory of personality development in the context of close relationships' (Howe 2001, p.194), owes much to the work of John Bowlby (Bowlby 1970, 1973, 1980) and later commentators, in particular, Mary Ainsworth (Ainsworth and others 1978) and Vera Fahlberg. Fahlberg (1988) defines attachment as 'an affectionate bond between two individuals that endures through space and time and serves to join them emotionally' (p.13). She goes on to note that (p.13):

> A strong and healthy bond to a parent allows a child to develop both trust in others and self-reliance. The bond that a child develops to a person who cares for him or her in their early years is the foundation of their future psychological, physical and cognitive development and for their future relationships with others.

In other words, attachments form the basis of our later psychological integrity and our capacity to engage in rewarding and reciprocal social and emotional relationships. As Howe explains (2005, p.4), '… the basic force that brings about and helps shape our mental landscape is the brain's programmed urge to interact with others.'

Bonding is the process by which attachments are made. It starts before birth when a parent forms mental images of the new infant and begins to develop expectations and hopes for its future. From the moment of birth onwards, bonding proceeds as a consequence of a mutually reinforcing cycle of events that is part of many routine parent–child interactions. These interactions involve touch, sound and visual stimuli appropriate to the child's stage of physical and cognitive development. A typical successful interaction might occur, for example, when an infant is hungry or uncomfortable. S/he shows this by moving or crying. While in this state, the infant is unable to perceive anything else of the world. The carer notices and accurately meets the need or otherwise satisfies the child. The child feels better, is quietened and content. The parent is gratified by the response. The infant is able to perceive the world around him- or herself again and subsequently becomes aware of further needs and so the cycle continues, as in Figure 5.1. It is not only the child who might initiate these positive interactions, so too might the carer(s). For example, in the case of an infant, the carer might 'coo' or talk to the child, which may elicit a smile, which encourages the carer to 'talk' more, and so on.

Figure 5.1 Arousal–relaxation cycle

There are many reasons why the bonding cycle may not be initiated or might be disrupted. It may be that the carer is not attached to the child for reasons relating to the nature of the pregnancy; the circumstances in which the child was conceived; a difficult birth or because of postnatal depression. Alternatively, it may be that the baby may have been born prematurely or with a medical condition that prevents the parent from entering into the child's routine care on a regular or sufficient basis for the virtuous circle described in Figure 5.1 to develop. It may be that the personality of the child too might influence the development of attachments (see, for example, Buss and Plomin 1984; Belsky and Rovine 1987).

Mary Ainsworth and others (1978) and later commentators developed a typology (see Figure 5.2) of different styles or patterns of attachment that varied according to:

- the sensitivity of the carer to the needs of the baby

- the degree of acceptance (or rejection) on the part of the carer of the demands made on him or her by the baby

- the degree of 'co-operativeness' that develops between the carer and the child

- the degree to which a carer is available to (or ignores) the needs of the baby.

Secure Attachment (Type B)

Securely attached children are less likely to cry or show signs of anxiety in the company of their primary carer, although they may cling to them in the presence of a stranger. If separated (for a short period) from their carer, such children will show distress and will respond positively upon their return. Carers' behaviour towards the child will usually be observed as positive and encouraging. Securely attached children develop positive feelings about themselves and experience their caregiver as available.

Anxious Avoidant Insecure Attachment (Type A)

Children who experience their carers as consistently rejecting of them come to regard themselves as of little worth. Such children will show very little distress at the absence of their carers and may completely ignore them upon their return. They may show little difference in their general responses to their primary carer and a stranger. Their carers may be observed as cold, angry or 'distant' in their interactions with the child.

Anxious Resistant or Ambivalent Insecure Attachment (Type C)

Where a child's significant carer responds to the child inconsistently and unpredictably, the child comes to regard him- or herself as dependent and poorly valued. Such children tend to cry more, are less responsive to or even rejecting of physical contact. These children will be anxious ahead of any separation from their carer, very distressed during such an absence and ambivalent about renewing contact upon their return.

Disorganized Disorientated Insecure Attachment (Type D)

Such patterns of attachment are often found in association with children who have suffered significant harm. They will have experienced their carers as frightening or threatening and themselves as helpless and of little worth. Such children may show a wide range of contradictory patterns of behaviour in their interactions with their carers.

Figure 5.2 Patterns of attachment

Fahlberg (1985) notes the several deleterious effects of lack of normal attachment. These include:

- poor development of conscience

- poor impulse control and lack of foresight

- low self-esteem

- poor interpersonal skills and relationships

- lack of emotional awareness and sensitivity

- reduced cognitive ability

- some general developmental problems such as poor verbal skills and difficulty in aural comprehension.

The potential for poor attachment histories in the case of parents under stress to be the precursor of child abuse has been noted by Howe (2005, p.5):

> It is one of the features of maltreatment that when the child's attachment system is activated, the parent's attachment system also becomes activated, triggering a range of fragile defensive mental processes, which when breached lead to highly dysregulated care-giving responses. Faced with a needy, vulnerable or distressed child, the maltreating parent feels disorganized, out of control, and without a strategy to deal with his or her own emotional arousal, or that of his or her child. The result is abuse, neglect or both.

One should note, however, that attachment theory has been criticized (see Gambe and others 1992, p.29) for its euro-centricity in that the theory moves from a 'universal concept of attachment to a context bound view' that emphasizes the importance of a primary caretaker and the child's developing sense of autonomy. This does not take into account different cultural patterns of child rearing which may involve multiple caretaking and a more positive evaluation of interdependency over individualized autonomy. Dominelli (2007) argues that judgements concerning the quality of attachment and the processes through which it occurs are ultimately qualitative ones, made from the perspective of a specific culture.

SEPARATION

The separation of a child and its carer can occur for many reasons and it is important to understand normal as well as less adaptive reactions to separation. Separation behaviour will vary, depending on the nature of the child's attachment to the primary carers; the nature of the primary carers' bonding to the child; the child's past experiences of separation; the child's perceptions of the reasons for the separation (especially whether the child views him- or herself as responsible for the separation); the circumstances of the move itself; the environment to which the child is moved and the environment from which the child was moved. Reactions will also vary according to the 'age and stage' of the child.

Each of these factors is, to varying degrees, susceptible to sensitive social work intervention, whatever the age or circumstances of the child. For example, providing space and time for the 'parting message' from a child's caregiver to be fully articulated and understood by the child; enabling the child to develop a 'coherent' sense of his or her own history and enabling some continuity of relationships with those from whom a child is separated (see Fahlberg 1994) will always be important considerations. We will return to the question of maintaining links with parents below.

Separation is not just an issue for the child, of course; the experience is shared, in some way, with the parents. Schofield and others (2010) in their research on the experience of parents whose children were fostered found that these often vulnerable adults had considerable difficulty in overcoming their feelings of loss, grief and anger, especially when these were mixed with feelings of regret and guilt. They had to readjust their own sense of identity as parents in the context of the shame and stigma associated with losing their children in such circumstances and in a context where there was little public sympathy on display. Schofield concludes that even though the range of parents' capacity to manage their feelings was very wide, all of them needed 'social workers to be both empathetic and active communicators about and between the children and the parents' (Schofield and others 2010, p.16). This is not simply in the parents' interest:

> For most fostered children, resolving feelings about their birth family is an absolute necessity in order to thrive in placement. To the extent that parents themselves can contribute to this process, the social worker's goal for the child can be best achieved by facilitating the contribution from parents. (Schofield and others 2010, p.16)

It's a great pity we didn't do this very well in Steve's case.

ATTACHMENT, SEPARATION AND THE LOOKED AFTER CHILD

It will often be the case that looked after children will have had less opportunity in the past to form strong attachments, particularly if their childhood is characterized by family breakdown or successive moves within the care system.

However, given that the function of attachment behaviour is ultimately self-protective, both physically and psychologically, it may be the case that the prospect of enforced separation may come to represent sufficient threat to force children into reliance on what limited attachments they already have. Hence a child may well cling to an abusive parent and exhibit hostility to the worker, who, in such circumstances, may represent the greater threat as far as the child is concerned. Where normal prior attachments do exist, workers must be careful not to misinterpret reactions to separation. It is not uncommon for children to react aggressively during separation and apparently to lose interest in their former carers or the prospect of a return home as part of the normal self-protective response.

Goldman (1994) has identified four psychological tasks with which a child or young person may be faced when adjusting to loss or separation:

- *Understanding*: this involves regaining cognitive control of the crisis that a separation or more permanent loss can bring about.

- *Grieving*: this is a complex and often lengthy process (see Jewett 1984) that does not apply only in the case of bereavement and which may involve a child moving through a number of phases in which s/he will demonstrate feelings that others will find very uncomfortable and distressing. These might include anger, denial and disbelief, depression and despair before the child is able to 'integrate' the experience of the loss.

- *Commemorating*: finding ways to remember the person from whom they are separated.

- *Going on*: looking to and investing emotionally in the future.

The importance of the separation experience to the subsequent process and outcomes of intervention cannot be under-estimated. In a review of the research literature on admissions to residential care, Bullock, Little and Milham (1993, p.16) concluded that the 'secondary problems' associated with 'separation and strained relationships':

> ... can so preoccupy the child and his or her carers that the primary problems necessitating the child's removal from home are neglected... Indeed, the problems separated children experience as they try to preserve the continuity of their personal and family relationships may overwhelm any benefit that might reasonably be expected to accrue.

How far this process of adjustment is facilitated may, to some degree, depend on the nature of the new attachment relationships that the young person may need or chose to make. Walker (2008) has identified ways in which foster carers' (and, we would suggest, child and family social workers') own experiences of attachment might influence their interactions with children for whom they are responsible. Where there remain unresolved attachment issues for the carer, he suggests that this could have a decisive effect on the choice of specific placement. Moreover, quoting Dozier (Walker 2005, p.53), Walker notes that even those carers who had resolved any outstanding attachment issues of their own, 'tended to respond in kind to the child's behaviour. Thus when a child behaved in avoidant ways, foster carers tended to respond as though the child did not need them; when children behaved in ambivalent ways, foster carers tended to respond angrily.' It may be the case that your experience of attachment and loss will also influence the nature of your own responses to children and young people who may have had less than ideal attachment histories of their own. In your involvement with a child or young person experiencing a temporary separation or the more permanent loss of a significant carer, you will need to recognize and respect the child's progress through the always-difficult process of managing these transitions and honestly reflect on and manage the nature of your responses in terms of your own attachment history.

EXERCISE 5.1: SEPARATION

It is difficult and possibly too intrusive to ask you to reflect on your attachment history and your possible responses to separation. We are not in the room with you and we are not able to support you if the feelings such an exercise might arouse become distressing. Nonetheless, we think that it is important at least to undertake a 'thought exercise' with you that, while it has no consequences in the 'real world', may still help you to empathize and understand what the separation experience can be like. Read through the steps in the exercise below and then answer the questions that follow. The exercise depends for its effect on you engaging with it as seriously as you can. Imagine that the choice we are about to offer you is a real one.

1. *Step 1.* Take out your mobile phone and put it on the table in front of you. If you don't have a mobile phone, write down a list of the members of your social or family network with whom you are most regularly in contact. Also, make a list of your favourite music and place your photo album and diary on the desk.

2. *Step 2.* Now imagine that you have to hand your mobile (or lists, etc.) to us. You don't know us, of course, but don't worry, because we promise to give you an entirely new mobile phone in exchange for yours. In fact, we

will give you a much more expensive phone (photo album, diary, etc.). It really will be the best phone available; it will be a considerable material improvement on your old phone.

3. Of course, it will not have your old 'contacts', music or photos on it but we will give you some new ones. We will also give you some new music to listen to and a whole new set of diary dates. We will even take new (better quality) photos for you.

4. *Step 3.* Take your phone off the desk and put it out of sight, ideally take it into another room.

QUESTIONS:

1. Would you hand your mobile over on these terms?

2. Why/why not?

3. What might you look forward to with your new phone?

4. What would you miss most from your old phone?

5. How long was it before you went and fetched your phone?

POINTS TO CONSIDER

1. In circumstances such as those described in Steve's story, what could you have done to improve on our response?

2. How might the experience for parent and child be different if the separation is at the request of one of them rather than at the insistence of someone else?

3. What might be the long-term effect of a traumatic separation on the child's and/or the parent's relationship with the worker(s) or agency implicated in the separation?

4. What might be the emotional cost to the workers involved in the separation of a child and its parent(s)?

5. What strategies, both productive and unproductive, might workers, parents and children adopt to protect themselves from the confusion and pain of a traumatic separation?

6. Is it possible to take all of the pain and confusion out of any enforced separation?

COURSE TEXT: PARENTING AND THE LOOKED AFTER CHILD

Once the vitally important and often very difficult decision has been taken to separate a child from its carers, either by agreement or by order of a court, a significant proportion of the tasks and duties associated with parenting that child will fall to the local authority. We have seen already (Unit 3) how complex and demanding the task of parenting can be, even within the relatively narrow confines of the family. Parenting becomes even more challenging when it falls to the elected members, managers, social workers, teachers, health professionals and all the other individuals and departments that make up a local authority. Parenting of this sort is sometimes referred to as 'corporate parenting' and the following Study Text explores some of the challenges that this form of parenting presents.

i STUDY TEXT 5.2: CORPORATE PARENTING

The Children Act 1989 does not define parenting, as such. It does however define parental responsibility as 'all the rights, duties, powers, responsibilities and authority which by law a parent of a child has in relation to the child and his property' (s. 3 (1)). It is beyond the scope of this book to provide a full account of what is implied by 'parental responsibility' and how it might be acquired, transferred or terminated (but see Brammer 2009). For our purposes, it must be sufficient to note that a local authority will obtain parental responsibility upon the making of a care order.

The parental responsibility attaching to a care order effectively gives the local authority the power to assume the day-to-day parenting of a young person. It does however, specifically exclude the right to determine the child's religion, to appoint a guardian, to agree to placement for adoption, to change the child's surname and to arrange the child's emigration (s. 33). It is very important to note that the making of a care order does not extinguish the parental responsibility of anyone else (except those who hold parental responsibility exclusively by virtue of a residence order), although it does give the local authority the power to determine how far others may exercise their parental responsibility.

In the case of children and young people accommodated on a voluntary basis (under s. 20, CA 1989), parental responsibility is undisturbed and does not pass to the local authority, even in part. The local authority will rely on the 'in loco parentis' provision of s.3 (5) which allows it to 'do what is reasonable in all the circumstances of the case for the purpose of safeguarding or promoting the child's welfare'. What this means, in effect, is that the local authority will in most cases share parental responsibility for looked after children with others although, in the case of children in care by virtue of an order under s. 31 (and s. 38) it is in a position to determine how far others will exercise theirs.

The Children Act 1989, as amended by the 2002 Adoption and Children Act, the 2004 Children Act and the 2008 Children and Young Persons' Act, sets out the duties that the local authority has towards a looked after child. As well as the more obvious requirements to 'safeguard and promote' young people's welfare and to provide them with accommodation (s. 22(1) and s. 22A), the Act makes clear that placement with a parent (or someone with parental responsibility, as defined by the 1989 Act) or other relative is the preferred option provided that this is consistent with the child's welfare (s. 22C (3) and (7)). This is sometimes referred to as 'kinship care'. The Act further requires that where a placement cannot be with a parent or other relative, then the placement should allow the young person 'to live near' his or her home, that it should not disrupt the young person's education and that s/he is placed alongside his or her brothers and sisters (s. 23C (8)).

These and other provisions of the Act, especially in relation to care planning and parental contact with children in care (see Study Text 8.2), reinforce not only the key rehabilitative principles of the 1989 Act but also stress the importance of continuing engagement with a child's family of origin.

This is made clear in the *Guidance* that accompanies the Act (DCSF 2010e § 1.5):

> Parents should be expected and enabled to retain their parental responsibilities to and to remain as closely involved as is consistent with the child's welfare, even if that child cannot live at home either temporarily or permanently... Continuity of relationships is important and attachments should be respected, sustained and developed.

The *Guidance* goes on to note (§ 1.6) that:

> ... parents should be encouraged to exercise their parental responsibility for their child's welfare in a constructive way and that where compulsory intervention in the family is necessary it should where possible, support rather than undermine the parental role.

This commitment to ensuring 'continuity of relationships' sits alongside a new understanding of the importance of permanence in the lives of looked after children, especially those in care. In the past, permanence was particularly associated with adoption although over recent years, the term has come to have a much wider application. The revised *Guidance and Regulations* associated with the Act make a distinction between (DCSF 2010e, § 2.3):

emotional permanence (attachment), physical permanence (stability) and legal permanence (the carer has parental responsibility for the child) which gives a child a sense of security, continuity, commitment and identity.

The *Guidance* makes it clear that 'permanence provides an underpinning framework for all social work with children and families from family support through to adoption.' (We shall see in Study Text 8.2 how a 'permanence plan' is central to the whole process of placement, planning and review in the case of looked after children.) There is strong research evidence to support this position (see, for example, Beek and Schofield 2004; Schofield 2002; Sinclair and others 2007; and Timms and Thoburn 2006). Bullock and others (2006) in their review of the literature on what promoted a sense of permanence both for children, young people and those looking after them included not only placement stability, the capacity of carers to cope with disturbed behaviour and continuity of education but also the following (p.9):

> … minimising destructive interference from birth relatives; enabling the child to reach a *modus vivendi* with their birth parents so that they are not torn in their own minds between yearning and rejection.

In other words, a positive engagement with birth parents may actually contribute to a sense of permanence for the child or young person, even if the plans for the child do not necessarily include an imminent return home (see also DCSF 2010e, s. 2.4).

We do not pretend that the model of inclusive parenting that the legislation requires (and that research evidence suggests is the most effective) is easy to achieve. We still know relatively little of how children themselves make sense of the relationships that they maintain with their parents and any substitute carers with whom they might be placed. One study (Heptinstall, Bhopal and Brannen 2001, p.14) reported that 'no matter how inadequate or unavailable their parents may be, they still form an important part of children's own representations of family life'. Siblings too were important to fostered children in that they 'represented continuity in the face of considerable disruption and change'. This study concluded (p.15):

> Children may have unrealistic and idealised views of their families, but these images remain important… Children in general do not necessarily talk about their family relationships nor their feelings of family change, much less explain them. As well as taking account of the context and manner in which children reveal information, it is important to pay attention to what is *not* said and to consider the meaning of these silences.

We would remind you again of our conversation with Steve. We cannot forget either that the families of children who are looked after will be facing significant challenges of their own that will not simply be resolved once a child becomes looked after by the local authority. It would be unhelpful to over-generalize about the families of looked after children; each is unique but research on the characteristics of families who are subject to care proceedings (see Brophy 2006; Hunt, Macleod and Thomas 1999; Masson and others 2008) does provide an indication of the complexity and severity of the problems that will still need addressing. For example, Masson and others (2008, p.80) reported that 31.5 per cent of mothers of children subject to care proceedings had mental health problems; 38.6 per cent had alcohol problems; 33.2 per cent had accommodation problems; 51.1 per cent had suffered domestic violence, 52.4 per cent had chaotic lifestyles and 58.7 were reported not to have co-operated with children's services departments. We have noted also how the process of separation can be enormously problematic for parents, as it can be for children.

As well as requiring intelligent, sensitive, painstaking and skilled direct work, parenting a looked after child, especially in such a way as birth parents are positively engaged, will require a strong commitment from the rest of the local state in order to support the social worker. As the 2006 government Green Paper, *Care Matters: Transforming the Lives of Children and Young People in Care*, that started a renewed policy interest in looked after children, stated (DfES 2006a, p.31): 'as the corporate parent of children in care the State has a special responsibility for their well-being. Like any good parent, it should put its own children first.'

The subsequent White Paper, *Care Matters: Time for Change* elaborated (DfES 2007); being a corporate parent (s 1.20),

> is about more than providing food and shelter: a good corporate parent must offer everything that a good parent would provide and more, addressing both the difficulties which the children experience and the challenges of parenting within a complex system of different services. This means that children in care should be cared about, not just cared for and that all aspects of their development should be nurtured.

The White Paper set out what it described as the 'components of effective corporate parenting' (DfES 2007, p.21) and these have been developed subsequently by the National Children's Bureau (see Hart and Williams 2008; see also guidance on co-operation arrangements for Children's Trusts (England only), DCSF 2010b.) While the regulatory and administrative arrangements described above apply in full to England only, the principle of clear lines of accountability for looked after children, the importance of listening directly to looked after children in relation to their experience of being looked after, the supply and use of accurate information on the progress and outcomes for children looked after and a strong strategic focus to ensure the joining up of services around the child would probably prove invaluable in any context.

However, translating strategic intent into practical reality is rarely straightforward. The following exercise is intended to sensitize you to some of the difficulties of deciding which aspects of parenting are to be taken on by whom and how relationships between all parties need to be actively considered and maintained when a child is placed in a substitute family care setting.

EXERCISE 5.2: REBECCA'S STORY

Re-read that part of Unit 3 dealing with 'good enough parenting' (Study Text 3.2) and the following account of Rebecca's placement with foster carers and answer the questions that follow.

The Griffith family is registered as a short-term foster carer for babies and very young children. The Griffiths have two children of their own: Bethan aged ten and Michael aged six. One day a social worker telephones and asks if the family could possibly stretch to taking a seven-year-old girl, Rebecca, who has been removed from home. Her 13-year-old sister has made allegations against her father of serious sexual abuse. The Griffiths agree to accept Rebecca on a temporary basis. They know that it means making up a bed in Bethan's small bedroom but the family are confident that she will not object.

Rebecca arrives. She lived in one of the large housing estates on the edge of town; one of the most economically and socially deprived communities in the area. Rebecca is dirty, ill clad, and has nits. She is carrying a small bag of unwashed clothes. She is brought in by her mother and the social worker. Mum looks unwell and harassed. She does not speak during her short stay at the house. Rebecca seems unperturbed by her departure. Rebecca's mother is moving into a hostel later that day on the far side of town. There is no obvious means of contacting her there and no arrangements are made for Rebecca's mother to visit her at the Griffiths'.

During the next few days and weeks, the Griffiths find clothes for Rebecca that Bethan has grown out of. It becomes difficult to recognize this smart, clean and smiling Rebecca as the child who first arrived on the Griffiths' doorstep. She settles well into a new school and is beginning to form a relationship with Bethan. There has been no contact between Rebecca and her mother.

Rebecca's father has started to ring her up on a daily basis. He appears to talk to Rebecca as if she were an adult. He cries and says that he is missing her.

Rebecca is very distressed after these calls. The social worker is trying to arrange supervised contact with Rebecca's father, who can, it has been alleged, be very violent. In the event, contact takes place in the residential unit where Rebecca's sister lives. (Up until now, Rebecca has been prevented from having any contact with her sister as a police investigation has begun into the allegations of abuse made against their father.) The first contact session does not go well and the girls' father accuses everyone, the Griffiths included, of stealing his daughters from him. Rebecca refuses to attend any more contact sessions. Her father is still ringing daily. Rebecca asks to see her mother.

Rebecca continues to live with the Griffiths as care proceedings are begun. A social worker is visiting to talk to Rebecca about the sexual abuse. The Griffiths tell him that Rebecca is telling Bethan and Michael what happened to her and Bethan has already asked whether her daddy would ever do such a thing. The Griffiths are not involved in the counselling sessions with the social worker although they comfort Rebecca when she has dreams afterwards. The final hearing is due shortly and a case conference is to be held within a few days.

TASKS

1. How are the various roles and tasks of parenting Rebecca being allocated between the Griffiths, the local authority and Rebecca's parents? How should they be allocated?

2. Describe what you think the appropriate relationship should be between:

    a. Rebecca and each member of the Griffith family

    b. each member of the Griffith family and members of Rebecca's birth family

    c. the social worker and Rebecca, her birth family and the Griffiths.

3. What are the advantages/disadvantages of maintaining Rebecca's family links in this situation?

POINTS TO CONSIDER

1. Has Rebecca been placed *in* or *with* the Griffith family?

2. How might the Griffiths' parenting of their birth children be affected by Rebecca's arrival?

3. How much of a voice in decision making would/should a foster carer have in situations like this?

4. What are the differences in the kind of parenting provided by a foster carer and the kind of parenting usually provided by a child's birth family?

5. What responsibility does the social worker have for the effects of this placement on each member of the Griffith family?

6. What motivates people to become foster carers? Would you consider becoming one? Why/not?

COURSE TEXT: SPECIAL PESSIMISM

While it is the case that fostering has become the dominant form of substitute care, for the remainder of this Unit, we will be placing rather more emphasis on residential care, for two reasons. First, popular and professional interest in residential care has been more intense during recent years than for many years previously, as we explore below.

The second reason is a more personal one. It is our experience that field social workers and other professionals tend to undervalue, or even discount, residential care as a learning resource while in training and, more importantly, they tend to disregard residential care as a viable resource in practice. Few become engaged in the continuing debate about the role, function and future of residential care. This is a wide-ranging and important debate encompassing attitudes and values as well as substantial changes in the population of looked after children and in the range and type of provision available. In our practice, we see little to persuade us that the conclusion reached by the Department of Health and Social Security in 1985 (p.46) does not apply still:

> Virtually all social workers appear to view admission to care very negatively. They see it as a last resort and as a sign of failure to prevent the break up of families. They are also worried about what the care experience will do to children and parents. Residential care is looked on with special pessimism.

i STUDY TEXT 5.3: 'LOVE AND PROTEIN': POLICY AND PRACTICE WITH LOOKED AFTER CHILDREN

Reference has already been made to the 2006 and 2007 Green and White Papers that signalled a renewed policy interest in services for looked after children. In fact, professional and policy interest in this particular group of children in need had grown throughout the 1990s in the light of increasingly robust evidence of the relatively poor outcomes for children looked after away from home, especially but not exclusively, in respect of their educational achievements. This was accompanied by a growing awareness of the rise in expenditure on looked after children (HOC 2009, s. 13 ff. esp. Figure 3) set in the context of a steady decline in numbers from the late 1970s through to the mid 1990s.

In the 1990s too a number of residential care 'scandals' achieved prominence and both the Utting (1997) and Waterhouse (2000) reports led to an increased emphasis on adoption as a route out of care and both were influential in the passing of the 2002 Adoption and Children Act. In September 1998, the then Department of Health had launched the Quality Protects programme (known as Children First in Wales). This was part of a larger agenda of the New Labour government in the UK that should be seen alongside the publication, in November 1998, of the White Paper *Modernising Social Services* (Department of Health 1998). Drawing on the findings of a series of critical Joint Reviews[5] of local authority services, the White Paper spelled out the government's commitment to the 'third way for social care' that would move the focus 'away from who provides the care, and [place] it firmly on the quality of services experienced by, and outcomes achieved for, individuals and their carers and families' (Department of Health 1998, s. 1.7).

One of the specific outcomes of the broad 'modernizing agenda' was the development of key indicator sets and the development of targets, often set in relation to national minimum standards, introduced, in the case of looked after children, through the Care Standards Act 2000. The Act also introduced more bureaucratic regulatory and inspection regimes (see Humphrey 2002, 2003 for a critical perspective on the effects of an 'audit culture' on children's services at the time and Parton 2009 for a wider discussion of the bureaucratization of welfare practices).

Early reviews of the Management Action Plans that local authorities (in England) were required to produce as part of the regulatory and funding arrangements of Quality Protects and other 'modernizing' initiatives, demonstrated, at best, very uneven progress (see, for example, Department of Health 2001). Research (see Brandon and Thoburn 2008) was also suggesting that the emphasis on adoption had in some areas been at the expense of improving standards in other forms of substitute care. Together, these factors were influential in the launch, in March 2002 of the Choice Protects initiative. Initially focussing on the development

---

5   Joint Reviews of social services departments were carried out by the Social Services Inspectorate and the Audit Commission, combining a regard for professional standards and value for money.

of foster care, Choice Protects was supported with government funding from December 2002 (LAC 2202(19): DOH 2002d).

However, evidence of any improvement in outcomes for looked after children remained disappointing, again particularly but not exclusively in relation to placement stability and educational achievement (see Social Exclusion Unit 2003). The 2006 Green Paper, *Care Matters: Transforming The Lives of Children and Young People in Care*, recognized that progress had been insufficient (DfES 2006a, p.i):

> The life chances of all children have improved but those of children in care have not improved at the same rate. The result is that children in care are now at greater risk of being left behind than was the case a few years ago – the gap has actually grown.

In its review of progress, the House of Commons Children Schools and Families Committee (2009) found it 'dispiriting to consider just how intractable serious deficiencies in the care system have been' over at least 60 years (s. 26). Similar reflections have led researchers, with apparently ever increasing urgency, to ask such questions as 'Can the corporate state parent?' (Bullock and others 2006), 'Is the Care System Failing Children?' (Forrester 2008); and 'Looked after children: Can existing services ever succeed?' (Little 2010).

The Children and Young Persons' Act 2008 is a further step towards putting a legislative and policy framework in place to try and provide a positive answer. It makes provisions to improve the stability of placements and to improve the educational experience and attainment of young people looked after, particularly those who are about to leave care (see DCSF 2010d). Other guidance and regulations, such as that in relation to improving the health and well-being of looked after children (DCSF and DoH 2009) are also intended to drive up expectations and outcomes. Although it is too soon to judge the benefits of these additional provisions, the evidence for improvement across the National Key Indicators that are part of the National Performance Framework for Local Authorities and Local Authority Partnerships (in England) (Department for Communities and Local Government 2007) continues to present at best a slow moving picture. For example, in 2009 (DCSF/ONS 2009):

- NI 62: Stability of placements of looked after children: number of placements
  - 10.7 per cent of children had three or more placements during 2009. This figure has decreased steadily from 13.7 per cent since 2005.

- NI 63: Stability of placements of looked after children: length of placement

- ○ 67.0 per cent of children who had been looked after for two-and-a-half years or more had, in the past two years to 31 March 2009, lived in the same placement or their combined adoptive placement and preceding placement. This percentage has increased gradually since 2005 when the percentage was 62.9 per cent.

- NI 66: Looked after children cases which were reviewed within required timescales

  - ○ 90.9 per cent of children had their cases reviewed within the required timescales during 2009. This percentage has increased from 78.9 per cent in 2006 but there has been little change compared to the previous year (90.0 %).

Perhaps not surprisingly, the Care Matters Ministerial Stocktake Report 2009, while acknowledging progress, still takes the view that 'we need to go much further and faster' (DCSF 2009a, p.1).

Progress has been disappointingly slow in producing revised National Minimum Standards for children's homes and foster care to replace those first introduced in April 2002 by the Care Standards Act. These have an important potential for improving direct practice as well as being the basis for future inspection of services for looked after children (Ofsted 2010). The draft of the Standards on children's homes (DCSF 2010a) was only issued for consultation in August 2010. The twenty-eight draft standards include a welcome and increased emphasis on 'The child's wishes and feelings and the views of those significant to them' (Standard 1) and 'Promoting positive behaviour and relations with staff and others' (Standard 2) (see Figure 5.3).

STANDARD 1 – *The child's wishes and feelings and the views of those significant to them*

OUTCOME

- Children's views, wishes and feelings are known by staff and are reflected in all aspects of their care except where it would not be in the best interest of the child to do so.

- Children are helped to understand why, within reason, when their views, wishes and feelings are not reflected in their care and understand how to complain and get help and support.

- The views of others with an important relationship to the child are gathered and acted upon where appropriate.

STANDARD 2 – *Promoting positive behaviour and relations with staff and others*

OUTCOME

- Children have the support and encouragement they need to behave appropriately taking into account their individual circumstances.

- Children's behaviour is managed appropriately.

- Children can enjoy sound relationships with staff and others in the home based on self-esteem, self-worth and mutual respect.

Figure 5.3 Draft National Minimum Standards for Children's Homes (DCSF 2010a)

There is insufficient scope in a short Study Text such as this to describe the research evidence on the outcomes for children and young people who become looked after. What is important to note however is that there is a broad consensus (see for example, Thoburn 2007) to support Bullock and others' conclusion (2006, p.18) that the available evidence reveals that there is 'much success in what the state does for separated children and suggests that a lot of the criticisms are unjustified'. Critically, Bullock notes (p.11):

> The important message from research is that the factors predicting the success of long-term substitute placements are similar to those that predict successful parenting in ordinary families. Thus, the tasks to be undertaken and the qualities necessary to do them are virtually the same. But some children in care also need other things that rarely arise in ordinary families, such as managing contact with relatives, therapeutic help and protection from harm. So successful corporate parenting is more likely to require something extra rather than something different.

In other words, positive outcomes for looked after children are perfectly possible through the provision of competent parenting and negative outcomes are by no means inevitable. We would agree with Sinclair (2010) who suggests that while the policy, legislative and service framework provide a more or less permitting context for our work, we need to be 'much clearer about the crucial importance of practice and the difficulties of ensuring that it is uniformly good' (p.12) if we are to serve looked after children well.

This is certainly the view of some looked after children and young people. In an enormously perceptive and sensitively reported survey of young people's opinions on 'life in children's homes' undertaken by the Children's Rights Director for England (Ofsted 2009), it was the staff who were the 'best thing' (p.4). The experience of living in a children's home was described by one young person very succinctly as 'You get love and protein.' Not surprisingly in the light of what we have explored in this Unit, young people put 'missing your family' as the worst thing about living in a children's home. As always, in our experience, the young people reported a balanced, realistic and often humbling account of their experiences, warts and all. On the other hand, Gaskell's study of care leavers leaves no room for complacence (Gaskell 2010, p.146). Gaskell reports that 'the main framework through which these young care leavers understood their welfare needs and service use was that of a perceived lack of care' (p.145). This arose partly from their pre-care experiences 'that dominates their childhoods' and which can build up barriers to the development of trusting relationships but also because of their experiences 'of a lack of care within the context of constraints on service provision, rather than a direct lack of caring on the part of individuals themselves.' (*ibid.*)

To take what we believe to be a realistic position, we end this Study Text with some comments made by June Thoburn. She notes (2007, p.512):

> ... removal from home of a child who may be in need of protection may solve one set of problems but makes the child vulnerable to a new set of hazards...if temporary removal does become necessary, a course has to be steered between excess optimism and excess pessimism about the likely outcome for the child.

That course is one that you will help to steer.

PERSONAL OBJECTIVES

There can be no doubt that there has been an intense policy interest in the quality of services for children looked after away from home since the late 1990s. As yet, progress towards meeting the aims of the policy framework that has been put in place has been, by general consensus, at best, uneven. One might argue that this is because insufficient time has been allowed for the various policy initiatives to take effect. This is undoubtedly the case in some respects. However, the deficiencies of the 'care system' have been well known for many years and little of what has been put in place can be described as radically new, although it is the case that policy has never been so explicitly stated nor carried the authority of central government to the same degree. We would simply remind you of the danger of relying on systems and procedures without taking into account those who have to operate them. A personal commitment to make the policy work 'on the ground' is important too.

We will look shortly (Exercise 5.3) in a little more detail at what we mean by this. For now, we want to pass on something that we sometimes say to our students: 'What is wrong with social work practice currently, is our fault. What will be wrong with it in ten years' time will, to some degree at least, be yours.' What will you do to help improve both the process and the outcomes of being looked after?

EXERCISE 5.3: DAVID'S STORY

There are few 'smoking guns' in social work. What we mean by this is that very often the failure to look after children adequately does not lie in the 'gross failures' of the statutory or regulatory framework, stark deficiencies in our professional knowledge base nor even in the inadequacies of the network of provision available to children. Very often they reside in the 'small carelessnesses' to which each of us is prone. Consider the following account of one young person's experience of being looked after and answer the questions that follow:

Day One – Friday Night

A telephone call from the Emergency Duty Team is received at Paddlebrook Residential Unit at 1.00 a.m. It is a request for a placement for a 15-year-old young person. He had been missing from home for a few days and upon his return, his mother had been afraid to let him in. Father is out of town at the moment. A neighbour called social services after David was seen 'wandering the streets'. His mother refuses to have him home until father gets back and agrees to the social worker providing accommodation for David.

David asks the social worker to take him around to his uncle's, who lives across town, as he will look after him. The social worker refuses to do so as he says it is too late to obtain the necessary approvals and besides, uncle hasn't been 'police checked'. At 2.00 a.m. the 'out of hours' social worker brings David in and then leaves almost immediately. He leaves behind details of the young person's name and his address.

The 'sleeping in' residential social worker deals with the admission, much to his annoyance, as he has to be on shift again in the morning. He makes his feelings very clear to the waking night staff. With David in the room, he takes the opportunity to complain about how the emergency social worker had dealt with the whole business. A member of the night staff gives David a quick physical examination. David is told that he is just looking for bruises and any signs of infection. No toothbrush, soap or towel can be found for David, who is looking quite grubby and dishevelled. A bed has to be made up and there is a problem finding a full set of bedclothes. Eventually David is sent up to bed without supper or a drink, his clothes are taken from him, his pockets emptied and his clothes taken down to the laundry.

Day Two – Saturday Morning

David stays in bed waiting to be told he can get up. He can't find his clothes. A log entry is made that David wouldn't get up. David is given a tracksuit belonging to some past resident and comes downstairs. He has missed breakfast. A social worker who had called to collect another young person, and who specializes in home finding, is told all about last night's admission. This discussion takes place in the office with all but one member of staff present. This member of staff comes in to the office at one point and complains about being left with the kids all morning. David sits and watches TV. At lunchtime, David refuses to eat the food that is offered to him. He approaches a member of staff whom he addresses as 'Sir', much to everyone's amusement, and says he doesn't like it. He is told to 'like it or lump it' by the member of staff who had 'admitted' David the precious evening. A confrontation then ensues in which David loses his temper and swears at staff. A log entry is made for the afternoon staff to be especially vigilant as David is clearly 'potentially violent'.

At 6.00 p.m. David 'absconds'. At about 6.30 p.m., David's father turns up at the residential unit. He says that he has only just found out where David was put last night. He asks to see his son. He is told that this can only happen with the social worker's permission and the area office will be open on Monday. He is sent on his way. At approximately 7.30 p.m. David returns to the unit in a calm frame of mind. He says he has been to see his uncle who would look after him until his father gets home. He offers to cook his own tea but permission is refused.

At 9.30 p.m., David leaves the unit again without permission. He is reported to the police at 10.00 p.m., as per the authority's guidelines. He is returned to the unit at 11.15 p.m. by the police. He has been glue sniffing with two other residents from the unit and is to be interviewed in the morning about the theft of glue from the local garage. He is argumentative and difficult and is manhandled into his room.

to 'role-play' the situation with a pre-selected and prepared student volunteer. Be aware however, that watching someone have their contacts, photos, music, etc. 'deleted' in front of you can be equally affecting and trainers will need to be sensitive to the reactions of the rest of the class. Quiet consideration of the issues raised is, in our view, a better way for participants to explore the issues raised by this exercise.

Exercise 5.2: Rebecca's Story

The case material can easily be adapted to provide the scripts to role-play the imminent case conference. Questions about role, task, status and power emerge quite naturally in most simulated (and many real) case conferences. An interesting variation can be introduced if the case conference (or a simulated family conference) is asked to make arrangements for the termination of Rebecca's placement. The issues around separation as well as role and task are even more complex at this point. Alternatively, the exercise material can be used to explore attachment and loss behaviours.

Exercise 5.3: David's Story

Participants could be asked to use the material generated by the exercise as the basis of a procedure manual or good practice guide for field and residential workers. Alternatively, participants could be asked to write an information leaflet either for children and young people looked after or for their parents. A larger group, suitably divided, could be asked to do both. It is instructive to note the points of similarity and difference that inevitably emerge.

UNIT 6

Child Abuse

OBJECTIVES

In this Unit you will:

- Explore child abuse from an emotional, a thinking and a moral perspective.

- Begin to learn how child abuse is defined and classified.

- Learn how to make an initial response when child abuse is alleged or suspected.

📖 COURSE TEXT: CHILD ABUSE AND YOU

No qualifying or newly qualified social worker should be solely responsible for cases involving child abuse. The development of knowledge and skills in this area should form part of a social worker's post-qualifying experience and training. But, even though we assume that you are at an early stage in your professional development, it is important to begin preparing yourself for work in this area as soon as possible, for you may find yourself confronted with child abuse much earlier in your career than you anticipate. You may already have a statutory duty to respond to allegations of abuse as part of your job or during training. Your preparation must precede your professional obligations and it is never too early to start. This Unit is intended to develop your awareness and understanding of what is meant by 'child abuse'. Many of the themes introduced in this Unit are developed in Unit 9, which explores key elements of child protection practice.

We have suggested several times already that *you*, *your* attitudes, *your* values and the knowledge that *you* bring to a situation, are important influences on both the processes and the outcomes of social work with children and families. We begin this Unit by exploring what agenda you bring to work in the area of child abuse.

Any number of radio, television or newspaper headlines reporting an incident of harm to a child, the conclusions of the latest serious case review or the findings of a public inquiry into a child death would serve to demonstrate the significant emotional impact of child abuse. In the UK, you would only have to remember the outrage widely expressed at the deaths of Victoria Climbié (2/11/1991 – 25/02/2000) or Peter Connelly ('Baby P'; 1/03/2006 – 03/08/2007) to understand that child abuse can raise powerful feelings in anyone, including the social worker. It is important to recognize the emotional impact child abuse has on you. Ignoring your emotional responses may interfere with the work you are trying to do. Once acknowledged, however, you can use your own emotional responses to practical effect. Exercise 6.1 will demonstrate what we mean.

EXERCISE 6.1: A PERSONAL ACCOUNT

The account below was written specifically for the purposes of this exercise by someone who had been abused as a child. Although it is very graphic in some ways, you will have to supply most of the details of what took place yourself.

Read the text, take a few minutes to think about it and then carry out the tasks below.

There are two things that I remember more clearly than anything: the fact that he could be so nice sometimes and not being able to stop thinking about it. Even days afterwards I'd think about what had happened while I was doing something else, like at school. After the physical pain had gone I still used to feel it, that it had happened – not always him doing it but the feeling afterwards and the certain knowledge that it would happen again. But then, it wasn't him, in my mind, it was two other people.

I still felt bad because I knew, somehow, that it shouldn't happen and I'd try things in my head, stupid things to try and make sure it wouldn't happen again. He was always so apologetic. I'd work out how to stay on the right side of him but, of course, I couldn't. I certainly didn't want anyone else to know, not then. You know, when you have not done your reading or your work for a class and you hope it's not you that gets asked but you know, you just know, that you will be, it's like that. You think people know already, you see, but you wish that they didn't.

If someone tells you that they love you and they're sorry then you want to believe them and you hope that it's all over. Maybe I should have done more to stop it. I think perhaps that I should but I didn't. I didn't know what he felt about me then and I don't think I do now. There is no excuse for what he did to me.

How I didn't talk about it, I don't know. What would have happened if it hadn't stopped, I don't know. You can't imagine what it did to my head when I was older. I was so angry and felt such a fool. I nearly died the first time this kid asked me out.

TASKS

1. Make a list of words to describe how you feel about what you have read.

2. Write down how you feel about the child concerned.

3. Write down how you feel about the adult involved.

4. Write down how you feel the child and the adult may have felt at the time of the abuse and now.

POINTS TO CONSIDER

1. Were you surprised by any of the feelings that the piece raised in you?

2. Which of the feelings that you had towards the child might be helpful to you from this point?

3. Which of the feelings that you had towards the child might be unhelpful to you from this point? For example, do you see how a feeling of anger may motivate you to work hard for this child? Do you see how anger might also cloud your judgement and make it more likely that you will make mistakes? Do you see how fear might prompt a 'fight or flight' response?

4. What might be the consequences for you of denying those feelings that you have described?

5. What might be the consequences either of showing or hiding your feelings from the child and/or the adult involved?

6. What reasons might there be for someone not wishing to acknowledge his or her emotional response to child abuse?

COURSE TEXT: THINKING RESPONSES TO CHILD ABUSE

While our initial response to an incident or account of child abuse might be an emotional one, social workers cannot confine themselves to a response at this level. You have to think too. You have to reach a considered, informed and intelligent understanding of what has happened so that you can respond effectively. You might view such a suggestion as unnecessary. Surely, everyone knows what child abuse is? At the extremes, we might concede that there is likely to be a fairly ready consensus as to what constitutes abuse. On the other hand, while the deliberate starving to death of a child is clearly abusive, in what sense is the 'quiet catastrophe' of 25,000 children under five dying each day, mostly from low cost, easily preventable causes, also abusive (UNICEF 2007, p.16)? Is it abusive that 101 million primary aged children in the world do not go to school (UNICEF 2007, p.16)? Risking children's health in dangerous working conditions is clearly abusive, but have you thought about where your morning coffee, your trainers or your household furnishings come from? Were they perhaps produced by one of the 211 million children aged 5 to 14 who are 'economically active', i.e. who are involved in some form of work across the world (ILO 2004, p.8)? We do not expect you, as social workers, to take on such geo-political issues (but we wouldn't discourage you!). Our point is that what we describe as abusive is, in fact, selective. An example from closer to home might help to make the point; would you agree with the chairman of the UK's Royal College of General Practitioners, who in a letter to an national newspaper on 8th August 2010, wrote that parents who smoke in cars or at home 'are committing a form of child abuse' (*The Observer*)? Even at this more familiar level, we believe there remains a challenging uncertainty about how child abuse is defined. Exercise 6.2 will demonstrate what we mean.

EXERCISE 6.2: IS IT/ISN'T IT ABUSIVE?

Read the following mini case studies and answer the question: 'Is or isn't it abusive?'

1. Wayne is six years old. He has some behavioural problems and is generally boisterous and disobedient. He threw a stone, narrowly missing his baby brother, and broke a downstairs window. His father made him pick up the glass. Wayne cut his hands but his father made him clear the whole room nonetheless 'as a lesson to him'.

2. John is 13. His father has a large collection of pornographic videos that he allows John and several of his schoolfriends to watch together. John's father has said that he is only making sure that the boys understand the facts of life properly and that there is nothing to be ashamed of in being so 'open' about sex.

3. Julie is 14 and has run away from a children's home. She is staying with a much older man who has provided her with a home, food and clothing, but she is expected to pay for her keep by having sex with him and working as a prostitute. Julie says that she prefers this life to the one she had in care and does not want to return.

4. Sandra has moderate learning difficulties. She has twin boys aged 11 months. She keeps several dogs and the house is very dirty and disorganized. Sandra goes out every Thursday night and leaves the twins with the 12-year-old boy from next door. Both twins are dirty and have urine burns and nappy rash. Both are underweight. Sandra says that she cannot afford to buy more nappies than she does and, as she does not have a washing machine, she cannot keep up with the twins.

5. Tom is 16. He is not very 'sporty' and prefers to spend more time with his books and computer than he does with young people his own age. He is very shy in the company of girls. Some of his classmates have begun calling him names. They say that he is 'gay'. Tom has begun to pretend to be ill in order to avoid going to school. He says that the name-calling is 'getting to him' and making him have suicidal thoughts.

6. Rosie is 16. Her parents are members of a strict religious sect. Rosie is made to dress very plainly and is not allowed to wear cosmetics, listen to music or watch TV. She is not allowed out alone other than to walk to school. Her parents searched her school bag and found a 'love letter' from a classmate. Rosie was locked in her bedroom and kept away from school for a week.

7. Megan is 13. She lives with her mother and stepfather and her two half-brothers. The boys receive almost all of their parents' attention. Megan is not included in family outings and is made to do a disproportionate amount of helping out with the household chores. She is often not allowed to eat with the rest of the family. She is constantly told that she is 'useless' and will never make anything of her life.

8. Alun and Mary live in a particularly run down and deprived area. They have more or less dropped out of school and their prospects of work seem practically nil. Both are very depressed at the prospect of a life on benefits

and say that the only pleasure they get from life is from sex with each other and alcohol. Both sets of parents allow them to sleep together. Both are 14. Alun's father is worried about the alcohol but feels he has nothing better to offer his son.

POINTS TO CONSIDER

1. When making your decisions, how far did the nature and degree of any harm done and the degree of responsibility of the adults involved influence you?

2. Were you influenced by the immediate or by the longer-term consequences of the possible abuse?

3. Were you influenced by how much control the adult had over the circumstances in which the possible abuse took place?

4. To what extent did the 'maturity' of the young people involved affect your decision?

5. Would the determination of abuse be different if you were to ask the children concerned? Or the adults?

6. Are you aware of anything in your own experience of childhood that might prevent you from recognizing abuse?

COURSE TEXT: DEFINING CHILD ABUSE

Some definitions of child abuse are provided later in this Unit. Defining abuse is not the same as explaining it, of course, and we address some of the issues that arise when trying to define abuse in Study Text 6.1.

i STUDY TEXT 6.1: DEFINING CHILD ABUSE

We have already explored in Unit 1 how childhood is socially constructed and re-constructed, mostly by adults and often for reasons that have little to do with the rights, needs or interests of children. It is increasingly recognized that the same is true of child abuse (see Gelles 1975 for the earliest articulation of this approach).

It is perfectly possible, for example, to trace an explanatory, therapeutic and analytical history of child abuse and child protection, just as it is possible to trace the sociological history of children. Arbitrarily, one might begin with the nineteenth-century concern with what has been called a 'narrative of the body' (Hendrick 1994) where the visible poverty, palpable squalor, physical illness and the depredations of harsh working conditions were to be remedied with cleanliness, godliness and the cottage home; through to the development of a 'narrative of the mind' where the psychic traumas of childhood are internal, individual and, latterly, sexual. History is not a linear process, however, and ideas from one period may last well into succeeding ones; and sometimes, of course, old lessons have to be re-learned. Nonetheless, it does not appear possible to extract the concept of abuse from the context in which it occurs and the climate of ideas in which it is defined (see also Butler 2000; Corby 2005).

At one level, the idea that child abuse is socially constructed is relatively unproblematic. Self-evidently, the socio-historical context will have an effect on how children are treated, for good or ill. Similarly, it seems reasonable to expect that the socio-cultural structures, processes and economic conditions of the time will condition society's response. However, there have developed two distinctive ways of thinking about the consequences of these apparently straightforward propositions that we need to consider. The 'weaker' form of the constructionist approach suggests that while, at the margins, there may be room for negotiation about what constitutes harm to a child, there is sufficient moral and social consensus about what we mean by abuse to allow scientific study to proceed and to allow international and trans-historical comparisons to be made. We might disagree about precisely where and on what terms the state might intervene in cases of child abuse but that is simply a matter of thresholds that will become easier to define once we understand more fully just what behaviours impact negatively on a child and his/her development; by and large, while our understanding of child abuse is in the process of being defined and re-defined (refined?) in a more focussed way, there is an operational consensus about what and what is not abusive.

To a considerable degree, this is the view that is reflected in many key policy documents that govern child protection practice in the UK and elsewhere. For example, in *Working Together* (DCSF 2010f), the authoritative 'guide to inter-agency working to safeguard and promote the welfare of children' (to which we will return in Unit 9), child protection is expressed as an evolving function of scientific inquiry (s. 9.1):

Our knowledge and understanding of children's welfare — and how to respond in the best interests of a child to concerns about maltreatment (abuse and neglect) – develops over time, informed by research, experience and the critical scrutiny of practice. Sound professional practice involves making judgements supported by evidence: evidence derived from research and experience about the nature and impact of maltreatment, and when and how to intervene to improve outcomes for children.

There is a much broader debate to be had that extends well beyond the confines of this book about the nature of scientific and ratio-technical 'truths' in social work (but see Butler and Pugh 2004). For our present purposes, it is sufficient to note that the temporal dimension to our understanding of child abuse is acknowledged in *Working Together* but that this is seen in the context of ever improving, better evidenced, diagnostic and interventive techniques.

The 'stronger' version of constructionism, suggests that not only is this view of science ('scientism') naive, but that it also fails to take into account socio-structural processes and the uneven distribution of power and social capital. By this reading, definitions of abuse and their associated child protection practices impose dominant cultural values on subordinate groups; for example, 'white, middle class values' on poor, working class parents, especially those from disadvantaged communities and ethnic minorities (see, in particular, Garrett 2002, 2003 and 2008). By this reading, with any particular definition of child abuse, it is important to ask *whose* definition it is and whose interests does it serve?

For example, until relatively recently, the child's account of abuse has had very little impact on how child abuse is understood and acted upon by adults. Where there is a cultural presumption against the capacity and competence of children and young people and where children hold positions of relative powerlessness, their definitions of harm are less likely to receive official sanction and to be acted upon by the state (see Butler and Williamson 1994). Bullying, for example, would almost certainly rate much more highly on children's hierarchy of abuse than it does on adults'. Certainly, the detrimental effects of bullying on a child's well-being can be very serious (Stassen Berger 2007; Reijntjes and others 2010). Similarly, as far as the children of marginalized groups are concerned, different standards of what constitutes harm may be applied. For example, the children of asylum seekers have been shown to exhibit 'high levels of mental and physical health problems' while detained in immigration centres in the UK:

> …as well as child protection concerns [being] detected, detained families had very limited access to appropriate assessment, support or treatment. The traumatic experience of detention itself also has implications for the sizeable proportion of psychologically distressed children who are eventually released from detention and expected to successfully reintegrate into British

society; while those children who are deported are returned with increased vulnerability to future stressors. (Lorek and others 2009, p.573)

It is not our purpose to persuade you to adopt either a 'weak' or a 'strong' constructionist point of view. However, we do see the merits in adopting *a* constructionist position. As Howe (1994) has argued, a constructionist perspective encourages pluralism in debates about the children and families with whom we work. It should prevent us too readily from adopting a 'one true way' attitude, whatever our 'one true way' happens to be. Similarly, a constructionist approach invites participation and inclusion in the debates about what constitutes abuse. It should sensitize you also to the power relations inherent in society and help you to think critically about your professional relationship with children and families. It also, according to Rex Stainton Rogers, provides an optimism and an expectation of change that can sometimes be missing from child protection work:

> That we no longer hang children, burn them as witches or brand them as vagrants is not the victory of a few reformers, it is the victory of a whole society which has overcome the constructions that made such actions possible. The killings and the maimings of children that our society still generates can also be consigned to the history book – by the same processes that have made possible the worlds in which we now live. (Stainton Rogers 1989, p.29)

Depending on your point of view and relationship to the events in question, your definitions of, and explanations for, abuse may be different from ours. What matters, however, is that in your reading about these issues (which will extend well beyond the confines of this particular book), you examine critically, carefully and comprehensively any definition, explanation or account that you encounter. Certainly not all, maybe not any, definitions of abuse are universally reliable, valid or exhaustive.

As we will explore more fully below however, by encouraging you to think critically, we do not want you to 'think yourself to a standstill'. As a social worker, you will be required to translate your thinking into action. What we do want to encourage you to do is to adopt a reflective, critical and intelligent approach to thinking about child abuse. Not only will this enable you to develop an open-minded approach to your own learning, it will also have direct practice benefits.

What follows is a short extract from a background paper, prepared for the Department of Child Protection in Western Australia (DCP 2008). It sets out the rationale for the *Signs of Safety* framework that is used locally (and in parts of Canada, New Zealand, Denmark, Sweden, The Netherlands, Japan and the

USA) to 'ensure consistent, evidence based child protection practice' in a similar way to that which *Working Together* seeks to do in England. The details of the framework are not our primary concern but the fundamental attitude that it describes to practice reflects many of the points that we have tried to make in this Unit so far (details of the references are included in the index to this book):

> In the contested and anxious environment of child protection casework the paternalistic impulse to establish the truth of any given situation is a constant. As Baistow and colleagues suggest:
>
>> Whether or not we think there are absolute perpetrators and absolute victims in child abuse cases, and whether or not we believe in a single uncontaminated 'truth' about 'what happened', powerful forces pull us towards enacting a script, which offers us these parts and these endings. (Baistow and others 1995, p.vi)
>>
>> The difficulty is that as soon as professionals decide they know the truth about a given situation this begins to fracture working relationships with other professionals and family members, all of whom very likely hold different positions. More than this the professional ceases to think critically and tends to exclude or reinterpret any additional information that doesn't conform to their original position. (English 1996)
>
> Eileen Munro, who is internationally recognized for her work in researching typical errors of practice and reasoning in child protection (Munro 1996, 1998), states:
>
>> The single most important factor in minimizing error (in child protection practice) is to admit that you may be wrong. (Munro 2002, p.141)
>
> Restraining an individual's natural urge to be definitive and to colonise one particular view of the truth is the constant challenge of the practice leader in the child protection field. Enacting Munro's maxim requires that all processes that support and inform practice, foster a questioning approach or a spirit of inquiry as the core professional stance of the child protection practitioner. (DCP 2010)

Acknowledging, using and managing the uncertainty that so often inhabits child protection work, rather than ignoring it or taking refuge in simple (and simplistic) explanations or definitions, is one of the most difficult steps in developing as an effective professional capable of working in this field. At the heart of good child protection social work lies critical thinking, reflection and the exercise of good judgement. The next exercise reinforces the point.

EXERCISE 6.3: DEFINING ABUSE

Below you will find six thumbnail 'definitions' of abuse (more detailed definitions are introduced in Study Text 9.1). Read them carefully and jot down, for each one, an example of what is being described. Then go back and read the mini case descriptions provided for Exercise 6.2 before completing the tasks set out below.

1. *Physical abuse*: where a parent (or somebody else caring for a child) physically hurts, injures or kills a child.

2. *Sexual abuse*: when adults seek sexual gratification by using children.

3. *Neglect*: where parents (or whoever else is caring for the child) fail to meet the basic essential needs of children (e.g. adequate food, clothes, warmth and health care).

4. *Emotional abuse*: where children are harmed by constant lack of love and affection, or threats.

5. *Deprivation*: where children's needs fail to be met or their potential and life-chances are damaged by social forces and/or institutions.

6. *Exploitation*: where individuals and social institutions (including institutions of the State) satisfy their own needs or purposes by inappropriately using children.

TASKS

1. Allocate each of the mini case descriptions to one or more categories of abuse.

2. Describe clearly your reasons for doing so.

3. Describe how adequate each definition is for each case.

4. Amend each of the thumbnail definitions to reflect your appreciation of the cases and your broader understanding of abuse.

And/or

5. Rank order the cases (using any criteria that you think appropriate) – first from the point of view of the child concerned and then from the (imagined) point of view of the editor of the local tabloid newspaper.

POINTS TO CONSIDER

1. Was it difficult to place particular cases in single categories?

2. What does this tell you about the phenomenon and the concept of abuse?

3. Whose definition of abuse counts for the most and why?

4. Whose definition of abuse counts the least and why?

5. How adequate is your own definition of abuse?

6. What are you going to do to improve it?

COURSE TEXT: RESPONDING TO ABUSE

As well as someone who is sensitive to their own and other people's emotions and who is developing their capacity for critical thinking, we assume that you are someone who wants to *do* something about harm to children. Despite the difficulties in responding to abuse at a purely human level and all of the intellectual challenges that come with trying to define abuse, you will also have to act to protect children. You will not be surprised to find that it is exceptionally difficult to work out in practice what 'protecting' a child actually means. Sometimes, for example, the removal of a child from his or her home will be protective. Sometimes such a separation will prove harmful. Ritchie (2005, p.276), for example, has suggested that 'the 21st Century is the time to break the umbilical cord of public care' on the basis that there is 'no evidence that public care reduces the risk of significant harm' (p.764) – but see Unit 5. At this stage in your professional development, you may not be in a position to make such judgements. That does not mean, however, that you have no obligation to respond to situations in which child abuse may have taken place. The final part of this Unit deals with responding to child abuse when you are least prepared for it and least expecting it.

Exercise 6.4 examines how you might react if a child was to disclose abuse to you.

EXERCISE 6.4: JANE'S STORY

Read the following case scenario and answer the questions. Complete each individual section before attempting the next.

Jo, a student social worker, is taking her daughter to Brownies and the Leader asks to have a word with her. She starts by apologizing and says that she knows that Jo is something to do with social services. 'Can I talk to you in confidence?' she asks, 'It's about Jane [another Brownie]. I'm very worried about the bruises she has on her face and arms.'

1. What would your response be to a request for confidentiality in a situation such as this?

Jo has a look and is appalled at what she sees. Jo asks Jane how she got the bruises.

2. Was this the right thing to do in the circumstances? If not, what else could Jo have done?

Jane starts to cry and says that she fell over. She begs Jo not to say anything to anyone else. She seems really upset. Jo is beginning to feel a bit embarrassed about all the fuss and wishes that she had not become involved in the first place. Jane is clearly relieved when Jo tells her not to worry; Jo is not going to say anything.

3. Is this how you might have reacted?

4. What are the possible consequences of Jo's decision not to tell a child protection worker?

Later that night, Jo realizes that the incident with Jane is bothering her. It gives her a restless night. The next day Jo mentions it to a colleague in the office where she is on placement who says that Jo ought to discuss it with someone from the child care team. Jo delays doing this all day and finally, at 4.45 p.m., she goes and talks to the child care team leader.

5. What are the consequences of this delay:

   a. if Jane's injuries were sustained from an assault?

   b. if Jane really had simply fallen down the stairs?

The team leader listens to Jo's description of the bruises and is very interested in the fact that Jane was distressed and begged Jo not to tell anyone else. The team leader decides that there is sufficient reason to investigate further.

6. What are the possible consequences now if:

   a. Jane has been abused?

   b. Jane has not been abused?

7. Could Jo have done anything else which might have assisted the investigation which will now take place?

POINTS TO CONSIDER

1. List some possible reasons for someone in Jo's position not wishing to 'get involved' (e.g. fear of looking foolish if suspicions are unfounded; painful memories of your own). Might any of these apply to you?

2. What might Jane be expecting from someone to whom she does tell her story?

3. What particular needs of the child should your response be directed towards meeting?

4. What particular rights of the child must your response respect?

5. Where might *you* turn for advice if you were to find yourself in a similar position to Jo?

6. What might inhibit you from seeking advice in such circumstances?

i STUDY TEXT 6.2: RESPONDING TO ABUSE

Unit 9 deals in more detail with the process of investigation and the co-ordination of responses following an allegation or suspicion of abuse in England (see DfES 2006b for a concise account of how the child protection 'system' operates in England.) The purpose of this Study Text is to help to prepare you for exposure to abuse when investigation is not explicitly part of your professional role. It begins with some direct advice on what you need to bear in mind should you find yourself in a similar position to Jo. This is presented in the form of a series of 'bullet points' in the hope that you will be able to easily absorb and recall what is required of you. We then consider how you might think about responding to child abuse in a more holistic and considered way.

AN INITIAL RESPONSE

As a student or as a volunteer or sessional worker, or even as a qualified social worker, you can do a great deal to prepare yourself for the unexpected discovery of possible child abuse by making sure that you are familiar with your agency's child protection procedures. All health and social care agencies in the UK *will* have detailed procedures and protocols in place that should be explained to you as part of your induction to working in that agency or to starting a placement as a student social worker. Almost every other kind of organization working with children, from church groups to sports clubs, *should* have such policies and procedures in place. It is your responsibility to know what is expected of you should you have cause for concern whenever you accept any position of trust or responsibility in relation to children. There is no possible defence for not finding out what your responsibilities are under your agency's child protection procedures. 'No-one told me' is not an excuse.

In your professional role, or even in a situation such as the one in which Jo found herself, there are certain principles that you should observe should you find yourself dealing with a child or young person where you have suspicions that he or she may have been abused:

- *Listen*: If someone, particularly the child directly concerned, begins to tell you about a possible abusive incident or series of events, don't just do something, sit there and listen. Do not 'cross-examine' the child or begin some form of quasi-investigation. Be particularly careful not to jeopardize any possible criminal investigation by, for example, asking leading questions or 'putting words into the child's mouth'.

- *Be supportive*: It is important that the child feels supported and that you do not transmit any of the anxieties that you may have to the child. You will need to balance any emotional response that you may have with an appropriate thinking response. Try to relate to and communicate with the child in a way that is appropriate to his or her age and understanding.

- *Don't judge*: It is vital that you do not patronize the child or otherwise seek to diminish what you are being told. Keep the information that you are being given separate from your interpretation of it. It may prove necessary to repeat what the child says to child protection workers later and it may be helpful to make notes of what you have been told, as soon as practicable after you have spoken to the child.

- *Don't make promises that you can't keep*: Particularly, do not promise a child unconditional confidentiality. Be honest and offer reassurance wherever possible. It is far preferable to say to anyone, child or adult, who asks you not to tell: 'I don't know what you are going to tell me. I may have to talk to someone else if I think you or someone else is in danger but, if I can keep what you tell me in confidence, I will.' A significant barrier to disclosure by young people to professionals is the fear that many of them have about the potential loss of control over decisions that affect them (see, for example, Ungar and others 2009). If you are honest with young people, right from the outset, a degree of trust and confidence can be developed and some of this fear can be reduced.

- *Don't dither.* Check out your concerns with a more experienced worker and report them to a senior worker in your agency, ideally your line manager. Delay, in Jane's case for example, could have led to the bruises, that is the 'proof', fading and the opportunity for her to be further harmed. Or, if she hadn't been assaulted, delay may have made it more difficult for her parents to convince the social worker that the faded bruises were the result of a fall.

We do not underestimate the challenge of responding in situations such as these. There are many 'reasons' why you might feel reluctant. The National Institute for Health and Clinical Excellence (NICE 2009) in its guidance, *When to Suspect Child Maltreatment*, includes a comprehensive list of 'potential obstacles to recognising and responding to possible maltreatment' (p.8). Although written with health care professionals in mind, it includes the following generally applicable 'obstacles':

- … fear of losing a positive relationship
- discomfort of believing, thinking ill of, suspecting or wrongly blaming a parent or carer
- divided duties to adult and child … and breaching confidentiality
- an understanding of the reasons why the maltreatment might have occurred, and that there was no intention to harm the child
- losing control over the child protection process and doubts about its benefits
- stress
- personal safety
- fear of complaints.

We imagine that several of these occurred to you during the last exercise. While understandable, such 'obstacles' cannot stand in the way of your professional obligations to the child or young person and their family. As a social worker, you have to accept the moral responsibility to act in such situations; to be proactive and to act authoritatively.

'MORALLY ACTIVE PRACTICE'

Nonetheless, we understand that for some of you, the question of 'how can I be sure?' is still awaiting an answer. You may have been disappointed to learn that we are not going to provide you with a 'check-list' that will tell you what is and what is not abuse and what is and what is not protective. What you do have to help you reach a judgement though is the potential of your emotional response and your capacity for critical thinking. Each has their part to play and both should inform the other. Both are essential to the exercise of professional judgement. It is true that an overly 'emotional' response (such as overwhelming anger) may inhibit your capacity to act effectively and a clear-headed approach to a difficult and challenging situation would be preferable. However, an over-reliance on a dispassionate, coldly logical response may obscure some of the clues that can arise through the use of intuitive as well as analytical reasoning. An experienced worker's sense that 'something is not quite right' should not be ignored and could form the basis for further investigation. Recent developments in neuro-psychology (see Isen and Labroo 2003) would suggest that emotions play a critical part in promoting flexibility in decision making and helping to provide creative solutions to problems as well as helping us to decide which is the preferred or desired outcome for any given set of circumstances. Far from seeking to exclude *or* privilege either cognitive capacity or emotional sense, you will need to be able to integrate both analytic and intuitive reasoning (see Munro 2008 for a fuller discussion of the relationship between the two).

As a social worker, you will also need to be able to answer to your professional obligations and this means practising in accordance with the core values of the profession:

> What is considered child abuse for the purposes of child protection policy and practice is much better characterized as a product of social negotiation between different values and beliefs, different social norms and professional knowledges and perspectives about children, child development and parenting. Far from being a medico-scientific reality, it is a phenomenon where moral reasoning and moral judgement are central. (Parton 1997, p.67)

The exercise of that 'moral reasoning and moral judgement' will be grounded in your own attitudes and values, as we have made clear throughout this book. They will also be informed by the standards of social work, as a profession. These standards may be embedded in 'codes of conduct', 'ethical codes' or in regulations governing registration as a social worker or fitness to continue in practice. There are limitations to such codifications, not the least being that quite often they are little more than a formal articulation of 'those distinctive attitudes which characterise the culture of a professional group' (Häring 1972, p.24). In other words, they display a 'considerable measure of self-interest' (Homan 1991, p.3) on the part of the professional group by which they are constructed (see Dawson and Butler 2003 for a fuller discussion of the place of codes of ethics in social care practice). Nonetheless, codes of conduct and statements of the ethics of the profession still constitute important points of reference when operating in conditions of extreme uncertainty such as in child protection social work.

In the UK, the BASW Code of Ethics (BASW 2002) is probably the best known. Other countries have similar codes such as the Australian Association of Social Workers (2002; Second Edition); the ACTS/ CASW Code in Canada (2005) or the very helpful Swedish *Ethics for Social Work* (ASSR 2006). In England, there is the General Social Care Council's 'Code of Practice' that sets the standards for entry to the register of social workers. There is also the IFSW's key 'Statement of Principles' (IFSW 2004). It would seem even here that there are choices facing us, even in relation to which ethical principles should guide our practice! (In fact, there is a considerable degree of correspondence between the various codes but see Gilbert 2009 for a comparison of the BASW and IFSW Codes and their relationship to the GSCC Code of Conduct.)

Rather than advocate the adoption of any particular 'code', we wish to persuade you to adopt Husband's concept of the 'morally active practitioner'. In articulating the struggle for an ethical pluralism that arises from his engagement with anti-racist practice, Husband argues for eternal moral vigilance in the form of the 'morally active practitioner' who would 'recognise the implementation of professional ethical guidelines as desirable and as being *permanently irreducible to routine*... Morally engaged practitioners could not hide within [a] professional ethical anaesthesia, but would retain their responsibility for their professional practice and its implications' (Husband 1995, p.87 – our emphasis).

We think that the phrase 'permanently irreducible to routine' could be applied not only to the moral dimension of child protection work but to the whole of social work practice with children and families. Emotion, intuition, reflection, cognitive ability, critical thinking and a clear values position are the bedrock of social work with children and families and none of these, we hope you would agree, are reducible to routine.

CONCLUSION

We have suggested in this Unit that a central element in working in this field is an acknowledgement of the essential uncertainty and ambiguity that surrounds child abuse. There are no simple check-lists that you can apply to determine whether abuse is taking place or not; there are no simple steps you can take to make the abuse go away or magically 'get better'. You will go on to learn how to understand, evaluate and reduce the risks for the child and the worker in child protection situations as your career develops, but you may find yourself involved long before you think you are fully ready. At this point in your professional development we would want you to think carefully about what you see or are told about child abuse and critically to evaluate and reflect on your wider reading. We want you to use your instinct and intuition; your capacity for critical thinking and to be directed by your own moral 'compass' and the core values of the profession.

But, most important of all, we want you to be ready to act when your suspicions are aroused. There can be no justification for simply turning away.

NOTES AND SELF-ASSESSMENT

1. Are there certain forms of behaviour that you would always categorize as abusive?

2. How does your understanding of abuse relate to your particular construction of childhood?

3. What are the major influences on your understanding of abuse?

4. Do all instances of child abuse require action?

5. What might stop you from responding to any abuse of which you become aware?

6. Do you know how to take the appropriate next step in responding to abuse in your particular post or practice placement?

RECOMMENDED READING

Munro, E. (2008) *Effective Child Protection* (Second Edition). London: Sage.

Corby, B. (2005) *Child Abuse: Towards a Knowledge Base* (Third Edition). Milton Keynes: Open University.

TRAINER'S NOTES

Exercise 6.1: A Personal Account

Encourage group members to share feelings, possibly by 'quickthinking' them on to a flip chart. You may wish to consider the range of feelings expressed and their intensity. Are there feelings that are commonly felt? Are some much more personal than others? (Group members should be reminded that they do not have to explain or 'justify' their responses.) One important aspect to consider is whether some of the feelings expressed would be helpful in working with a family where abuse was suspected. If so, to whom would they be helpful? In the exercise, for example, we note how anger can be both a negative and positive influence – negative in the sense of rendering a worker unable to hear the needs of the person who has been abused, positive in the sense of providing the energy to 'do' something in the face of other overbearing emotions. What other feelings among those you have elicited from the group might have similar double-edged effects?

Exercise 6.2: Is it/Isn't it Abusive?

A larger group could be broken down into pairs and the decisions compared and debated between sub-groups. A much more effective (but much more difficult to manage) way to proceed is to work in a large group and to take each case in turn and to proceed only when unanimous agreement has been reached. This has the advantage of making participants explore in fine detail their reasons for whatever view they hold and it makes visible the kind of disagreements that really do exist about the nature of various forms of abuse.

Exercise 6.3: Defining Abuse

This exercise can be used in a group in the same way as the preceding exercise. For Task 4, sub-groups or pairs can work together to produce definitions that can be debated and 'adopted' by the whole group. Task 5 is best done by two 'opposing' groups, who complete their rankings and then, in role, argue the merits of their case.

Exercise 6.4: Jane's Story

The case material can:

- be given to each student as it is and the whole group works individually on the answers

or

- be read out by the trainer, posing the questions in sequence and having group discussion

or

- be prepared as a booklet for use in small groups. The booklets would have a scenario and question on each page so that issues could be discussed before the next instalment was revealed on the following page.

The following are some suggestions for discussion 'prompts':

1. What would your response be to a request for confidentiality in a situation such as this?

    - You can't guarantee confidentiality.

    - It's difficult to say no.

2. Was this the right thing to do in the circumstances? If not, what else could Jo have done?

    - Depends on how it is done. Might be Ok if Jo is subtle but perhaps a bit overpowering for Jane who, after all, doesn't know Jo.

    - Perhaps better to talk only with the Leader and enable her to do the talking to Jane and pass on information to Jo.

3. Is this how you might have reacted? After all, the bruises could have been caused by a fall.

    - Has Jo the right to tell Jane that she will respect her confidence and not tell anyone else?

    - What do you think Jane might be feeling now?

    - How swayed are you by Jane's distress?

4. What are the possible consequences of a decision not to tell a child protection worker?

    - Jane might be more severely bruised tomorrow.

    - Jane might be too terrified to tell anyone in the future.

5. What are the consequences of this delay:

    a. If Jane's injuries were sustained from an assault:

        ○ Bruises will fade and 'proof' of harm will be more difficult to come by.

        ○ There will be more opportunities for Jane to be further harmed.

    b. If Jane had really simply fallen down the stairs:

        ○ Nothing for Jane but if the social services department decide, when they are informed, that there is a case to investigate the fact that there are faded bruises might make it more difficult for Jane's carers to convince the social worker that it was simply a case of a fall.

6. What are the possible consequences now if:

    a. Jane has been abused:

        ○ Jane may be protected from further abuse.

        ○ The perpetrator may be stopped from harming Jane or any other children in the household.

        ○ Jane will be given the opportunity to talk about what has happened to her, to let out some of her distress. This may be the start of action to repair any damage, mental or physical.

        ○ The family will experience disruption and investigation by outsiders.

    b. Jane has not been abused:

        ○ The family, of which Jane is a part, will experience disruption and stress.

        ○ Jane herself may feel guilty for setting the investigation in progress.

        ○ If Jane feels that she is not believed then the protection may seem more like persecution.

7. Could Jo have done anything else which might have assisted the enquiry?

    • Enabled the Brownie Leader to collect together clear information about what she had seen.

    • Written down what she had seen: time, extent, reasons given, Jane's comments, etc.

    • Told the Brownie Leader whom to contact and offered to go with her.

    • Been more honest with Jane and explained that she is very concerned about her bruises and the fact that she seems very frightened.

PART II

Developing Specialist
Knowledge and Skills

UNIT 7

Assessing

OBJECTIVES

In this Unit you will:

- Learn some practical techniques for gathering and ordering information as part of an assessment.

- Consider means to effectively engage children and families in the process of assessment.

- Develop a practical understanding of child observation.

- Begin work on an extended case study and consider the application of what you have learned to practice.

COURSE TEXT: IN THE BEGINNING

'In trying to understand a problem and how to solve it, you should always start at the beginning.' That sounds like the kind of common-sense advice that you might expect to find in a book like this. The trouble is that, in social work, the 'beginning' can be a very difficult place to find! Even if you are the first point of contact for people using the services of your particular agency, the situation that prompted the referral will have a history that extends beyond your introduction into events. All of the individuals, families or groups involved will also have complex, dynamic, discrete and interrelated histories. You and your agency have particular histories too. It might be more appropriate, although not very helpful, to seek the 'beginning' in the 'life, universe and everything' kind of question that we usually leave to philosophers or theologians. The truth is that a social worker's involvement in any child and family situation never occurs 'at the beginning'. You are always going to be joining in a sequence of events that is already in progress and which will continue long after your involvement has ended.

We make this very obvious point for two reasons: first, because some social workers and other professionals too easily forget that this is the case and assume that nothing of importance or interest could conceivably have pre-dated the events that have prompted their arrival on the scene; and second, because, ignorant of the past and uncluttered by too many facts, it is much easier to make superficial judgements about the situation of the child or family and how it is to be tackled. These judgements have much more to do with the assumptions and 'one size fits all' solutions that the worker brings to the situation than the circumstances of the child and family concerned and, as such, are usually inaccurate, unproductive, if not downright harmful.

The key to avoiding such self-evident (but not always obvious) poor practice lies in a commitment to the process of assessment. The reference to 'commitment' is deliberate. It is perfectly possible, though highly undesirable, to proceed to action without assessing the circumstances or context in which that action takes place. We can all be too busy, too stressed, or too confident in our diagnostic skills. We refer to a 'process' of assessment deliberately too. Assessment isn't an event. It is not something you do once to someone else and exclusively for your own purposes. Assessment is a continuous and mutual process of making sense of what has happened and what is happening now.

Many attempts have been made to define more fully what is meant by 'assessment' in social work. To some degree, every definition bears the mark of the time at which it was made. It should be remembered, for example, that modern forms of social work owe much to the scientistic endeavours of nineteenth century social reformers who sought to apply the rational calculus of the natural sciences to social problems. In social work, this produced a highly medicalized understanding of assessment as part of a 'casework' model of social work practice (see Lloyd and Taylor (1995) for an interesting account of the 'history' of assessment from Florence Hollis to the mid 1990s). Such definitions of assessment tended to cast the social worker very much in the role of 'expert'. Indeed, Seden (2001), in her account of the development of assessment in social work, notes that it was not until the 1970s that the ideological shift 'away from a diagnostic focus towards understanding the perspectives of the service user within a holistic and person centred framework' (p.9) took place. It is important to remember the historical specificity of any model or theory of assessment in order to avoid an uncritical approach to contemporary forms of assessment practice. We return to this point below.

As Seden (2001) has pointed out, more recent definitions of assessment tend to emphasize the inclusive and 'process' nature of assessment (see Milner and O'Byrne 2002; Smale, Tuson and Statham 2000). The *Framework for the Assessment*

of Children in Need and their Families (Department of Health and others 2000)
that we have introduced at various points already (in Units 1, 2 and 4) gives
particular emphasis to such an inclusive and focussed approach to assessment:

> Nothing can be assumed; the facts must be sought, the meaning attached to
> them explored and weighed up with the family. (p.13)

> Understanding what is happening to a vulnerable child… must necessarily
> be a process of gathering information from a variety of sources and making
> sense of it with the family and, very often, with other agencies concerned
> with the child's welfare. (p.14)

The purpose of this Unit is to encourage you to develop your understanding
of assessment as a dynamic, interactive and reciprocal process that will be of
equal use to you, the child and the family concerned and to do so with a critical
awareness of the model(s) of assessment that are available to you.

So, even if we can't really start at the beginning, where can we begin the
assessment? If assessment is to be understood in broad terms as 'making sense
of what has happened and what is happening now', the obvious place to start is
with the information that you have in front of you. Often the most immediate
and voluminous, if not necessarily the most accessible, source of information
will be in the form of a case file. Such files come in all sorts of shapes, sizes,
colours and degrees of organization. As a student or a newly qualified worker,
perhaps the majority of your work will be encountered, in the first instance, via
the case file.

As well as offering the foundation of a thorough assessment, a good working
knowledge of the file has other benefits too. For example, acquaintance with
the contents of the file should reduce the possibility that information previously
provided to your agency will need to be collected again. Sometimes this
information will have been gained at considerable cost to the service user. Your
ignorance of key events already known to your agency will convey an unhelpful
sense that what has been shared previously has been forgotten or discounted.
You will have more time available for the task in hand if you do not have to
trawl for information that your agency already possesses. Moreover, confidence
in you and your ability to help will inevitably be diminished if you make a point
of demonstrating that you have not had either the time or the inclination to
prepare adequately. The following Study Text demonstrates some ways in which
you might begin the process of assessment, by exploring how you can make
most use of such a file.

i STUDY TEXT 7.1: STARTING POINTS

One key dimension along which we ordinarily fix and structure our own experience is by reference to time. Many interventive techniques, particularly those derived from the psychoanalytic tradition of casework, rely on establishing a detailed and accurate chronology of events as a basis for interpreting and understanding current situations and motivations. Even if you do not intend to base your own practice in this tradition, establishing the order of events is a useful first step towards developing your understanding of the histories and processes in which you are becoming involved.

Most case files are, nominally at least, compiled in chronological order. However, while case notes may be sequential, they often cross-refer to other sections of the file – such as correspondence or reports, which may be ordered thematically or in relation to particular events. In reality, the 'timelines' can be very difficult to trace through even a relatively new file. You could begin to get a sense of past events simply by writing the year down on one side of a piece of paper and, using the file, writing down the significant events of that year alongside. Alternatively, with particularly complex family histories, you could use a card index record – this allows you a little more flexibility to add additional information as your assessment proceeds. You could also represent the information graphically, in the form of a flow chart (see Figure 7.1).

A second key dimension along which we fix and order our experience is by reference to patterns of relationships. The nature of relationships can also be a focus for specific interventions and is usually an important consideration in child and family work. One commonly used technique for representing relationships through time is the genogram. At its simplest, a genogram is little more than an annotated family tree. The annotations can include major family events, occupations, places of residence and even patterns of contact. The genogram uses conventional notation: a square represents a male; a circle represents a female; a triangle represents those circumstances where the sex is unknown (e.g. an unborn child or a distant relative) and a cross drawn through one of these figures represents a death. Lines show the strength of relationships between individuals: an enduring relationship by a firm line and a transitory relationship by a broken line. These lines can be crossed through by a single line in the event of separation or by a double line in the event of a divorce. When drawing a genogram, the children of a particular couple are usually entered according to age, starting with the oldest on the left. It can be useful to draw a dotted line around all of those living in the same household. Figure 7.2 illustrates the basic form of a genogram covering three generations.

1971	1972	1973	1975	1978
September 12. Born North-town. Twins! Me 5lbs 4 oz; Jane 5lbs.	Whooping cough. In hospital for 2 weeks. Jane also poorly.	Family moved house. Brother Matthew born. June 24th.	Started school; hated it. Started speech therapy, hated that too.	March, fell off my bike. Broke my arm.
1982	**1987**	**1989**	**1990**	**1991**
Started Grammar School. Jane went to girl's school. Mum and dad split up.	Took GCSEs. Did well. Jane didn't. She was very disappointed.	Took 'A' levels. Got into university. Jane didn't. She started nurse training but dropped out after a few months.	Dropped out of university. Joined the army.	Gulf war. Jane got married. Missed the wedding. Home on leave in September when I met Becky.
1992	**1994**	**1996**	**1998**	**2000**
February! Married Becky. Posted to Germany. Jane had baby son. Quite a year!	Back in UK. Infertility treatment started. Jane now has three children!	Make first contact with adoption agency. Social worker starts to visit.	Turned down for adoption. Problems with Becky lead to separation.	Divorce. Leave army. Unemployed for six months. Problems with drink start.
2004	**2006**	**2008**		
Hospitalized for six weeks with mental health problems.	Beginning to fit the pieces together again. Back in touch with Jane and her family. Start work again as a carer.	Start my social work training...		

Figure 7.1 The flow chart

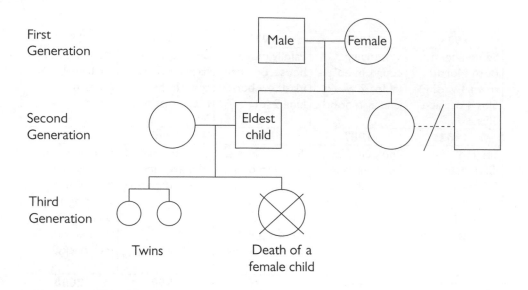

Figure 7.2 The genogram

At its best, the genogram can present complex family relationships in a very concise and accessible form. It can highlight themes and patterns that are echoed across the generations and it can serve to map key relationships and patterns of communication.

While the family is one important context in which to establish relationships, it does not provide a big enough picture (see Study Text 4.1). Individuals and families have relationships with individuals and groups around them and their particular household. Such groups, or 'systems', can include neighbours, school, friends, health services, and so on. One way of representing the various affiliations and the nature of a family or individual's relationships to the wider community is the ecomap (see Figure 7.3). Ecomaps can be drawn for families or individuals. In either case, a circle in the middle of the page represents the key person(s). Around this, sometimes at distances intended to represent the 'closeness' of the relationship, other circles are drawn that represent important connections to other members of the family, particular individuals or groups. As with the genogram, the lines used to join the various circles can also carry additional information: a solid line can represent a strong relationship; a dotted line, a weak one and a hatched line, a stressful one. Arrowheads can be added at either or both ends of the line to demonstrate the 'flow' of information, interest or resources between the parties.

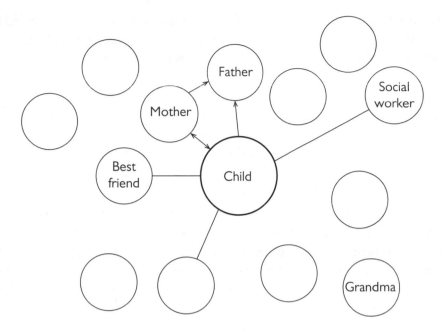

Figure 7.3 The ecomap

While we have presented each of these techniques as a useful means of sorting existing information, it should be clear also how they might be used in direct work, either to elicit further information on the basis of the gaps that show up in available data or to convey or interpret information that is not shared or understood by members of the family or individuals with whom you are working. Representing a child's journey through life as a railway line, for example, may allow opportunities for the child to reflect on who was waiting for him to arrive, who is travelling with him and where might his next and later destinations be. Conducting this exercise with a child and a set of marker pens is one of the better uses for flip chart paper that we have come across!

There are some obvious dangers in the process we have described so far, however. Files can be substantially inaccurate. They can be incomplete, outdated or record as factual what is merely conjecture. Frequently, simple mistakes, such as the failure to record a date of birth accurately, can be repeated over many years. Careful reading should help identify gross errors, but you should always confirm key information before acting upon it. This is an important route into the mutuality of assessment that we mentioned earlier. Sharing, comparing and reviewing the information that is the basis of your assessment is a vital part of the process of becoming engaged with the family with whom you are going to work.

The essentially subjective nature of any assessment needs to be acknowledged too, even where that assessment begins conventionally enough with the 'facts on file'. Cournoyer (1991) makes the point well in his account of the several stages involved in preparing to begin direct work. He describes what we have encouraged you to do so far as 'preparatory reviewing' and goes on to explore 'preparatory empathy' and 'preparatory self-exploration'. Preparatory empathy involves the worker imaginatively recreating the salient issues from the service user's point of view. This may heighten your sensitivity to the thoughts and feelings that others may have about the 'facts' of their life. Preparatory self-exploration is intended to identify the potential negative impact on the service user of the worker's characteristics, biases, emotional tender spots, 'unfinished business' and prejudices. It is also a very specific way of making explicit your commitment to anti-oppressive practice. Both preparatory empathy and preparatory self-exploration, however tentative, will demonstrate to you how much assessment is more of an interpretative art rather than an exact science and, as such, has always carried the indelible signature of its makers.

COURSE TEXT: A CASE IN POINT

If you are fortunate, many of the files allocated to you will contain a summary prepared when the case was closed or in anticipation of its transfer. What follows is a representation of such a summary, with the addition of a report of the most recent events that have led to the particular family involved presenting themselves at the Southtown children's services department. Assume that you are working in a child and family team in the children's services department and that the case is being allocated to you. Read through the file and then attempt the exercise that follows.

EXERCISE 7.1: GETTING TO KNOW YOU

Note: for the purposes of this exercise, and for all of those exercises that use this case material, the sequence of events is important. In order to ensure that this book has a 'shelf-life' we have adopted a particular convention regarding dates. Days and months are given in the usual way. The current year, however, is always 100. For example, in this exercise you are asked to assume that you are reading the file in early January 100. Michael, one of the characters in the case material, was born in June 90. This makes him nine years old for the purposes of this exercise; i.e. it is nine years from 6/90 to 1/100, from the year he was born to 'now'.

Assume that you are reading this file in January 100.

TAYLOR FAMILY CASE FILE

Background Information

Alison (1/3/89) and Michael (5/6/90) live with their mother, Tracy (2/2/73). Tracy prefers to be known as Tracy Taylor, her family name, since her divorce in June 96 from Ron Jones, Alison and Michael's father. No formal court orders concerning the children were made during the divorce.

Ron now lives in Northtown, some 140 miles away. He remarried 18 months ago. He has a newborn son, Wayne. Ron is an electrician by trade and it is believed that he has begun to build up a successful business with his cousin in Northtown. Tracy has had another child since the divorce, John (1/12/97). His father, Alun Evans, lives with Tracy and the three children at her council-owned house in New Estate, Southtown. Alun and Tracy have been living together for three years. No record exists of previous contact with Alun. Previous social workers do not seem to have seen him at all, although there is a note saying that Mr Evans would not meet the social worker as he had 'had enough of them when he was a kid'.

Tracy and Ron met when she was still at school. She became pregnant before she left and married Ron, four years her senior, just days after her sixteenth birthday. Her family has been known to the social services department for many years. She is one of six children, the eldest four of which, including Tracy, were the subject of care orders following the breakdown of her own parents' marriage in the summer of 79. Tracy and her three older brothers and sisters were fostered briefly in 80 as there was concern for the poor standard of care the children received from Mrs Taylor and their poor school attendance. The files relating to this period of Tracy's life have been lost and no further details are available.

When Alison was born Tracy found it very difficult to cope and moved away from her recently allocated council house in Old Estate, Southtown back to her mother's house, a few streets away. Ron went to stay with his parents in Northtown during this time (June to December 89), although he did make very frequent visits to Tracy and Alison. Mrs Taylor (senior) still lives in Old Estate. Tracy's father died in August 90.

In November 89 there were several anonymous telephone calls stating that the child living at Mrs Taylor's (senior) house was being neglected and that the house was in a filthy state. Two duty social workers visited and found the physical condition of the house appalling – the kitchen unhygienic, scarcely any food in the house, evidence of a recent fire in one of the bedrooms, a blocked toilet, broken glass all over the garden and dirty nappies spilling out of the bin.

Alison was clearly not well and, with Tracy's agreement, was admitted to hospital for a week. Ron visited regularly and Tracy stayed with Alison in hospital. At a child protection case conference called before Alison was discharged from hospital, it was decided, by consent, that Alison would be placed with foster carers while Ron and Tracy moved back into their former house in Old Estate. A support programme involving a family aide and regular visits from the social worker was initiated and it was not considered necessary to put a child protection plan in place. Within a month Alison was home and, with the right kind of support and practical assistance, the family settled down and social work attention eased off gradually.

The social worker was still visiting when Michael was born. This time Tracy and Ron were better prepared and, although Tracy did not have an easy time during the later stages of pregnancy and during labour (Michael was a high forceps delivery), the early weeks at home seemed to go very well. However, in the late summer of 90, the health visitor reported that Tracy was becoming very depressed and was unable to look after the children properly. Ron was not always around as he was working with his cousin in Northtown and the health visitor was becoming concerned for the children. In her opinion, Alison was developmentally delayed and Michael was not thriving as he should. Additional support, including help from staff at the local family centre, was put in place.

The situation did seem to be holding together but Ron was clearly very distressed by all that was going on. He decided that Tracy and the children should go with him to Northtown where his family would look after them and he could see them every day. He agreed to allow a social worker from Northtown Social Services Department to call in to see that all was well.

From September 90 until October 92, the children lived with Tracy, Ron and his cousin's family. According to a report from Northtown Social Services, who only visited once, the children were being very well looked after and both thriving. Tracy was not happy in Northtown for long, however, and had begun to spend longer and more frequent periods at her mother's house in Southtown.

In October 92, the family moved back to Southtown, this time to New Estate, which is on the far side of town to Old Estate and Tracy's mother. Ron had reluctantly agreed, although he kept his job in Northtown. A social worker visited and was more than satisfied with the welfare of the children but did note the tension in Tracy and Ron's relationship. As no help was requested in this regard, the case was closed.

The file has a note attached of a conversation with a probation officer, dated June 96, indicating that a welfare report had been written as part of divorce proceedings but that no further involvement was envisaged.

A further note from a health visitor announces the arrival of John but does not express any concern. No referral is made and so the file is not re-opened.

Current Situation

Tracy came into the neighbourhood office on New Estate during the week saying that she was at the end of her tether and very anxious about the safety of her children.

It would seem that Alison and Michael have been spending occasional weekends and most holidays with Ron since the divorce. All has not been going well recently, however, and Alison, in particular, has been complaining to her mother that she doesn't enjoy going to visit Ron. She particularly dislikes the way her brother Michael is treated so differently. According to Tracy, this is becoming increasingly obvious as they are growing up. Last time the children went to stay, Michael spent most of his time with his father whereas Alison was expected to spend all her time with Ron's wife and Wayne. She found it hard, particularly as Ron's wife seemed to dote on the new baby and ignore her. Michael, on the other hand, says that he enjoys being with his father, uncles and 'new brother'.

The situation has caused a lot of arguments between Alison and Michael, which has spilled over into arguments between Tracy and Ron. Ron has said that he is unhappy with the way that the children were being brought up and that they would have a better upbringing with him and his new wife and family. He is talking about 'going to court' to have the children live with him.

The situation at home is becoming unbearable and Tracy says that she doesn't know if she can keep going. She says it is affecting her relationship with Alun and she feels that John is getting a raw deal. Alun is not, apparently, very supportive and she feels he would probably want to see 'the back of' the two eldest. He has never liked Ron, according to Tracy, and is beginning to take it out on all of the children and on her. Tracy does not want to 'lose the children again'. She wants a social worker to come and help. Mrs Taylor (senior) is aggravating the situation, as she doesn't get on with Alun. The tension at home is rising and Tracy hinted to the duty social worker that 'something will break' if she doesn't get help.

TASKS

1. Establish the basis of this family's history in chronological order using the card index method described above.

2. Draw a flow chart for Tracy Taylor.

3. Prepare an ecomap for Alison. Include all the members of her family referred to in the case file.

4. Draw a genogram for the whole family.

QUESTIONS

1. How old was Alison when her parents divorced?

2. How old was Ron when Alison was born?

3. How old was Alison when she was first fostered?

4. How long did John live in Northtown?

5. How old was Alison when Michael was born?

6. How old was Michael when John was born?

7. How old was Tracy when her father died?

8. How long after the birth of Michael did Tracy's father die, and how long before she moved to Northtown?

9. How old was Tracy at the birth of each of her children?

10. How old is Tracy now?

11. How long was she married?

12. How old was Tracy when her parents divorced?

13. How old was she when she became pregnant?

14. How old are each of the children now?

15. What relation is Wayne to Alison?

16. Who are John's grandparents?

17. Who are Alison's grandparents?

18. How many maternal aunts/uncles does John have?

19. What relation is Alun to Wayne?

20. What relation is Alun to Alison?

POINTS TO CONSIDER

1. What are the key pieces of information in the file that you might want to confirm with family members?

2. Have you begun to form an idea of what gaps exist in your knowledge of this family? If so, list them.

3. From the information that you have, write down what impression you have begun to form of Alun and Ron.

4. Can you identify just how much of that impression is based on what you found in the 'file' and how much of it comes from preconceptions of your own?

5. Describe Tracy's history of involvement with your department. What might her expectations be of you and what you might do?

6. Write down what expectations you have of Tracy. Do your expectations focus on Tracy's potential weaknesses or on her strengths?

COURSE TEXT: ART OR SCIENCE?

After completing the previous exercise, most students are surprised by how much they have managed to 'learn' about the Taylor family. This experience, despite our earlier cautions, might lead them to think that the process of assessment can be reduced to a set of technical exercises or even simply to filling in a few forms. Nothing could be further from the truth. Any assessment will require, as well as the intelligent, structured and purposeful acquisition of information, the synthesis and analysis of that information and the exercise of professional judgement. Assessment remains both a 'scientific' and a 'reflective' process (Holland 2004).

The value of such technical devices as the ecomap or the genogram or the wide variety of other 'practice tools' that are available to social workers lies in the way in which they structure the process of gathering information and help to present it in such a way that it can be systematically reviewed and interpreted. You should note however, that there is rarely a consensus on what constitutes a reliable assessment 'instrument'. Debate extends beyond such matters as the reliability or validity of specific measures (such as a particular standardized psychological test). The broader frameworks in which they might be embedded can also be called into question. For example, we have thus far made references to various domains or dimensions of the *Children in Need Assessment Framework* as though these were relatively uncontroversial. This is not the case.

For example, Garrett in a series of articles reflecting both the *Children in Need Assessment Framework* and its predecessor, the *Looked After Children Assessment and Action Records* (Parker and others 1991) develops a radical critique of how such frameworks are 'awash with unexplored social and political meanings' (Garrett 1999, p.44). He sets such frameworks in the context of the de-professionalized and bureaucratized managerialist social work that he associates with the New Labour government of the UK from 1997 onwards. The normative elements that he sees in the *Children in Need Assessment Framework* go beyond the specifics of each side of the assessment 'triangle' (see Study Text 4.1). In Garrett's view, the *Assessment Framework* tries to establish an epistemological position that specifically excludes ideology; a kind of unexplored but powerful 'common sense' position. However, implicit in the framework, according to Garrett, is a set of assumptions about families and society that is highly individualist (rather than collectivist) and which leaves social work as 'merely to aid people as they hunker behind the rocks as the fiery tides of globalization wash all around them' (Garrett 2003, p.452).

You may or may not share similar views but, as we have already indicated, social work in all its forms and practices cannot escape its political context and content. To take an even starker example, had this book been written before May 2010, a great deal of it would, in all probability, have been set in the context of the *Every Child Matters* (ECM) policy framework that had been developed within government and championed by the Department for Children, Schools and Families since the publication, in September 2003, of a Green Paper of the same name (HM Government 2003).

The Green Paper was followed, ultimately, by the 2004 Children Act, and a 'national framework for local change programmes' published by central government (DCSF 2004). From it flowed a new service delivery structure ('Children's Trusts' – see Audit Commission 2008 for a review of the introduction and limited efficacy of Children's Trusts in England) and a whole new architecture of social work policy and practice, including an ambitious IT programme to manage and to aggregate case data (the 'integrated children's service' or ICS – see Broadhurst and others 2010; Gilligan and Manby 2008; and White and others 2010 for an account of the paradoxical impact of the ICS in practice which has, according to White at least 'disrupted the professional task, engendering a range of unsafe practices and provok[ed] a gathering storm of user resistance' (p.405)). A considerable financial investment was made in establishing a universal child surveillance database (ContactPoint) and countless areas of activity concerning children were brigaded under the 'every child matters' brand.

What was scarcely noted however (either by central government or by social work commentators) was that the ECM policy framework applied *only* to England. In Wales, children's policy was grounded in an explicitly rights based framework that pre-dated ECM and which would appear to have outlasted it. In Wales, policy has been guided by the 'Seven Core Aims' (WAG 2004), which are firmly rooted in the UNCRC; hence every young person has a right to:

- have a flying start in life

- have a comprehensive range of education and learning opportunities

- enjoy the best possible health and be free from abuse, victimization and exploitation

- have access to play, leisure, sporting and cultural activities

- be listened to, treated with respect and have their race and cultural identity recognized

- have a safe home and a community which supports physical and emotional well-being

- not to be disadvantaged by poverty.

These should be compared to the 'five outcomes' of the ECM framework, which intended that every child should (HM Government 2003, p.6):

- be healthy

- stay safe

- enjoy and achieve

- make a positive contribution

- achieve economic well-being.

The differences are subtle but important. In the ECM framework, as much is expected of children as for them; in the Seven Core Aims, the onus for ensuring the well-being of children rests clearly with civic society more broadly. We have noted the foundational differences in approaches to child welfare in more polemical terms elsewhere (Butler and Drakeford 2010, p.16):

> Where children and young people are thought of in terms of their needs rather than their rights; their vulnerabilities rather than their strengths; the problems that they cause society rather than the problems that society

causes for them; where policies are conceived and delivered reactively rather than in pursuit of an over-arching set of objectives (which are NOT the same as 'outcomes'); where services are delivered through a confused and constantly changing set of structures and professional networks; where there is a residualised model of the welfare state operating and where a rhetoric of consumerism, competition and 'business' rather than justice, equality and participation makes little sense to front-line workers; where practice is subsumed into performativity, performance management and risk avoidance, it would suggest also that there exists, in Westminster at least, a dominant political vision of childhood that is anxious, uncertain, pessimistic and lacking in imagination.

Again, we do not intend to persuade you to any particular point of view. We simply make the case that policy frameworks and the apparatus that they produce (including assessment protocols, tools and 'conceptual maps') vary and need to be understood in relation to their precise socio-political context.

What is perhaps more striking than any differences across jurisdictions is that within weeks of coming into office, the new UK government elected in May 2010, dismantled key elements of the ECM framework (e.g. ContactPoint), called for a review of child protection social work with a particular emphasis on reducing the time that social workers spent servicing the system (the 'Munro Review' – see Study Text 8.3) and almost immediately consigned the enormous ECM website to the archive!

While the structured and systematic gathering of information ('the science' of an assessment) is of vital importance, it is our view that its quality and usefulness lie also in the way in which information is analysed and reflected upon (the 'art' of an assessment). It is also the case that the 'politics' that shape the lives of children and families, also shape the practice of social workers and influence the tools, techniques and processes of any assessments that they are called upon to make. Do not only ask questions of the children and young people with whom you work, ask yourself also why you are asking such questions in the first place.

COURSE TEXT: BEGINNING THE ASSESSMENT

In England, the next stage in the process for the Taylor Family might involve the completion of a brief assessment, using the Common Assessment Framework (CAF). The CAF is a product of the ECM policy and practice framework. In essence, it is a framework and a process for identifying those children and young people whose needs cannot be met through the provision of universal services (such as schools or routine health services). Such children are said to have 'additional needs' as opposed to those children who have 'complex needs' (see CWDC 2010a), including child protection needs. The following diagram seeks to establish the boundaries more clearly:

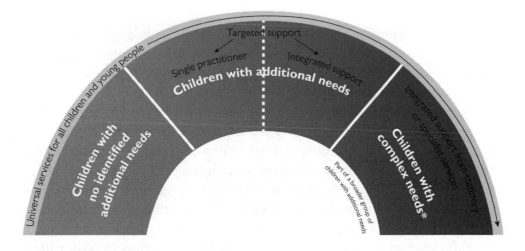

Figure 7.4 The Common Assessment Framework

The CAF is intended to provide a standardized protocol for everyone who may be part of the 'children's workforce'. It is intended that the CAF is completed by a 'lead professional' who may be drawn from a wide range of professional backgrounds. The assessment covers (although in far less detail) the three domains that form the basis of the 'assessment triangle' of the *Children in Need Assessment Framework* and is supported by standard pro-formas. In earlier iterations, it was intended to link the CAF (the eCAF) to the Integrated Children's Services IT infrastructure and to ContactPoint although these links have now been broken.

The impact of the CAF in practice can perhaps best be described as 'limited' (see Brandon and others 2006; Easton, Morris and Gee 2010). Whereas progress has been made in improving outcomes in some areas ('school attendance, engagement and aspirations, in physical health and self-confidence, in family relationships and in housing and financial support' Easton, Morris and Gee 2010, p.vii), there are 'challenges' still:

> The CAF process is not yet fully embedded in any one service locally. In some agencies and services there is strong reluctance to engage with or support the CAF process. Where there is engagement it can feel like an add-on process and workload can be a barrier.

The CAF is not always well understood and consistently applied. Questions raised include which groups should have an assessment, how does CAF relate to other formal assessments, should social care be involved and who has access to what information?

Given the uncertainty over the status of the CAF, its limited scope and some reservations over its effectiveness as well as its limited application within the UK, for the remainder of this chapter, we intend to focus on the *Children in Need Assessment Framework*.

The guidance to the *Framework for the Assessment of Children in Need and their Families* distinguishes between two levels of assessment and sets appropriate timescales for both. The expectation is that within one working day of a referral or of new information coming to light in relation to an existing case, the agency (usually the local authority social services department) will make a clear decision as to what it will do next. If the agency decides to gather more information, this constitutes an *initial assessment*. This is defined as 'a brief assessment of each child referred to social services with a request for services to be provided' (Department of Health and others 2000, p.31). Such an initial assessment should be completed within a maximum of seven working days and must address all of the dimensions of the *Framework for the Assessment of Children in Need and their Families*. The initial assessment will have regard to determining whether the child concerned is a child in need and what responses or services, if any, are required. The family must be informed of the conclusions of the assessment and, if a child is a child in need, of the plan for providing services.

If, after (or during the course of) the initial assessment, it becomes clear that the situation of the child is more complex and that a further, more detailed assessment is required, then a *core assessment* may be begun. A core assessment is defined as 'an in-depth assessment which addresses the central or most important aspects of the needs of a child and the capacity of his or her parents or caregivers to respond appropriately to those needs within the wider family and community context' (Department of Health and others 2000, p.32). A core assessment should be completed within 35 working days.

You should note that should a child protection concern arise at any point, subject to the additional procedures that apply in such circumstances concerning the convening of a strategy meeting and the consideration of any inter-agency action (these are explained in Study Text 9.2), the necessary assessment will take place (or continue, as the case may be) using the *Framework for the Assessment of Children in Need and their Families* although the pace and scope of the assessment may well change.

Bearing these timescales in mind and remembering what you have learned from Exercise 7.1, the following exercise is designed to encourage you to think through what is involved in undertaking an initial assessment, using the *Framework for the Assessment of Children in Need and their Families*.

EXERCISE 7.2: AN INITIAL ASSESSMENT

A senior colleague of yours has reviewed the notes on the Taylor family made by the duty social worker and has determined that an initial assessment of the family should be made. This task has been allocated to you.

TASKS

1. Drawing on the Taylor Case File and the information you reviewed in Exercise 7.1, make notes under each of the headings ('dimensions of assessment') of the *Framework for the Assessment of Children in Need and their Families*, setting out what you 'know', what you will need to verify and what gaps there are to be filled in your knowledge of this family. (You may wish to look back to Study Text 4.1 also.)

2. Using these notes, decide what topics, themes or issues you will want to explore with the Taylor family at your first meeting with them. (Of course, in a 'real situation', you would want to reserve some space to ensure that the family's priorities are also properly explored.)

3. For at least two of the topic areas you have prioritized, write down what questions you will need to ask, of whom, when and where, to inform your assessment. Make a list also of what other information-gathering techniques (other than asking questions) might be helpful in relation to the particular areas that you have chosen.

POINTS TO CONSIDER

1. Are you able to justify asking for all of the information that you intend to gather?

2. How would you explain to Tracy why you were asking for the information that you are seeking?

3. How would you explain to the children why you were asking for the information you are seeking?

4. How might you interpret a refusal to provide information?

5. How well able are you to articulate the standards against which you will be judging the information you gather?

📖 COURSE TEXT: CHILD AND FAMILY OBSERVATION

While we hope that the Taylors are beginning to 'come to life' for you, we realize that is impossible for us to create through the pages of this book, anything more than a very limited, two-dimensional sense of our fictional family. It is beyond our literary skills to provide you with enough details of family members' appearance; how they dress, their mannerisms or their tone of voice to give you a real sense of what they look or sound like; we cannot show you how their facial expressions change or how they stand when they talk to each other; we cannot show you where they live or what the living room or children's bedrooms look and feel like. In fact, the longer that we make this list of what we haven't been able to tell you, the more impoverished our actual account seems to be! It just shows how much more information might be gleaned from simply spending a few moments with a family and how much additional information about the 'micro-culture' of this particular family (see Study Text 2.2) is embedded in the fine detail of their daily interactions. Access to such subtle, rich and important detail can best be achieved through direct observation and it is to this that we now turn.

𝑖 STUDY TEXT 7.2: CHILD AND FAMILY OBSERVATION

In any meeting with the family, you are likely to be making informal observations about the home environment, the characteristic behaviours and attitudes of individuals and their interactions with each other. In this Study Text we wish to focus on those observations that you undertake with a more explicit aim in mind; where you are seeking to gather information about a specific aspect of parenting or a child's development, for example, and which are, to some degree, more structured and more formal.

The primary value of directly observing a child in a more focussed, purposeful way is that it provides the worker with much greater access to that part of a child and family's world that is non-verbal. Children in particular, may lack a suitable vocabulary to fully express themselves through words alone. Similarly, emotions and attachments can be expressed much more graphically through behaviour, proximity or facial expression, for example. Direct observation offers a window into the subtlety and complexity of human relations that is hard to match through the spoken word and, as such, is a potentially rich source of information to assist you through the process of assessment.

In most instances, we would suggest, your interest will be in a child's relationship with his or her primary carers and so your more structured, more in-depth observations will be of the child and the parent or carer together. Sometimes, your focus may be on the child's interactions with his or her peers; in which case your observations may be of the young person in a playgroup or classroom context. You may also wish to observe a child's progress towards meeting his or her developmental milestones; in which case you may actually want to observe the child (or infant) alone. For the purposes of this Study Text, we are going to concentrate on those circumstances where your purpose is to gather information on a child and his or her relationship with a parent in order to help you make an informed assessment of family functioning. There are instances where such information may be required for forensic purposes, to provide advice to a court that is considering making or varying an order relating to residence or contact or for evidential purposes in the case of care proceedings. In these circumstances, you may have to take child protection processes into greater account and there may be strictures on how you record your observations. Whatever the specific context, our primary purpose is to encourage you to see the value of developing the skills of child observation and to appreciate their value to the assessment process.

For the purposes of this Study Text therefore, we are assuming that you are looking to understand the family's routine, everyday and 'ordinary' ways of going about being a family. It is important therefore that individuals are able to behave as ordinarily as they can during the course of your observations. You will defeat the object of the exercise if family members put on a 'performance' in order to meet their understanding of your expectations or if they 'freeze' simply because someone is watching. Both of these are aspects of what is sometimes called, 'the observer effect'[6]. You can do much to allay any nervousness on the part of family members by making sure that you have carefully explained not just what you are doing by observing them but why you are observing them too. Remember that many families, with good reason, may be suspicious of your motives and in particular, may be thinking that you are only interested in what they do 'wrong' when you are observing them. They may even feel that you are

---

6   whereby the act of observing directly influences what is being observed.

trying to 'trick' them into revealing something about themselves that you may use to their disadvantage. Fully informed consent is a pre-requisite of the kind of direct observation that we describe here and that must be predicated on an honest explanation from the observer of what it is they are seeking to use the observation for.

How you record your observations can also contribute to the 'observer effect'. Conspicuous scribbling can be very off-putting and can very easily become the focus of a child's attention in particular. In fact, how to record your observations can be quite a challenge in itself. Unless you are videoing the interaction, you can be certain that you will definitely not be able to record everything! Not only will your attention wander from time to time, there will simply be too much detail for you to capture, some of which will escape you while you are making your notes. The task of recording will vary according to how you structure your observations.

For example, naturalistic or narrative observations can either be planned or occur spontaneously. In effect, these are forms of (almost) continuous observation, where the worker tries to write down everything s\he sees and hears, with perhaps 1 or 2 or 3 minute breaks, noted in the margin. One advantage of this method is that it requires little preparation; it feels natural, records a great deal and can give a very detailed picture of the subject being observed. On the other hand, you may be left with a large volume of data that may be difficult to analyse.

Methods that rely on sampling may reduce the burden of recording and may provide more focussed data. For example, event sampling concentrates on a particular behaviour such as a parenting problem or a child's response to instructions and records a specific behaviour's frequency and duration. Such an approach suits short, well-defined events and may be particularly useful in isolating specific 'cause and effect' patterns to problematic behaviours. However the observer must be able to recognize imminent events in order to record them and, more importantly, such approaches may provide a very partial account of a wider family dynamic.

One approach that is increasingly popular with social workers and social work students is the 'modified Tavistock Model' (see Fawcett 2009). In most instances, this involves a series of one-hour observations (usually no less than 6) of parent and child where the worker is encouraged to 'be' (as unobtrusively as possible) rather than to 'do' and to leave all of their recording until after the session is over. Once the session is complete, the worker notes what they saw and heard and records their interpretation of their observations. The worker should then discuss their findings with other workers, where possible, to identify other ways of understanding what they have witnessed and to test out their analysis.

In the case of naturalistic or narrative approaches, you might not choose a particular task or activity to observe. One of the best ways to enter the world of the child is through observing and developing an understanding of children's play, for example. By careful observation of a child at play, the worker can build a very detailed picture of a child by noting how he or she interacts with other children or adults (verbally as well as non-verbally), engages with toys, chooses which games to play and uses the room or space itself, both inside and outside. (See Beunerman 2010; Burghardt 2005; Masten 2001; Pellis and Pellis 2009; Spinka and others 2001 for a wider discussion on children and play.)

However, where your focus is more narrowly defined, you may suggest a specific task or activity as the subject of your observations. These could include key points of tension or difficulty in the family (such as mealtimes or bedtimes). Children generally respond most easily to unstructured observations – such as play or watching TV but you will need to be aware that in restricting your observations to such non-conflictual settings, you may be missing important aspects of family functioning.

Precisely where you undertake your observations needs to be a considered choice. Intruding on private space (such as a child's bedroom or even garden) may well influence the process and outcomes of an observation as much as observing the child and family at the local children's centre. Choice of location should be influenced much more strongly by its acceptability to the child and family than by the worker's convenience or preferences.

Creating the optimal conditions for effective and productive direct observations will be helped if you:

- are clear about what you are doing

- are honest about why you are doing it

- share your interpretations with others, especially the family concerned

- are sensitive to your own attitudes and values and how these will influence your interpretation of what you observe

- make a conscious effort to judge any 'observer effect', including the effects of location

- do not let your recording take precedence over your observation.

We hope that the next exercise will help you to see the benefits of developing your observational skills.

EXERCISE 7.3: OBSERVING THE TAYLORS

Using the example of the Taylor family, design an observation you could conduct with the family that would provide you with additional information for your assessment. In doing so, consider the following questions:

1. Which members of the Taylor family would you want to observe, and why?

2. When and where would you want to observe them?

3. Which observation method would you choose to use and why?

4. How would you explain the observation to the children and family?

POINTS TO CONSIDER

1. What would worry you most about conducting an observation, being able to remember facts or accurately recording your observations?

2. What aspects of your own life or personal history do you think might impact on how you conduct an observation or how you make sense of the material you observe?

3. How would you explain to children that you wanted to observe them but not join in with their play?

4. How do you feel about being observed yourself?

CONCLUSION

We have only hinted at the practicalities of undertaking an assessment and said even less of the agency context in which it will take place. Our intention has been to encourage and enable you to reflect upon the process of assessment and to recognize that it is a negotiated one. There are many different routes to 'make sense of what has happened and of what is happening now', some more formal and codified than others. Assessment is the foundation for planning and so for direct work, but it is an interpretative process throughout. Assessment is a complex and demanding task that should never be reduced to routine, certainly not to an exercise in form-filling; especially if you are ever tempted to take the 'forms' for granted. Assessment requires thoughtful preparation and creativity in your approach to practice. Moreover, it requires a critical and reflective practitioner who is prepared to take great pains to gather reliable assessment data, including from direct observation, and who is prepared to subject that data to careful analysis.

One of the real rewards of social work is encountering the real-life histories of the real live people you will work with. Each and every one of the complex biographies through which you pass should be treated with respect and your attempts to make sense of them for the purposes of your work should be approached with some humility.

NOTES AND SELF-ASSESSMENT

1. How would you explain to a ten-year-old what you mean by 'assessment'?

2. How comfortable are you articulating the theories that inform your work?

3. Who should 'own' the assessment?

4. How easy to assess are you?

5. How would you feel about being assessed by a social worker? Write down why you feel as you do.

6. What aspects of your own life or personal history would you find most difficult to introduce into an assessment being made of you?

RECOMMENDED READING

Holland, S. (2004) *Child and Family Assessment in Social Work Practice.* London: Sage.

Helm, D. (2010) *Making Sense of Child and Family Assessment: How to Interpret Children's Needs.* London: Jessica Kingsley Publishers.

TRAINER'S NOTES

Exercise 7.1: Getting to Know You

Task 1 is best done individually as each member of the group will need a thorough knowledge of the 'file' for subsequent work. Tasks 2, 3, and 4 are best distributed among the group – the resulting material can then be shared with other group members and retained for use in later sessions. This works well if the material is prepared using flip chart paper. The 'twenty questions' can be used to test the group's knowledge of the case after a simple reading of the file (i.e. before attempting any of the tasks) and then again after the tasks have been completed. This is usually a powerful demonstration of how much information can be gleaned from only a few pages after a little less than an hour's work. We have deliberately not supplied any answers to the questions as we do not want anyone (including the trainer) to take a short cut to a working knowledge of the case.

Ignoring information gaps, forming impressions based on personal prejudices or over-emphasis on weaknesses and the priorities of the worker are common faults among newly qualified workers and group members should be encouraged to illustrate the discussion with material drawn from their own experience.

Exercise 7.2: An Initial Assessment

This exercise is intended as a summarizing or reinforcing exercise. It can be used most effectively to integrate practice and classroom study if, instead of preparing an assessment using the Taylor case, a real case from group members' own experience or current practice is used. This can be combined with a skills rehearsal exercise around the presentation of formal assessments. Instructions can be given as follows:

This exercise is intended to provide opportunities for you to share your practice experience with your colleagues and to benefit from the practice experience of others; to encourage you to reflect on the relevant skills that you possess or need to develop; to provide you with an opportunity to rehearse your skills in communicating your assessments to others.

For the (next) session prepare a five-minute presentation (no more and no less) of a case or incident of which you have direct knowledge that has involved you in the process of assessment of a particular child or family situation.

Structure your presentation as follows:

1. Describe the particular situation and circumstances that gave rise to the assessment that you made and some indication of what conclusions you have or are beginning to form about the child/situation.

2. *Either* identify the skills that you used in making the assessment *or* describe any particular technique(s) that you used that might be of interest to your colleagues.

3. Identify what this piece of work has taught you about assessment that you would want to pass on to others.

Exercise 7.3: Child and Family Observation

Rather than suggest a simple modification to the original exercise, in this instance we want to introduce two real exercises in observation that we believe are particularly helpful to students in demonstrating the power of observation and how observation is affected by the observer ('observer effect').

Walking Observation 1: Ask the students to get into pairs and go for a walk outside. Depending on the time you have available for the class you can suggest between a 10–20 minute walk. After forming pairs, ask the students to no longer talk to each other. They must go for a walk without verbal communication with each other or anyone else, or using other signals. Ask them to just observe everything (internally and externally) they become aware of. On return to the class ask the students to write down everything they observed still in silence (again depending on the time available you can allocate between 5–15 minutes to this). Then ask the students to compare notes with their walking partner, looking for areas of similarity and difference in their observations.

Walking Observation 2: Repeat the above exercise but when the students return to the room they are asked to complete the list of questions on their table in front of them (some suggestions below). We have often placed a number of toys in the room at the start of the lecture and not made any reference to them until the students are asked to describe them (while they are out of the room the toys are removed from sight). Many students do not 'see' them at all, others have confidently remembered a toy purple shark as a green elephant producing opportunities for rich discussions about accurate observation and how easy it can be to just 'fill in the gaps' or guess with all of the risks associated with guesswork.

Walking Observation Questions

- How many people did you observe?

- How many people were alone?

- How many under the age of 20?

- How many people were laughing?

- How many people were sad?

- How many people were eating or drinking?

- How many people were sitting down?

- What toy was in the classroom?

- How would you describe the weather today?

- How many cars did you observe?

- Which one of you 'led' the walking observation?
- Who walked faster?
- Which one of you is taller and by how much?
- Describe the shoes the other person is wearing.
- What colour eyes do they have?
- Was there anything that made you laugh?
- Did you observe anything that made you think?
- Give examples of some of the random thoughts that crossed your mind.
- Give examples of some of the feelings you noticed.
- Is there anything about the exercise that has surprised you?

UNIT 8

Planning

OBJECTIVES

In this unit you will:

- Consider the relationship between assessment and planning.

- Learn about the process of goal setting.

- Learn about the statutory basis for planning in respect of looked after children.

- Explore the basis of relationship-based social work.

COURSE TEXT: WONDERLAND

Even if you don't know the story of *Alice in Wonderland*, you may have heard of the Cheshire Cat. Alice is lost in a wood and is anxious to find her way out. She sees the Cheshire Cat sitting in a tree and decides to ask his advice. She asks him which path she should follow. He replies that it rather depends on where exactly she wants to go. Alice says that she doesn't much mind where, at which point the Cat interrupts and tells her that it doesn't matter which way she chooses then. Alice completes her question: '…so long as I get somewhere'. 'Oh you are sure to do that', replies the Cheshire Cat, 'if you only walk long enough.'

Alice's uncertainty about where she is now, her sense of urgency to get somewhere and her apparent unconcern for just where that 'somewhere' turns out to be familiar feelings for many social work practitioners. What Alice needs is a plan! Not just a two-dimensional map of Wonderland, although with that she could at least work out which paths lead where, and she would know a little better where she had been and what might be waiting around the next corner. Her progress through Wonderland would, at least from that point on, be a more rational and predictable one.

A simple map wouldn't help her decide her destination, however, and it wouldn't necessarily tell her whom she might meet on the way or of any short cuts or delays; for that she would need to draw on her wider knowledge and experience. She would need to make a series of informed decisions that would take her further towards where she wanted to be – she would have to engage in a process of rational and purposive decision making to really make progress through the wood. It is this process of rational, purposive decision making, or planning, that is the subject of this Unit.

To give a more practical illustration, consider the point at which we last left the Taylor family. Once you had decided your priorities and approach, especially to seeing and talking to the children (see Exercise 7.2), you would then have to think about the actual process of carrying out the assessment. There are a number of questions you would need to consider at this point: Whom are you going to consult? Whom will you want to speak to in person? In what order will you see people? Where will you meet them? Who will you see together and who separately? What would be a good time to see the children? After school? What if that conflicts with mealtimes? And so on.

You could simply answer each question as it arose and proceed on that basis. You may even be able to complete an assessment in this way. Some social workers do. There is considerable evidence stretching back a long time (e.g. Department of Health 1991b; Department of Health and Social Security 1985; but see also Roach and Sanders 2008) to suggest that a great deal of social work in respect of children looked after has taken place in a planning vacuum. Alternatively, you could organize, prioritize, take positive decisions about what you will do and *plan* the assessment. So, a competent assessment requires planning too. Like assessment, planning is also a continuous process that needs to be kept under review and one that overlaps with later phases in the social work process, such as intervention. But, accepting that planning cannot be easily divorced from other elements in the social work process, what can we say about planning to help establish a clearer sense of what the term implies?

Planning begins with the identification of the planning required; with the question 'planning for what?' – the answer to which usually derives from the nature of the assessment that is underway. During the assessment stage, some preliminary decisions must be taken about the immediate future and about the expected direction of events later on. Indeed, in an emergency, decisions often have to be made and action taken before the situation can be even partially assessed. But, these kind of situational responses are not plans in the sense in which we intend; this would imply that planning is far too reactive a process. In our view, planning is itself a form of causality; it is about *making* things happen rather than simply responding to events as they occur. So, while planning is inextricably bound up with the assessment phase (assessments need to be planned too), it is not coterminous with it. While the assessment phase may well be on-going and may well be revisited and revised during the course of the social work involvement, there is a very general sense in which it is concerned with what *has* happened in the past or *is* happening now. Planning is about what *will* happen in the future – understood in the instrumental sense of what it is that those involved intend to happen.

It might be helpful to see how the general point we are trying to make applies in a specific social work context, namely in the case of looked after children. For reasons that will become clear shortly, we will explore in more detail later in this Unit the formal regulations and guidance that structure planning in relation to looked after children. *The Children Act 1989 Guidance and Regulations. Volume 2: Care Planning, Placement and Case Review* (DCSF 2010e) indicate that a care plan should (§ 2.29):

- describe the identified developmental needs of the child and the services required to meet those needs, including services to be provided to family members

- describe why a particular placement has been chosen

- include specific, achievable, child-focussed outcomes intended to safeguard and promote the welfare of the child and identify how progress will be measured

- include realistic strategies and specific actions to bring about the changes necessary to achieve the planned outcome

- clearly identify and set out the roles and responsibilities of family members, the child's carers and practitioners (including for example GP, nurse and designated teacher), and the frequency of contact of those practitioners with the child, his/her carer and/or family member; and

- describe the contingency arrangements if the proposed ... plan for the child is not achievable, in order to reduce delay.

It is not necessary to fully understand all that is implied in this list (but see Study Text 8.2 following) for our present purposes. However, it should be clear, even from a superficial reading, that planning for looked after children is about purposeful decision making, grounded in a thorough assessment and with specific outcomes in mind.

Before the Cheshire Cat could answer Alice's question, Alice would have to have had a much better idea of where she was intending to go; to have a sense of what the purpose of her journey was. To put this another way, she needed to define her 'goal' and it is to the question of goal setting that we now turn.

i STUDY TEXT 8.1: GOAL SETTING

What do we mean when we use the term 'goal'? Among the definitions offered by the *Shorter Oxford Dictionary*, two seem particularly apt for our purposes: 'Goal: the object of effort or ambition, or the destination of a (difficult) journey'.

It would seem that goal setting is an almost universal human activity with well-established socio-psychological benefits. For example, studies in the field of 'cognitive self-regulation' (see Zimmerman 2001) would suggest that goal setting improves learning and the acquisition of skills and has positive effects on behaviour in the classroom. Social exchange theorists (see Cook and Rice 2003) also suggest that positive engagements with others and the building of social networks (including networks of support) can be enhanced through the positive reinforcement and sense of self-efficacy (a belief that an individual can make things happen) that comes from achieving self-directed goals. According to social learning theory too (see Bandura 1997), goal setting can be an important part of achieving the kind of behaviour an individual is seeking to model and acquire. There is even emerging evidence in the field of neuroscience that would suggest that goal setting, especially in older children and young people, can help to 'hard-wire' such processes in the brain and improve cognitive skills for a lifetime (see Blakemore and Choudry 2006; Giedd 2004).

Goal setting has been an intrinsic part of many approaches to social work and has increasingly found expression in the development of so-called 'brief' or 'solution focussed' therapies and approaches to counselling. Goal setting has also been central to a number of 'task-centred' forms of practice (see Teater 2010 for a detailed contextual and practical account of a wide range of social work methods and theories). The following is typical of what might be regarded as almost a social work orthodoxy; Hepworth and Larsen (1982) note that goals serve the following functions in the helping process:

- Goals provide direction and continuity to the helping process and prevent needless wandering.

- Goals facilitate the development and selection of appropriate strategies and interventions.

- Goals assist practitioners and clients in monitoring their progress.

- Goals serve as outcome criteria in evaluating the effectiveness of specific interventions and the helping process.

Moreover, the process of goal setting with service users would seem to contribute substantially to the effectiveness of the helping process itself. Goal setting is motivational. Knowing that there is at least the possibility of arriving somewhere you want to be can bring a renewed sense of optimism and confidence for both service user and worker, whatever form of intervention is being pursued.

But what exactly do we mean by the term 'goals'? What kind of appropriate 'destinations' might be defined as goals, to continue our metaphor? Goals are not to be expressed in global terms. They cannot be generalized to the level of life, the universe and everything. To be useful, goals must remain specific to the current person/situational circumstances. Hence, statements such as 'to make X better', 'happier' or 'better able to cope' are not goals so much as pious intentions. Goals must reflect the nature of the issues that originated the social work contact in the first place; for example, 'to improve the quality of parenting', 'to increase participation in social groups', 'to improve verbal communication' or 'to relate more comfortably with the opposite sex'. In this way, goal statements, although somewhat abstract, are still rooted in the circumstances (person/situation dynamic) that bring the social worker and the service user together. Goals expressed at this level of generality should be distinguished from objectives or aims, which Anderson (1984) describes as 'statements of intended accomplishments that are specific, attainable, appropriate and measurable' (p.488). In other words, objectives are the steps we take along the path to reaching our goals.

A well-constructed objective statement will answer the five key questions of who, what, to what extent, when and where:

- *Who?* The objective statement is often made with reference to the service user. This does not necessarily imply that the identified service user is the only object of any objective statement. For example, if the social worker is engaged with a family, it is important to specify whether the objective is to be attained by all family members, specific family members or by other people altogether, including representatives of outside agencies.

- *What?* The task here is to formulate statements that are specific to the desired outcome. For example, such a statement as 'To get Chris to attend school' is inadequate. Does that mean just once more or every day for the next two terms? Without this degree of specificity, how can one begin to evaluate progress? To blur this distinction between specific outcomes and more generalized statements of intent can be very tempting. To promise a court 'To get Chris to attend school' leaves plenty of room for negotiation if at any point you have to report back. It also lets you off the hook in other ways in that lack of specificity allows you to set, in effect, very low-level objectives. Getting Chris to attend school once in the next two years may satisfy your objective statement but it does little for Chris's educational development.

- *To what extent?* Answers to this question do not have to be set only in positivistic, numerical terms. Other formulations are possible: for example, 'to stop drinking alcohol on my own' describes a specific context rather than any quantitative element. Nevertheless, whether expressed in qualitative or quantitative terms or any combination of them, the message is one of specificity.

- *When?* This question addresses when the expected outcome is going to occur. The period will need to be realistic in order to achieve a balance between motivation and setting a course for inevitable and avoidable 'failure' judged by not meeting arbitrary deadlines.

- *Where?* Often, problematic behaviours occur in specific settings or at specified times during the day. Answering this question of the objective statement tells everyone where to look for the expected outcome.

It should be noted that despite the apparent deterministic approach reflected in the above, the goal setting process should be a mutual and negotiated one. Just as with assessment, goal setting is not something done to service users by social workers. It should, wherever possible (see Study Text 8.3), be part of an agreed process whereby worker and service user determine the path that they will take in order to get out of 'the wood' together. In order for you to practise what is involved in the goal setting phase at the transition from assessment to planning, we want to return to the Taylor family, to catch up on events and to begin the process of planning with them.

✏ EXERCISE 8.1: GOAL SETTING

First, read the next instalment of the developing case of the Taylors and then attempt the tasks that follow.

It is now just over a week since Tracy Taylor called into the office. You have been able to make just a brief couple of visits to the family since receiving the referral. This means that, unfortunately, you have not been able to make very much progress with your assessment. Indeed, you have been overtaken by events once more, as the following case notes reveal.

TAYLOR FAMILY CASE FILE

The weekend following your last visit, Ron came down to collect Alison and Michael. Alison refused to go. There was a very heated discussion on the doorstep, which ended in a fight between Alun and Ron. Ron eventually left without the children, who had witnessed the fight and who were very distressed. On the Sunday, Alun and Tracy also came to blows over the situation and Tracy left with the three children and went to stay with her mother. You have visited Mrs Taylor's (senior) house and spoken to Tracy and the children.

Tracy is adamant that she will not go home to Alun and does not want to try and remove him from the family home at this point. The tenancy is in his name. Unfortunately, she is aware also that she cannot stay where she is indefinitely as the children are already getting on their grandmother's nerves and the tension is beginning to mount. Tracy feels that she could manage John but cannot cope with Alison and Michael, who have not stopped quarrelling since they arrived at Tracy's mother's house. Michael blames Alison for what has happened and is being very loud and aggressive. Alison is being very sullen and keeps bursting into tears.

You have already phoned Ron but he has made it clear that he cannot have Alison and Michael stay with him, except at weekends. Wayne has been poorly over recent weeks and his wife has been very upset at what happened over the weekend. His family have advised him to consult a solicitor to resume the formal care of the children but he seems reluctant to do so. He is prepared to talk about the children and does want to see that they are well looked after. At the moment, he cannot offer accommodation.

Tracy is asking that the older children 'get looked after by a foster family' for a while until things settle down. You have contacted the placement unit and they have told you that they do have two 'short-term beds' with the Williams family. The Williams, who run a small-holding, live about six miles out of Southtown. The only other option is to place the children in a residential unit, Brummell Drive. This is a small unit, due for closure shortly, that is more used to dealing with older children.

You have not had very much time to get to know the children. Michael appears to be very fond of his father and protective of both Alison and John. His relationship with his mother is being tested but you feel that there is a strong bond. He is probably appearing braver than he feels at the moment. You know that he is doing very well at school and is very keen on football and computer games.

Alison, although older than Michael, seems emotionally much less mature. She is very 'clingy' with mother and seems to think that dad is trying to break them up. She seems resentful of John. Both children speak very harshly of Alun, whom they are clearly in no hurry to see again.

John is very quiet for his age and seems to you to be rather small. He is not particularly sociable and does not seem able to walk unaided, preferring to crawl still. He has very little language and is still in nappies. You have been meaning to have a word with the health visitor but have not been able to yet. You were beginning to be worried about him before this last episode occurred and recent events have not lessened your concern.

Mrs Taylor (senior) is blaming the whole world for what is happening and switches from being very aggressive towards you, Tracy and the children to being utterly indifferent. She leaves you in no doubt whatsoever that the children cannot stay with her. Tracy and her mother insist on foster care for the children. Tracy will not allow them to go to any of her brothers and sisters as 'most of them have got social workers already'. Mrs Taylor (senior) tells you bluntly 'I know what is right for my grandchildren and I know that you have to listen to what I say. I want them fostered for a week or two till we can get things sorted out.' In the circumstances, you are inclined to agree.

TASKS

(Although you should assume that the children will need to be looked after by the local authority for at least a short period, do not, at this stage, be too concerned with the formal processes of planning for children looked after – we will examine these in more detail in Study Text 8.2. Instead, think in terms of the longer-term objectives that you want to achieve with this family, given their current circumstances.)

1. Drawing on your answers to Exercise 7.2, but adding relevant information contained in these case notes, begin to plan for the immediate future of these children.

2. Identify clearly what it is you are planning for and prepare statements of the goals you intend your plans to achieve.

3. Identify the specific objectives that you intend to achieve on the way to the overall goals that you have determined.

POINTS TO CONSIDER

1. Have you included goal statements in respect of where the children will live and who will parent them?

2. How well do you think your goals will meet the needs of the children?

3. How well do you think your goals will meet the wishes and feelings of the children?

4. How well do you think your goals will protect the rights of the children?

5. How well have you reflected the needs, wishes and feelings of all the adults involved in the goals you have chosen?

6. Are your statements of objectives 'specific, attainable, appropriate and measurable'?

COURSE TEXT: INFORMED DECISION MAKING

We made the point earlier that Alice's decisions (and yours) will need to be informed as well as purposive ones. The capacity to plan is clearly influenced by the worker's professional skill and knowledge. You cannot plan for what you do not know or, to put this more positively, the more extensive your knowledge base, the more options you might be able to build into your plans.

What counts as knowledge of and for social work is perhaps rather more controversial than you might imagine (see Osmond 2005; Shaw 2008). The idea that it might be more helpful to think in terms of 'knowledges' (in the plural) rather than knowledge (in the singular) may seem rather odd at first but it is a familiar idea to sociologists (and philosophers!). Long, Grayson and Boaz (2006) have provided a brief taxonomy of social work knowledges, which extends from (p.208) 'tacit, experiential knowledge arising from everyday practice, to the knowledge embodied in rules and regulations, to the formal codified knowledge arising from research into social work issues'. They then proceed to try and construct a means to assess the 'quality' of such knowledges. This is a complex and contentious task as the question of the 'quality' of knowledge can be linked to the issue of the relative status of different kinds of knowledge. In particular, the question arises as to which forms of knowledge, (after Foucault 1980), are dominant and which are 'subjugated'. This is a large and complex debate and it is very much a live issue in social work where it surfaces in discussions around 'evidence based practice' (EBP).

The immediate origins of EBP are usually traced (see Gibbs and Gambrill 2002) to the 'research–practice gap' in medicine; that is to say, to the realization in the United States that medical practitioners did not have access to research findings and consequently their formal knowledge base was commonly out of date and not easily remedied by programmes of continuing professional education. This could lead to the continuing use of interventions/treatments that, at best, had little or no demonstrated efficacy or, at worst, were positively harmful.

Possibly the most widely quoted definition of EBP was derived in this context:

> Evidence based practice is the conscientious, explicit and judicious use of current best evidence in making decisions about the care of individual patients, based on skills which allow the doctors to evaluate both personal experience and external evidence in a systematic and objective manner. (Sackett and others 1997, p.2)

The 'fit' between a model of EBP that has been derived from the 'natural' sciences and a form of welfare practice that operates in a field where problems are defined socially rather than scientistically is immediately problematic. The sheer complexity of a 'social' problem may also militate against naturalistic forms of explanation and may defy generalizability. In part this is because a 'social' problem is one capable of a wide range of subjective definitions as well as a range of more 'objective' accounts. Social problems have 'meaning' in a way that naturally occurring phenomena do not, at least not intrinsically so. Gould (2010, p.94) has even suggested that the term 'evidence' is itself 'too saturated with positivist associations to be permissible within the social work lexicon'. He goes on to describe how qualitative approaches (as opposed to the 'gold-standard, quantitative, randomised control trial that has come to dominate some forms of EPB') have the potential for (p.106) representing 'the perspective of those on the receiving end of interventions' and so present a challenge to received notions of what constitutes 'expertise' as well as 'knowledge'.

Indeed, in the UK, the development of EBP in social work draws on several different traditions and not just those derived from the natural sciences and scientistic positivism. It references behavioural social work (see for example, MacDonald 1994, 1998; MacDonald and Sheldon 1992) and the empirical practice movement (Bloom 1993; Fischer 1993; McGuire 1995; Reid 1994). It has been modified and applied by the Centre for Evidence-Based Social Care at Exeter University, with the main emphasis being upon seeking the practical goal of 'what works'.

Of course, 'what works' is also a controversial question, especially where debates about EBP cross over into debates about managerialism and the bureaucratization of practice (see Butler and Pugh 2003 for a fuller discussion on the way in which certain forms of EBP have been pressed into service in support of the 'modernizing' agenda of recent UK governments). As Webb notes, if EBP is understood strictly in terms of a 'formal rationality of practice based upon scientific methods' it is a short step to seeing how it might be employed to 'produce a more effective and economically accountable means of [delivering] social services' (2001, p.58). Whereas we might be able to build a ready consensus around the ideas of what we mean by 'effective', our ideas of what we mean by 'economically accountable' may differ quite sharply.

As far as the planning process is concerned, its intimate relationship with the use of evidence (in the form of knowledge drawn from empirical research) has been identified by Hudson (2009, p.157):

> [EBP] emphasises the use of research throughout the problem-solving process, including assessment, setting goals, planning and implementing interventions, and in evaluating the process and outcomes of these interventions.

However, Hudson (2009) takes a very broad view of what constitutes EBP, recognizing how taking a too 'narrow, rationalistic and inductivist approach to knowledge building' (p.170) conflicts both with the value orientations of most social workers and breaks down in the face of the complexity of social and personal problems. Instead, he argues that by accepting the moral responsibility to base practice on solid empirical evidence, social workers should not reject 'the role of professional judgement, clinical intuition, or other forms of transrational knowledge development'. He concludes (p.172):

> Conceived in this manner, EBP can avoid becoming a technology and instead becomes a kind of dynamic art or dance that is informed by and grounded in multiple sources of evidence and in the reflective use of self. Most important for students, seasoned practitioners, and social work educators is the on-going development of what might be regarded as a type of wisdom, involving situational awareness and metacognitive capacities of self-reflection, as well as creative ways of integrating these with empirical and theoretical knowledge, and grounding them on ethical decision making and core social work values.

As well as being a 'dynamic art or dance', however, social work operates within certain constraints, not least those imposed by agency practice and available resources. It also operates in the context of the administrative, regulatory and legislative rules that not only 'govern' social work but which also, to a very substantial degree, define it in practice.

We have seen at several points in this book already how the 1989 Children Act frequently provides the immediate context for practice in this field. As well as the Act itself, the statutory *Regulations* and *Guidance* that accompany it can greatly influence the form and content of direct work. Without wishing to influence the 'goals' you have begun to formulate with/for the Taylor family, we suggest that you may have recognized that you will shortly have to plan for the children being looked after by someone other than Tracy. The following Study Text is intended to locate your planning with the Taylor family in the context of *Guidance and Regulations*.

Note: Before you read the following Study Text you may wish to re-read Study Text 5.2, which deals with the general duties that a local authority has in relation to a child that it is, or is proposing to, look after.

i STUDY TEXT 8.2: CARE PLANNING

THE PRINCIPLES OF CARE PLANNING

We noted above that *The Children Act 1989 Guidance and Regulations. Volume 2: Care Planning, Placement and Case Review* (DCSF 2010e) sets the formal context in which planning for looked after children must take place. The *Guidance* (G.) re-articulates many of the principles on which the 1989 Act is said to rest and which we have introduced at several points already. You would probably wish to be reminded of the following however (G. § 1.5):

- Time is a crucial element in work with children and should be reckoned in days and months rather than years.

- Parents should be expected and enabled to retain their responsibilities and to remain as closely involved as is consistent with their child's welfare, even if that child cannot live at home either temporarily or permanently.

- Continuity of relationships is important and attachments should be respected, sustained and developed.

- A change of home, carer, social worker or school almost always carries some risk to a child's development and welfare.

- All children need to develop their own identity, including self-confidence and a sense of self-worth.

These principles, which we regard as at least of equal importance as the fine detail of the formal *Guidance and Regulations*, have been restated and expanded by SCIE/NICE as part of the advice offered on *Promoting the Quality of Life of Looked After Children and Young People* (2010). SCIE/NICE's specific recommendations are premised on a number of 'principles and values', including (SCIE/ NICE 2010, p.11):

- Putting the voices of children, young people and their families at the heart of service design and delivery.

- Encouraging warm and caring relationships between child and carer that nurture attachment and create a sense of belonging so that the child or young person feels safe, valued and protected.

- Helping children and young people to develop a strong sense of personal identity and maintain the cultural and religious beliefs they choose.

- Supporting the child or young person to participate in the wider network of peer, school and community activities to help build resilience and a sense of belonging.

We feel that it is important to bear these principles very much in mind as you consider the formal requirements of the *Regulations* and *Guidance* set out below.

THE CONTENT OF CARE PLANS

A care plan is required for every looked after child (*Regulations* (R.) § 4 (1–2)). Where possible, this should be an agreed plan (R. § 4 (4–5)) and be put in place before the young person is placed outwith the care of his or her parents. The plan must indicate not only how the young person's current needs will be met but also contain details of the longer-term plan for the upbringing of the young person (R. § 5 (a)). This part of the plan is referred to as the 'permanence plan'.

Guidance defines permanence in terms of 'emotional permanence (attachment), physical permanence (stability) and legal permanence (the carer has parental responsibility for the child) (G. § 2.3) and describes the objective of planning for permanence as to help provide a young person with a 'secure, loving family to support them through childhood and beyond'. It must be understood that 'permanence' does NOT equate to adoption and the *Guidance* is clear that permanence can be achieved through a return home to a child's birth family (see Farmer, Sturgess and O'Neill 2008 for an evaluation of those factors associated with a successful reunification of looked after children with their parents), kinship care, short or longer-term foster care or adoption. Permanence in this sense implies providing young people, irrespective of their placement or the point that they have reached in their 'care career', with a real sense of belonging, of being cared for and a sense of stability and predictability in terms of both where and with whom they live (see Study Text 5.2 for an indication of the research evidence in support of the importance of permanence in securing improved outcomes for looked after children).

Research by Beckett and McKeigue (2010) provides an important reminder that this sense of permanence needs to be engendered right from the beginning of the time that a young person becomes looked after, even during the court process itself (where this is relevant). Lengthy and inexplicable delays in decision making, frequent changes of placement and the consequent disruption of routines in the case of younger children and any form of continuity in terms of peer and social networks for older children, frequent changes of social worker and an air of not knowing who is actually 'in charge' of events make for a bewildering experience for young people, 'as they are ferried to and fro, day after day, between a bewildering variety of adults with a bewildering variety of agendas and in a bewildering variety of locations' (p.11). (See Jones and others 1991, for an account of the longer term impact of placement instability on a young person's capacity to form relationships.) Beckett and McKeigue stress that while it is clearly necessary to reassure a young person that his or her future needs are being taken seriously, it is also important to begin to take care of young people 'in the here and now' (p.14).

You should be aware that as well as the Care Order, there are other ways whereby legal permanence can be secured. These include Residence Orders, adoption and a new order, introduced by the Adoption and Children Act 2002, of special guardianship. Each order confers parental responsibility on the holder and adoption uniquely removes parental responsibility from the birth parent(s), extinguishing their legal relationship to the child. Special guardianship may prove to be particularly useful where a child is placed with relatives. Prior to its introduction the Prime Minister's Review of Adoption (PIU 2000) noted its suitability for:

> Local authority foster parents, relatives, older children who do not wish to be legally separated from their birth family, children cared for on a permanent basis by their wider family, and certain minority ethnic communities with religious and cultural objections to adoption.

Caselaw has subsequently confirmed that each case will be considered on its own facts, applying the welfare principle to decide on the most appropriate order, (Re AJ (Adoption Order or Special Guardianship Order) [2007] EWCA Civ 55). When making any of these orders, the court will also consider whether a contact order needs to be made.

As well as giving a general but purposeful sense of being looked after, the care plan must also set out the arrangements for meeting the young person's specific health needs ('the health plan') and his or her education and training needs ('the personal education plan'). The 'health plan' (R. Sch. 1 § 1) must include information in relation to the young person's:

- state of health including [his or her] physical, emotional and mental health

- the young person's health history including, so far as practicable, his or her family's health history

- the effect of the young person's health and health history on his or her development

- existing arrangements for the young person's medical and dental care including:

  ○ routine checks of the young person's general state of health, including dental health

  ○ treatment for, and monitoring of, identified health (including physical, emotional and mental health) or dental care needs

  ○ preventive measures such as vaccination and immunisation

  ○ screening for defects of vision or hearing, and

  ○ advice and guidance on promoting health and effective personal care.

Regulations also require an assessment of the young person's health as soon as practicable after placement and at regular intervals thereafter (R. § 7).

The 'personal education plan' (R. Sch. 1 § 2) must contain information in relation to the young person's:

- educational and training history, including information about educational institutions attended and the young person's attendance and conduct record, academic and other achievements, and special educational needs, if any

- existing arrangements for the young person's education and training, including details of any special educational provision

- any planned changes to existing arrangements for the young person's education or training and, where any changes to the arrangements are necessary, provision made to minimise disruption to that education or training

- leisure interests.

(See also R. § 10, which sets out further considerations in the case of older children to avoid or to minimise disruptions to a young person's education.)

In addition, the care plan must include details of how a young person's emotional and behavioural needs are to be met; how his or her 'identity' needs (including religious, race, cultural and linguistic considerations) will be addressed and how his or her family and social relationships will be maintained (including specific arrangements in those cases where contact between a young person and his parents is being denied or restricted); how his or her social presentation and self-care skills will be developed (see Parker and others 1991, for a full account of why these particular dimensions of need are included here.)

THE PLACEMENT PLAN

The Children and Young Persons' Act 2008 received Royal Assent on the 13th November 2008 and contains several provisions intended to extend and improve services to looked after children. Critical for our current purposes is the duty it places on local authorities (s. 8 of the 2008 Act substitutes a new series of subsections (22A ff.) into the 1989 Children Act in place of s. 23 of the 1989 Act) to secure appropriate accommodation for young people whom it is looking after (see Study Text 5.2). How far local authorities in England and Wales are able to meet this statutory requirement remains at issue but the point is that each local authority *should* have at its disposal a sufficient range of placements to meet the specific needs of those children for whom it has the day-to-day care.

To ensure an appropriate match between the young person and a specific placement, *Regulations* require the preparation of a 'placement plan' that sets out how the arrangements being proposed will contribute to meeting the young person's needs (R. § 9). Further details of what needs to be included in the placement plan are set out in Schedule 2 of the *Regulations*. Central to the placement plan is a clear account of how 'on a day-to-day basis' a young person will be cared for and how his or her welfare 'will be safeguarded and promoted' (R. Sch. 2 § 1). Arrangements for contact with parents (and relevant others) will also need to be set out in the placement plan as well as detailed arrangements for meeting the health and educational requirements of the young person's health and personal education plans.

The *Regulations* go on to describe in more detail the specific arrangements to be made, depending on the type of placement envisaged, including placement with parents (§ 15–20 and Sch. 2 § 2 and Sch. 3), a kinship carer (see R. Sch. 4) or a foster carer (R. § 21–23).

REVIEWING THE CARE PLAN

Grimshaw and Sinclair (1997) distinguish between planning ('a developing sequence in which the objectives of the plan and the current needs of the child are reconsidered on the basis of changing circumstances and fresh experiences' p.246) and review ('a process of considering the whole care plan, concluded by a final child-centred meeting and the completion of all the pertaining records' p.250). S. 26 of the 1989 Children Act provides for Regulations to be made governing the conduct and timing of reviews and the details of how these are to be conducted are also to be found in *Guidance and Regulations Volume 2* (§ 32–38). Key points to note are that a first review should take place within 20 days of a young person becoming looked after; the second within 3 months after that and subsequent reviews should take place at intervals of no more than 6 months. In addition, the *Regulations* are clear that no 'significant change' in a child's placement should be made without a formal review (R. § 32).

Critical to the review process is the Independent Reviewing Officer (IRO) as it is the IRO who will (usually) chair the formal review meeting and who will monitor the progress of the young person and the implementation of their care plan.

THE INDEPENDENT REVIEWING OFFICER

The role of the IRO was established following a House of Lords judgement, which indicated that a local authority might be vulnerable to a challenge under the Human Rights Act 1998 where it failed in its duty towards a child. Moreover, the judgement expressed concern that some children might have no adult to act on their behalf in such circumstances (see DCSF 2010c § 1.15 ff. for a full account of the statutory framework under which the IRO operates). The role and function of the IRO is set out in statutory *Guidance* (DCSF 2010c) that makes clear that the IRO's 'primary duty is to quality assure the care planning and review process for each child and to ensure that his/her current wishes and feelings are given full consideration' (DCSF 2010c, § 1.21). The 'primary task' of the IRO is to 'ensure that the care plan for the child fully reflects the child's current needs and that the actions set out in the plan are consistent with the local authority's legal responsibilities towards the child' (DCSF 2010c, § 2.10). (See Study Text 10.1 for the specific role of the IRO in respect of care proceedings.)

Both the *Guidance and Regulations* that we have described here and the additional statutory *Guidance* issued for IRO's (DCSF 2010c) provide a detailed framework through which the principles of care planning can be given effective expression. However, we should not imagine that we can design procedures that are better than those who have to work with them. In other words, in our view, the motive force in care planning will remain, the commitment that the social worker shows to practising in a way that is consistent with the principles that we set out at the beginning of this Study Text.

EXERCISE 8.2: PLANNING FOR PLACEMENT

In the event, the only placement available for the Taylor children is with the Williams family.

1. Review your plans for Alison and Michael and revise as necessary. Your review should include a consideration of all of those matters required by the Children Act 1989 and associated *Regulations* and *Guidance*.

2. Set out the sequence of events that will be necessary to put your plans into effect.

3. Using the diary sheets (see Figure 8.1) construct a timetable to operate alongside the plan that indicates the order in which tasks will be undertaken.

POINTS TO CONSIDER

1. What are the specific goals and objectives that your plan sets out to achieve?

2. What are the main tasks that:

    ○ the foster carers

    ○ the parents, and

    ○ the social worker

3. need to undertake in order to achieve these goals and objectives?

4. Is the timescale that you have determined appropriate to those goals and objectives?

5. What contingency plans have you made and does everyone know what these are?

6. What help do:

    ○ the foster carers

    ○ the parents, and

    ○ the children

	Week 1	**Week 2**	**Week 3**	**Week 4**
M				
T				
W				
Th				
F				
Sat				
Sun				

Week 5
Week 6
Week 7
Week 8
Week 9
Week 10
Week 11
Week 12

Month 4
Month 5
Month 6
Month 7
Month 8
Month 9
Month 10
Month 11
Month 12

Figure 8.1 Diary sheets

7. need to prepare for the admission?

8. Who will be responsible for, and involved in, planning for these children's longer-term future?

📖 COURSE TEXT: AFTER PLANNING?

There remains very little research of any substance that directly bears on the care planning and review process (with the notable exceptions of Grimshaw and Sinclair 1997 and Thomas and O'Kane 1999), although as we have indicated at several points, there is good empirical evidence to support the importance that should attach to both permanency planning and placement stability. There has, to date, been no comprehensive evaluation of the work of the IRO, for example. Nor has there been, to our knowledge, any comprehensive review of local authority care planning processes and the outcomes these produce for young people (although see Roach and Sanders 2008 for some indications of how vagueness in objective setting and delay still haunt the practice of care planning).

However, alongside the 'evidence' (or lack of it) and the 'systems' put in place to structure our practice (no matter whether these are honoured more in the breach than the observance), there is also the matter of the 'dance'; the very human encounter that is at the heart of the social work process. In a book such as this where there is simply no opportunity to present a detailed account of the variety of social work methods available to social workers, we wanted to reserve the final part of this chapter to at least raise your awareness of the fundamentals of relationship based practice. We do so here for two reasons. First, relationship based practice is developing a new momentum in response to some of the alleged dehumanizing aspects of some iterations of EBP and the managerialism that is sometimes associated with it or with the 'modernizing' agenda of recent years. Second, it is important to lay the foundations for the next stage in the social work process, namely intervention and, in our view, the relationship that develops between a social worker and those he or she works with and which remains a critical factor in bringing about change.

𝑖 STUDY TEXT 8.3: RELATIONSHIP BASED PRACTICE

Wilson and others (2008) have suggested that relationship based practice has several key characteristics: a recognition that each social work encounter is unique; an understanding of human behaviour as complex and multifaceted and a recognition that people have both conscious and unconscious components to their thoughts, feelings and behaviours. Relationship based practice therefore focuses on both the internal and external worlds of people and is grounded in the complexities of self and in human relations. What characterizes relationship based work is the emphasis that is placed on the professional relationship as the medium through which the practitioner can engage with and intervene in the complexity of an individual's life and internal and external worlds. The social worker and service user relationship is acknowledged to be an important source of information for the social worker to understand how best to help, and simultaneously this relationship is the means by which any help or intervention is offered. Given what we have said about the rise of certain forms of EBP already in this chapter, such a model of practice may seem somewhat out of place these days.

However, times, as ever, may be changing. One of the first acts of the new government that came to power in the UK in 2010 was to establish (on the 10th June) an 'independent review of child protection in England'. This review was to be led by Eileen Munro and is now usually directly associated with her by name. In her interim report, Munro describes the nature of the problems that are facing contemporary child protection practice, and, by implication, child and family social work more generally. Some of the challenges she sees as associated directly with previous attempts at reform, which 'have not led to the expected improvements in frontline practice'. Indeed, according to Munro, 'there is a substantial body of evidence indicating that past reforms are creating new, unforeseen complications' (Munro 2010, p.5).

In particular, Munro identifies the disadvantages (and some benefits) that have arisen as a result of the dominance of 'technocratic' approaches to child protection practice over recent years. She contrasts such approaches with a 'socio-technical' approach (§ 1.21), which

> ... assumes the individuals involved and how they work together are just as important as any analytical problem. There is no presumption about consensus regarding the problem: aims might be hard to agree on, and implementing change may require support from a range of partners. This approach does not undermine the value of rigorous analytical thinking, but argues for a balance of abstract analysis and consideration of human relations.

In other words, the problems and challenges that the social worker faces (alongside the child and family concerned) may be less clear-cut than some more 'naturalistic' or positivist paradigms might suggest, as might be the potential 'solutions'. The social worker will have to engage more than their analytical capacity in the helping process; they will also have to engage at a more 'human' level; through their relationship with the service user.

The re-discovery of the human dimension to practice and the critical importance of the social work relationship through which it is mediated precedes Munro, of course (see Houston 2003) and has arisen from practitioner expertise and experience and from a more widespread 'recognition that technical-rational knowledge offers only a partial insight into and explanation of the complexity of human behaviour' (Howe 1997). In many ways, the relationship has remained the foundation of social work practice since the development of social work as a modern form of welfare practice, reflecting its origins in psychotherapeutic 'casework', despite its periodic eclipse by other practice paradigms and policy regimes. Koprowska (2007), has made the case that 'there is a growing body of evidence that supports the long-held belief that therapeutic relationships can be reparative' (summarized by Schore 2003) and Sudbury has argued that 'a core component of social work is the ability to respond to people's emotional needs, to their impulse for emotional development' (Sudbury 2002, p.150). In examining a range of different social work methods and interventions, Teater has also demonstrated that the relationship between social worker and client is 'a crucial factor in the effectiveness of social work interventions' (Teater 2010, p.7) and refers to Rogers' (1957) core conditions for developing a positive therapeutic relationship between social worker and client; namely, the social worker needing to demonstrate: genuine concern, warmth, empathy and unconditional positive regard.

Children and young people have identified a similar range of components to an effective helping relationship.

Luborsky in Horwarth and Greenberg (1994) reported a number of more subjective feelings that the service user needs to feel in order for the relationship to be most effective, including, feeling the social worker is warm and supportive, believing the intervention is helping, feeling that there is some change from the intervention, feeling some rapport with the social worker and that their values are respected.

Children value social workers who:

- Listen – carefully and without trivializing or being dismissive of the issues raised

- are available and accessible – maintaining regular and predictable contact

- are non-judgemental and non-directive – accepting, explaining and suggesting options and choices

- have a sense of humour – it helps build rapport

- are straight talking – with realism and reliability; no 'false promises'

- can be trusted – maintain confidentiality and consult with children before taking matters forward.

Figure 8.2 The Complete Social Worker
Source: Department of Health (2000, p.46) (Crown Copyright)

However, while we would agree with Munro that 'building strong relationships with children and families with compassion is crucial', we would agree also that 'trust needs to be placed with care' and that a degree of 'respectful uncertainty' (§ 1.29) towards families, particularly in relation to child protection practice is also advisable. This can be reinforced through effective supervision but it can also be developed through self-aware and self-reflective practice (see Schön 1991 for a detailed account of what is meant by 'reflective practice') that recognizes both the emotional and rational components of practice and which makes both of these the objects of the social worker's honest and critical scrutiny.

Developing an effective helping relationship is not easy and requires a degree of personal commitment as well as a set of 'relationship skills'. The following exercise should help you understand the nature of the challenge.

EXERCISE 8.3: BUILDING A RELATIONSHIP

Look again at the qualities that children and young people say they value in social workers (Figure 8.2).

In relation to Alison, Michael and John, write down how you might be able to demonstrate each of these qualities.

POINTS TO CONSIDER

1. When you listen, are you simply looking for the next opportunity to talk? Or are you listening to help you frame the next question to ask?

2. What can the children teach you?

3. Would you give the children your mobile phone number? Why/why not?

4. Who is 'in charge' of helping this family?

5. Are you prepared to tell the children what is about to happen to the degree that they will be left in no doubt over the likely sequence of events?

6. How far should the children rely on you?

CONCLUSION

In his book *An Introduction to Social Work Theory*, David Howe (1987) reviews the literature that describes what the users of social work services perceive as effective help. He is in no doubt that service users often feel confused, threatened and angered by the social worker who is vague or uncertain about his or her role and purpose (p.6):

> Both social workers and clients should know where they are and where they would like to go. If you do not know where you are, you will not know in which direction to move. If you do not know where you are going, you will not know when you have arrived. Drift and a lack of purpose in much social work practice suggests that many social workers have little idea of place in their work with clients. Thus a sense of location and a sense of direction should structure practice.

If you are to prevent you and the children and families becoming lost in the wood like poor Alice, never venture far without a plan of where it is you are seeking to go.

NOTES AND SELF-ASSESSMENT

1. Do you think that social work really is about 'making things happen'?

2. Do you think that planning of the sort described in this Unit might rob social work of its creativity and spontaneity?

3. How 'planned' would you say your life is? What might this suggest about your attitude to planning?

4. Given the statutory basis of much social work in this area, how free to plan are you?

5. How good are you at 'sticking' to a plan?

6. Think about some of your own relationships; which would you describe as 'good' and which 'poor'? List some of the things that make these relationships either good or poor for you.

RECOMMENDED READING

Ruch, G., Turney, D. and Ward, A. (eds) (2010) *Relationship-based Social Work: Getting to the Heart of Practice.* London: Jessica Kingsley Publishers.

Teater, B. (2010) *An Introduction to Applying Social Work Theories and Methods.* Milton Keynes: OUP.

TRAINER'S NOTES
Exercise 8.1: Goal Setting

A larger group can be subdivided with two groups asked to plan on behalf of each child separately and a third on behalf of both children together. Subsequent discussion should be aimed at reconciling any differences. Once agreed, it is helpful to ask participants to role-play presenting the plan in summarized form (i.e. 'bullet points'), either for the purpose of a simulated case conference or for discussion with the children and parents concerned. It is a useful corrective for over-ambitious plans if the trainer consistently asks participants how they will achieve what is being proposed as well as when.

Exercise 8.2: Planning for Placement

For the purposes of Tasks 2 and 3, a larger group can be subdivided in order to provide a contrast between ideal solutions (i.e. unlimited time, no bureaucratic hurdles, etc.) and the practical task of planning in practice. Discussion should focus on the acceptability of the compromises that will have to be made.

Exercise 8.3: Building a Relationship

A larger group could begin by 'quickthinking' of ways of demonstrating the necessary qualities for establishing an effective relationship with a child or young person. These could then be rehearsed in the form of a role play – one each for Alison, Michael and John. The trainer should pay particular attention to any age and gender differences that emerge in the role play and engage the groups in discussion about what implications these may carry for relationship based practice.

UNIT 9

Child Protection

OBJECTIVES

In this Unit you will:

- Develop your understanding and awareness of child abuse.

- Develop your capacity to recognize and respond to abuse.

- Learn how child protection processes, services and systems are organized and administered.

COURSE TEXT: SOME BASICS

We have attended child protection case conferences where, to use a phrase that one of our former line managers used to use, the family were not so much social worked as 'social worked over'. In other words, where the experience of being 'protected' was itself a damaging one. The experience of being 'protected' can be made better or worse by the manner in which it is achieved.

The point has, perhaps, best, and most famously, been made in the UK context by Lord Justice Butler-Sloss in her report of the child abuse 'scandal' in Cleveland (Cleveland Report 1988). Butler-Sloss LJ noted, after criticizing some aspects of professional practice undertaken as part of a child protection intervention, that a 'child is a person and not just an object of concern' (Cleveland Report 1988, p.245). A child's longer-term interests, dignity and sense of identity, already made vulnerable by the process of abuse, must be preserved through any process of child 'protection'. As such, child protection practice must be firmly embedded in the attitudes, values and practices of social work with children and families more generally. Child protection is a *specialist* field but it is not to be understood as a *separate* one where the familiar 'rules' don't apply.

Hence, this Unit, while focussing on child protection processes and practice, will do so in the context of knowledge, skills and values that have a more general application. We have chosen to do this not only because it would be absurd to try and compress a comprehensive account of practice in child protection into a single chapter but also because we believe that there are dangers if social workers and other professionals think about child protection in terms which isolate it from a broader understanding of social work with children and families. In working through this Unit, therefore, we do not want you to jettison all that you have learned about good social work practice just because you are engaging with 'child protection'. No single chapter can take you very far into an understanding of the complexities of direct work in this area (we purposely omit any reference to post-abuse work as this is well beyond the scope of a book such as this) but we do want you to begin your journey with a positive regard for what you already know rather than with misgivings about what you have yet to learn.

We should perhaps say at this point why we have persisted with the terms 'child abuse' and 'child protection' rather than the more fashionable terms, 'maltreatment' and 'safeguarding' in this Unit and throughout this book. We do not have any particular objections to the term 'safeguarding', when it is properly applied, but it has come to have a rather unhelpful and somewhat limited meaning, in our view. To talk of 'safeguarding' is to talk of the systems, processes and protocols that have been put in place by professionals. It describes what *we* do rather than what has happened to the child and it does so usually in a way that is largely unintelligible and therefore inaccessible to the children and families with whom we are working.

The term derives from s. 17(1) of the 1989 Children Act and the general duty that this imposes on local authorities in England and Wales:

> to safeguard and promote the welfare of children within their area who are in need.

It is vitally important to note that there is no comma in the text of the Act between 'safeguard' and 'promote welfare'. The duty is one to *both* safeguard *and* to promote welfare; not to 'safeguard, and (maybe later or as an afterthought) promote 'welfare'. The Act is clear in its intentions that any action taken to safeguard a child should also be one that promotes his or her welfare. Eileen Munro has put this very neatly: '… the aim [of child protection systems] is not just to *minimize* the danger to children but to *maximize* their welfare' (Munro 2008, p.1 – original emphasis).

Where 'safeguarding' is used as a (not very helpful) shorthand for 'safeguard and promote', then we would regard its use as (just about) acceptable. However, where it is used to force a virtual comma between the duty to safeguard *and* to promote such that the focus is exclusively on the minimization of danger to the exclusion of the maximization of welfare, then its use is positively unhelpful.

The position that we take is entirely consistent with that taken in *Working Together* (DCSF 2010f – see Unit 6 and Study Text 9.2, below). Here, safeguarding and promoting the welfare of children is unambiguously defined as (§ 1.20):

- protecting children from maltreatment

- preventing impairment of children's health or development

- ensuring that children are growing up in circumstances consistent with the provision of safe and effective care

- and undertaking that role so as to enable those children to have optimum life chances and to enter adulthood successfully.

Working Together goes on to note (§ 1.21 ff.) that:

> Protecting children from maltreatment is important in preventing the impairment of health or development though that in itself may be insufficient to ensure that children are growing up in circumstances consistent with the provision of safe and effective care. These aspects of safeguarding and promoting welfare are cumulative... Child protection is a part of safeguarding and promoting welfare.

We continue to use the term 'child abuse' because we regard this as simply more descriptive than the newspeak 'safeguarding issues' or 'safeguarding concerns', both of which we find regularly in use among social workers and social work students. We use it in preference to 'maltreatment' to retain the focus on the experience for the child and to retain a sense of the differential possession of power that is inherent in the social relations between children and adults and which is very often implicated in the process of abuse itself.

Whatever term you prefer, the important point to remember is that working with children who have been abused is not altogether different from other kinds of work with children and their families; the knowledge, skills, principles, values and forms of practice that you will rely on in one context will support you in the other. Working to protect children from abuse requires a holistic awareness of the needs and rights of children and the careful, reflective and informed exercise of professional judgement on the part of the social worker (and others) involved – as with every other piece of work undertaken with a child or their family.

The following exercise, based on developments with the Taylor family, should demonstrate to you what you already know about 'protecting' children.

TAYLOR FAMILY CASE FILE

Despite the careful arrangements that you made for the children, you have had to revise your plans once again. Ron could not bring himself to consent to Alison and Michael being provided with accommodation and decided to exercise his parental responsibility and make arrangements of his own. With Tracy's blessing, and with the informed consent of both Alison and Michael, the older children have gone to live with Ron and his wife and child in Northtown. Supervision by the local social services department has been arranged and you have been invited to monthly review meetings with the children, Ron and the area social worker. The children are to have unrestricted contact with Tracy.

All of this has happened very quickly and the children moved to Northtown on 19 February. Tracy and John continued to live at Mrs Taylor's (senior) house on Old Estate. At first everything seemed to be going along well: the older children had settled down in Northtown and were making good progress in school and at home and Tracy seemed to be on good terms with her mother. Tracy said that she didn't really need your help and your visits declined to no more than once every three weeks.

In early May the local health visitor telephoned to say that she had recently seen John at the GP's request. The GP had noted that John was being brought to the surgery very frequently with a succession of minor childhood ailments. The GP indicated that she thought John 'wasn't being very well cared for' and that 'he looked a bit on the thin side'. You visited the home on 14 May. The house was dirty and very disorganized. Tracy told you that John was 'off his food and had the runs'. When asked about the state of the house, Tracy said that Alun had started to call around and was being very difficult and that the stress she was feeling meant that she had 'let things slide a bit'. Her mother, according to Tracy, 'couldn't be bothered', leaving more for her to do than she could manage. There had been a minor fire in the kitchen recently that made matters look worse than they were, according to Tracy. You arranged for the repair of the kitchen and for the temporary re-connection of the gas supply, which had been turned off two months ago because of unpaid bills. You also arranged for a cash payment to enable Tracy to stock up with food. Tracy agreed to attend the local child health clinic on a weekly basis and accepted your offer of referral to the local family centre where John could attend 'toddlers' club' and Tracy could meet other women in her position who might be able to offer advice and support.

On 3 June, the health visitor informed you that Tracy had not kept a single appointment at the clinic. On the same day that the health visitor had been in touch, Tracy turned up at your office (while you were out) and left a message to say that she wasn't getting on with the health visitor and asking that you visit her. You tried, on four occasions over the next three weeks, to see Tracy but she was never in at the times at which you had agreed to call. On the last day of June, during evening surgery, Tracy called at the clinic to see the health visitor. The health visitor had left for the day but Tracy was seen briefly by the practice nurse who said she would pass on a message to the health visitor in the morning. John had not attended any of the toddler sessions that you had arranged for him.

In the first week of July, an anonymous caller informs your duty office that a young child had been left unattended in the garden for most of the day. He was crying and there didn't seem to be anyone looking after him. The address given was Mrs Taylor's house in Old Estate. You visit and find Tracy at home. You tell her what you have been told. Tracy explains that she has been away for a few days with Alun and that her mother was supposed to be looking after John. Tracy tells you that Mrs Taylor (senior) has taken John out in his buggy. They both return while you are still there.

John is still clearly very distressed. Mrs Taylor explains that 'he must have caught the sun' and that he's just 'hot and bothered'. Tracy accuses her mother of not looking after John. She responds that Tracy shouldn't have gone off and left him like she did and an argument develops between the two. Each accuses the other of failing to look after John properly. Tracy shouts at John that this wouldn't have happened if it wasn't for him. John is sitting silently in his buggy, watching what is going on around him.

You intervene in the argument between the two women. You observe that John is sitting in a very dirty nappy and that his buggy is filthy and very smelly. Neither Tracy nor Mrs Taylor seems prepared to do anything about this. Tracy says that she will see to John after you've gone. You notice that he has a number of what appear to be bruises on his arms with two much darker ones on each arm, just below the shoulder. You ask Tracy how he got them and she explains that Alun had been playing 'aeroplanes' with him. Mrs Taylor (senior) asks Tracy whether Alun had been around the house, as she never wanted to see him again. Tracy says that she hadn't seen Alun and it was the boyfriend of a friend of her's who had been playing with John.

You ask Tracy to meet you at the clinic in the morning. She doesn't keep her appointment but does see the duty doctor later in the day. The doctor is clear that John is underweight for his age and that he is suffering from moderate sunburn and impetigo, aggravated by urine burns.

EXERCISE 9.1: SAFEGUARDING AND PROMOTING

Having read the account of developments in the Taylor family, complete the following tasks. Today is 3 August.

1. Write down what you consider to be John's primary needs at this point.

2. Assuming that John's needs are as you predicted, identify the ways in which these might be met.

3. How far does your answer to (2) adequately safeguard and promote John's welfare?

POINTS TO CONSIDER

1. Which of John's needs must be met in order to 'safeguard' his welfare?

2. Which of John's needs must be met in order to 'promote' his welfare?

3. Write short definitions of what you understand by the terms 'safeguard' and 'promote', in order to clarify their meaning for you.

4. Do you consider John to be an abused child? If so, at what point did this case become a 'child protection' one? Be clear about your reasons.

5. Would such a determination make you revise your plans for investigating John's situation further?

6. Would such a determination make you want to revise your plans for meeting John's needs?

COURSE TEXT: RECOGNIZING CHILD ABUSE

John's situation is now (probably) an abusive one in that he appears to be suffering or likely to suffer significant harm (see Study Text 10.1 for a detailed explanation of 'significant harm' – for present purposes, you can take the phrase at face value). Your answers to the questions posed by the last exercise, and to the points that you have been asked to consider, have probably raised new and more pressing concerns for you. John almost certainly needs a more immediate and direct form of protection now. Even so, in safeguarding John's welfare from this point on, it will be vital to ensure that we also continue consciously and actively to promote it.

As suggested in Unit 6, child abuse rarely presents itself in a dramatic or easily identifiable form. Families where child abuse occurs may not be immediately distinctive from other families with which you are working. Sometimes, especially in the case of neglect, what has been a chronic family situation, such as that described in the Taylor file, may shift catastrophically into some other more readily defined form of abuse. Indeed, in Unit 10, we will see that this is what happens in this case. However, at this stage we clearly will need to investigate John's situation further. We will also need to do so fully conscious of the potential threats to John's welfare from the circumstances he is now facing.

It is perhaps another one of those things that goes without saying (and which therefore needs to be said!) that the potential effects of child abuse are serious. There is an established literature on this subject (see Hanks and Stratton 2007 for a useful review) that continues to expand and to increase in specificity and sophistication. For example, in a period of little more than a year, the leading journal in this field, *Child Abuse and Neglect* reported research on the relationship between physical and psychological violence in childhood and later mental health (Greenfield and Marks 2010); child abuse and the risk of poor physical health in adulthood (Chartier, Walker and Naimark 2010); sexual abuse and later risk behaviours such as alcohol abuse (Schraufnagel and others 2010); the effects of childhood abuse on subsequent socio-economic well-being (Zielinski 2009) among a range of other papers on the consequences of abuse. For the purposes of this Unit, we will have to be content with the summary of the potential effects of childhood abuse provided in *Working Together* (DCSF 2010f: § 9.3):

> The immediate and longer-term impact can include anxiety, depression, substance misuse, eating disorders and self-destructive behaviours, offending and anti-social behaviour. Maltreatment is likely to have a deep impact on the child's self-image and self-esteem, and on his or her future life. Difficulties may extend into adulthood: the experience of long-term abuse may lead to difficulties in forming or sustaining close relationships, establishing oneself in work, and to extra difficulties in developing the attitudes and skills necessary to be an effective parent.

It is important to note however, that this is a summary (although later paragraphs of *Working Together* do provide more detail). As such it is a generalized statement. These effects will not hold true for all children in all circumstances. As a professional in the field, we expect you to develop the kind of differentiated and sophisticated awareness that comes from reading the research literature rather than relying on summaries of the sort provided in *Working Together* and in this book. These can be helpful in providing you with a general orientation to the subject but they are not sufficient on their own to provide you with the knowledge base that you will require to act with confidence and authority as an effective child and family social worker. That is a career-long commitment.

In the following Study Text, we will introduce some further detail to the 'categories' of abuse that we introduced you to in Unit 6. We will also raise with you some of the factors that are associated with the incidence of child abuse. In thinking about abuse in 'categories' you must guard against any assumption that abuse neatly falls into such categories in reality. Each can overlap the other; sexual abuse can involve physical abuse; physical abuse can involve neglect and emotional abuse can be present in the context of any other form of abuse as well as occurring on its own. We are describing abuse to you in terms of categories for the purposes of exposition only. Real life is much more complicated.

i STUDY TEXT 9.1: RECOGNIZING CHILD ABUSE

In answering the question 'What is abuse?' *Working Together* (§ 1.32–1.36) defines four forms or categories of abuse: physical, emotional, sexual and neglect. Brief definitions are offered of each form of abuse and the first three of these are reproduced below (see Figure 9.1). In each case, we have added further detail of how such abuse might manifest itself to the assessing social worker or other professional. The additional detail is taken from guidance issued to heath professionals by the National Institute for Health and Clinical Excellence (NICE 2009), introduced in Unit 6 but we have *excluded* indicators that specifically require a medical assessment (such as fractures or internal injuries). Moreover, as the NICE guidance makes clear, any 'alerting feature' (p.10) is to be assessed fully and in context. No determination of abuse can be reached without a thorough process of listening, observation, recording, consultation and evaluation ('considering, suspecting or excluding' maltreatment, to use the model described in the NICE guidance).

The taxonomy of presenting features in the guidance is NOT offered as a simple check-list to assist in a simplistic diagnosis. Rather, its purpose is 'to raise awareness and help healthcare professionals who are not specialists in child protection to identify children who may be being maltreated' (NICE 2009, p.4). NICE is clear that no guidance can or should 'override the individual responsibility of healthcare professionals to make decisions appropriate to the circumstances of the individual patient, in consultation with the patient/ or guardian or carer' (NICE 2010, p.i). This quotation is a reminder too that the determination of abuse is a multi-disciplinary process and that under no

Table 9.1 Alerting features

Working Together Definition	Physical Features (NICE Guideline 89)
Physical abuse	
… may involve hitting, shaking, throwing, poisoning, burning or scalding, drowning, suffocating, or otherwise causing physical harm to a child. Physical harm may also be caused when a parent or carer fabricates the symptoms of, or deliberately induces, illness in a child.	*Bruises*: esp. in shape of a hand, stick, tooth mark, grip or implement; multiple bruises or bruises in clusters; bruises of a similar shape and size; bruises on any non-bony part of the body or face *Lacerations (cuts)*: multiple or symmetrical cuts; on areas usually covered by clothing *Burns or scalds*: in the shape of an implement (e.g. cigarette, iron); on any soft tissue area that would not be expected to come into contact with a hot object (e.g. the backs of hands, soles of feet).
Emotional abuse	
… is the persistent emotional maltreatment of a child such as to cause severe and persistent adverse effects on the child's emotional development. It may involve conveying to children that they are worthless or unloved, inadequate, or valued only insofar as they meet the needs of another person. It may include not giving the child opportunities to express their views, deliberately silencing them or 'making fun' of what they say or how they communicate. It may feature age or developmentally inappropriate expectations being imposed on children. These may include interactions that are beyond the child's developmental capability, as well as overprotection and limitation of exploration and learning, or preventing the child participating in normal social interaction. It may involve seeing or hearing the ill-treatment of another. It may involve serious bullying (including cyberbullying), causing children frequently to feel frightened or in danger, or the exploitation or corruption of children. Some level of emotional abuse is involved in all types of maltreatment of a child, though it may occur alone.	*Parent–child interactions*: negativity or hostility towards child; rejection or scapegoating; developmentally inappropriate expectations of or interactions with a child, incl. inappropriate threats or methods of disciplining; exposure to frightening or traumatic experiences, including domestic abuse; using the child for the fulfilment of the adult's needs (for example, children being used in marital disputes); failure to promote the child's socialisation.

Table 9.1 Alerting features cont.

Working Together Definition	Physical Features (*NICE Guideline 89*)
Sexual abuse	
involves forcing or enticing a child or young person to take part in sexual activities, not necessarily involving a high level of violence, whether or not the child is aware of what is happening. The activities may involve physical contact, including assault by penetration (for example, rape or oral sex) or non-penetrative acts such as masturbation, kissing, rubbing and touching outside of clothing. They may also include non-contact activities, such as involving children in looking at, or in the production of, sexual images, watching sexual activities, encouraging children to behave in sexually inappropriate ways, or grooming a child in preparation for abuse (including via the internet). Sexual abuse is not solely perpetrated by adult males. Women can also commit acts of sexual abuse, as can other children.	There are a number of physical signs that may be associated with sexual abuse but most of these are not usually accessible to the social worker and need careful consideration by a paediatrician. They include injury to genital area (these are often minor but inconsistent with accidental injury), vaginal or anal soreness, discharge or bleeding, presence of a sexually transmitted disease, soft tissue injury to breast, buttocks or thighs, love bites and semen stains and/or pubic hair on skin or clothes. Behavioural clues are more difficult to detect and are open to a wider range of interpretations that rely on greater practice experience. These include a preoccupation with sexual matters and compulsive sexual behaviour. Most children are curious about sexual matters but overtly sexualised behaviour, attempts at simulating sexual acts, persistent masturbation in public or anatomically detailed drawings by younger children should be taken as possible causes for concern.

circumstances should social workers attempt quasi-medical diagnoses of physical or other symptoms.

However, as a qualifying social worker, you too need to be aware of some of the alerting features of abuse and you too must not be tempted to think that from simply observing any one of these features (or even a combination of some of them) you can reach an immediate and final conclusion. The process of assessing abuse is an extension of the core social work processes of assessment that we introduced to you in Unit 7.

While the process of risk assessment in relation to potential abuse is a complex one (but see Munro 2008, p.58 ff.), it is important to have an 'alerting' sense of the familial context in which abuse may occur. There is a measure of agreement over the characteristics of carers who are more likely to abuse their children (assuming that you take a 'weak constructionist' point of view – see Study Text 6.1). These have been summarized by Thoburn (2010, p.9), according to whom these carers may:

- be isolated, without extended family, community or faith group support

- have been abused or emotionally rejected as children or had multiple changes of carer

- have a mental illness and/or a learning disability, especially if no other parent or extended family member is available to share parenting, and combined with a child who is 'hard to parent'

- have a personality disorder

- have had several partners often involving an abusive relationship

- have an alcohol or drug addiction and do not accept that they must control the habit for the sake of their child's welfare

- have aggressive outbursts, a record of violence, including intimate partner violence

- have obsessional/very controlling personalities, often linked with low self-esteem

- have been in care and had multiple placements or 'aged out' of care without a secure base (potentially mitigated if they had a good relationship with a carer, social worker or social work team who remained available to them through pregnancy and in early parenting)

- be especially fearful of stigma or suspicious of statutory services, including those from communities which consider it stigmatising to seek state assistance, immigrants who have experienced coercive state power before coming to the UK, or because of their own experience of poor services as they grew up.

Thoburn goes on to note that some children and young people have characteristics which, when combined with one or more of the above parental characteristics, make them more vulnerable to continuing harm; they include:

- children born prematurely and/or suffering the effects of intrauterine drug and/or alcohol misuse, which can make children fretful, hard to feed and unresponsive

- children with disabilities or other characteristics which make them hard to parent or 'unrewarding' in the eyes of parents who lack self-esteem and confidence

- individual members of sibling groups 'singled out for rejection' and/or targeted for abuse

- children returning home from care, especially if they suffer the loss of an attachment figure (usually a foster carer) – several recent studies have demonstrated that children who return to a parent following more than a short period of planned care are more likely to be re-abused than those who remain in permanent foster care, are placed with relatives or are adopted

- teenagers (many of whom have suffered from unrecognised or un-responded to abuse or neglect) who engage in risk-taking or anti-social behaviour.

For the remainder of this Study Text, we have chosen to focus on neglect. We do so because it is one of the most difficult forms of abuse to detect and because of our belief that social workers, and others, face some of the greatest difficulties in recognizing and responding to neglect. Notwithstanding this, neglect is also the most frequently recorded category of abuse for the purposes of official statistics. In 2008, neglect at 16,300 in the UK, counted for over 45 per cent of all case conference categorizations (36,000) (ONS 2010a, Table 8.21) – see Study Text 9.2 for further details on how abuse comes to be recorded under various categories. By describing this particular category of abuse in more detail, we will help you to understand better the limitations of the 'category' approach to recognizing child abuse.

NEGLECT

Working Together (DCSF 2010f) defines neglect as:

> the persistent failure to meet a child's basic physical and/or psychological needs, likely to result in the serious impairment of the child's health or development. Neglect may occur during pregnancy as a result of maternal substance abuse. Once a child is born, neglect may involve a parent or carer failing to:
>
> - provide adequate food, clothing and shelter (including exclusion from home or abandonment)
>
> - protect a child from physical and emotional harm or danger
>
> - ensure adequate supervision (including the use of inadequate caregivers); or ensure access to appropriate medical care or treatment.
>
> It may also include neglect of, or unresponsiveness to, a child's basic emotional needs. (p.39, para 1.36)

Any difficulty in recognition has to be understood against the background of the very broad range of a child's emotional, psychological and physical needs, many of which are age specific. Accordingly, universally reliable indicators of neglect are as elusive as any comprehensive definition of the process itself. Moreover, neglect is often about things undone rather than things done, acts of omission rather than commission, and non-events are that much more difficult to observe, of course. Horwath (2007) collected over a dozen definitions of neglect from authoritative sources that differed from each other to some degree but which led her to offer the following synoptic definition (p.38):

> Child neglect is a failure on the part of either the male and/or female caregiver or pregnant mother, to complete the parenting tasks required to ensure that the developmental needs of the child are met. This should take into account the age, gender, culture, religious beliefs and particular needs and circumstances of the individual child. This failure may be associated with parenting issues. It has occurred despite reasonable resources being available to enable the carer/s to complete the parenting tasks satisfactorily. Whilst neglect is on-going, one-off incidents and episodic neglect can affect the health and development of a child.

This definition makes it clear that neglect is a function of parenting; it moves beyond the simple attribution of blame and it is set in the context of providing support and resources to parents and carers. Horwath further distinguishes between medical neglect; nutritional neglect; emotional neglect; supervisory neglect; educational neglect and physical neglect. In contrast, Howe (2005) describes neglect in terms not so much of the form it takes as the mode in which it operates. He describes 'disorganized neglect'; 'emotional neglect'; 'depressed, passive and physical neglect'; social deprivation and chronic neglect, including 'institutionalised care' and compound cases of abuse and neglect (physical abuse and neglect; drugs, depression and domestic violence and child sexual abuse). (See also Hanks and Stratton 2007; Minty 2005; Spencer 2005 for further discussion on the definitions and categorization of neglect.)

However defined, neglect can only be identified by comparison with the circumstances and development of the non-neglected child. In terms of general development, particularly in the case of infants and children under five, there are recognized standards against which any individual's progress or lack of it can be measured. Where a child's general development is delayed other than for medical reasons (non-organic failure to thrive), although this is usually the province of the health visitor, the social worker still has an important role to play. You should be concerned if a young child suffers repeatedly from chronic diarrhoea, recurrent and persistent infections, voracious appetite or no appetite at all; thrives while away from home and/or has a general delay in acquiring such skills as sitting, crawling, walking and talking.

In behavioural terms, a neglected or emotionally abused child may be unresponsive to social stimulation and avoid eye contact. Such a child may also exhibit excessively 'clingy' behaviour developed through lack of confidence and any sense of emotional or physical security. There may be signs of self-stimulating behaviour, such as head banging or rocking. Most striking of all (and not confined to neglect or emotional abuse) is the child who distances her- or himself from others and observes whatever is happening in an attitude of 'frozen watchfulness', ready to respond to a blow or a threat but not actively engaged with what is going on around him or her.

Older children may appear more obviously dirty, smelly and unkempt. They may rush around, unable to concentrate on anything for very long and may have great difficulty in playing with other children. They may also be 'touch hungry' and seek physical contact, even from strangers. There may be additional signs of self-stimulating behaviour, including self-harm. At school, there may be apparent signs of learning difficulties and poor peer relationships as well as social and emotional immaturity (see NICE *Guidance* 2010, p.22 ff.).

While neglect is a difficult area conceptually and definitionally, this is not the most salient challenge in relation to practice with children who are neglected. Research has shown that our collective tolerance of the neglect of children can be far too high and that the comparative neglect of neglected children by those professionals whose job it is to protect them needs to be carefully examined (Horwath 2005; Minty and Patterson 1994; Reder, Duncan and Gray 1993).

It is possible to suggest a number of explanations for the failure to see abuse, even if signs of the neglect are obvious:

- In our work generally, and in child protection specifically, we are too much concerned with the actions and behaviour of adults and too little concerned with the consequences for children. Few of us would tolerate a urine-soaked mattress, infestation or prolonged cold and hunger for ourselves or those close to us for a moment longer than we could avoid, yet both child death enquiries and serious case reviews would seem to indicate that we will accept excuses from adults for the neglectful treatment of some children.

- We avoid confronting neglect through misplaced cultural relativism. We console ourselves with the thought that 'Children around here all live like that. They may be scruffy, but they're happy!' *All* children have a right to adequate standards of care and a right to our protection.

- We confuse neglect with poverty. It is true that, in the context of structural poverty, the potential for children to lead impoverished lives on a grand scale is disturbingly high. The fact of structural economic inequality and the consequences of poverty provide a bleak background against which to identify particular instances of neglect. Nevertheless, it is a dangerous fallacy to locate the responsibility for neglect other than with a child's carers. Responsibility is not, of course, the same as blame. Poverty attracts the attention of the authorities as parents are forced to ask for financial or other assistance; poverty forces cruel choices on parents and increases the stress of parenting. However, many children and their parents achieve 'good enough' parenting despite the grinding poverty that is the lot of too many parents and children.

- Linked with this idea is also the 'fear of the flood': this is the very real anxiety that were anyone to move the current threshold of tolerance of neglect, personally and organizationally, we would be overwhelmed.

We also avoid neglect through falling in with the general sense of hopelessness that can infuse such cases. This sense of hopelessness arises because of the elusive nature of much neglect, which often leaves the social worker with no specific behaviour or clear circumstances to work with to bring about change. Indeed, long-term interventions may seem wholly unproductive as they attempt to address the personalities of the carers or else rely inappropriately on 'support services' that maintain, rather than reduce, the problem. In other words, neglect cases can seem deeply unsatisfying in professional terms and their hopelessness can easily become ours.

📖 COURSE TEXT: SIMPLE ANSWERS TO COMPLEX PROBLEMS?

Another of our line managers used to tell us that 'There is always a simple answer to a complex problem – and its usually the wrong one!' In recognizing abuse, you will also have to recognize that it is an 'elusive hazard' (Kates 1985). Almost each and every sign of abuse can have an innocent explanation. Certain medical conditions can produce bruising, skin discolouration and fractures. The most unlikely accidents do happen. All children collect bruises and other signs of injury as part of the routine business of being a child and, although there are patterns of difference between accidental and non-accidental injuries, there are exceptions to almost every rule. None of the 'alerting features' that we have described above, taken in isolation, can be considered as conclusive evidence of abuse. Nonetheless, it is important to recognize that the absence of proof in child abuse is not proof of absence and you must always give serious thought and proper consideration to any alerting feature of possible abuse.

In particular, your concern should be heightened in those situations where there has been a failure or reluctance to seek appropriate medical advice or assistance, where the account of the injury or other indication is not credible in terms of the child's age and stage of development or where the account changes when closely examined or when carers give inconsistent accounts of the same series of events.

However, the essential uncertainty which remains at the heart of child protection practice need not lead you to over-predict abuse or to fail to recognize it when it is happening. Whether your strategy is an optimistic one (which rushes to find or accept innocent explanations for indications of abuse), whether it is a pessimistic one (which finds evidence of abuse in innocent, if unfortunate, circumstances) (Dingwall 1989) or whether it is a balanced one will be a function of how acute are your observations, how extensive and current is your knowledge base and how far you have consciously developed the capacity to exercise your professional judgement. It is only through the exercise of that judgement that the determination of abuse can be made. The next exercise should illustrate what we mean.

EXERCISE 9.2: SIGNS OF NEGLECT

Read over the case notes for the Taylor family in this Unit and in Units 7 and 8 and then:

1. Write down those alerting features of the possible abuse and/or neglect of John that you find in the case notes.

2. Try and construct a completely innocent explanation for each of the features you have listed in (1).

3. Make a list of the additional information you might need to verify or refute your suspicions of neglect and/or other forms of abuse.

POINTS TO CONSIDER

1. How confident do you feel now about whether John is being abused?

2. How much additional information would be required to make you more sure?

3. How confident would you need to feel before you decided that matters should be further investigated or action taken?

4. Do you think that, in the circumstances, what is happening to John was probably inevitable and as such, unavoidable?

5. Who is responsible for the standard of John's care?

6. What might prevent you from seeing evidence of neglect or other forms of abuse?

COURSE TEXT: FRAMEWORKS FOR CHILD PROTECTION

In Unit 6, we briefly introduced the *Signs of Safety* child protection framework alongside the *Working Together* framework that governs practice in England. Our point then was simply that there is more than one legislative, regulatory and policy framework governing work in this area. Indeed, in some cases, there are none. In Germany for example, partly stemming from deeply embedded suspicions over the role of the state in the collection of data on families that is rooted in recent and more distant historical contexts, there is no mandatory reporting of child abuse, no national data collection and no established collaboration between the child welfare and healthcare system. In fact, even within the UK, there are significant differences in the governance arrangements operating across the devolved administrations, largely consequent on differences in legislation and/or the organization and structure of children's services (see AlEissa and others 2009 for a brief review of 10 national 'child maltreatment systems').

Moreover, even within single countries, systems for surveillance and child abuse data management for example, are subject to radical change as governments change. In England, the May 2010 general election was swiftly followed by the ending of the ContactPoint database (a database on every child in England) in which a significant political and financial investment had been made by the previous government and an immediate review of social work and frontline child protection was announced ('The Munro Review' – June 2010). With technology comes ideology and in a thinly disguised criticism of the ICT arrangements (the 'integrated children's system') that had been advanced as central to effective child protection (in England) by the out-going administration, Professor Munro, possibly signalling a significant change in the direction of child protection policy and practice, is reported as saying:

> Social workers have one of the most difficult jobs in the world and we really need to look at how we can ensure children are at the heart of what they do. Less time in front of computers and filling in forms and more time working with vulnerable children, young people and their families, many of whom so desperately need the support of a good social worker. (Press Notice; DfE 10 June 2010)

We have already alerted you to the need to adopt a critical approach to any given 'framework' for practice in Unit 7. The same injunction applies here. The current, national and local framework for managing and regulating practice is precisely that – current, national and local. That is not to say however that it is something to which you need only pay passing attention. As we made clear in Unit 6, it is a professional obligation on your part to know, understand and be able to follow your local procedures. In what follows, we provide a very brief account of the framework provided in *Working Together*. For those of you in England (and to some degree, in Wales), it is your point of reference; for others it can be a point of comparison. We have focussed on the more 'stable' elements of the framework, many of which have stood the test of time in that *Working Together* has been in existence (in a variety of forms) since its origins in the case of Maria Colwell (Colwell Inquiry Report 1974) in the 1970s.

i STUDY TEXT 9.2: WORKING TOGETHER

LOCAL SAFEGUARDING CHILDREN'S BOARDS

The subtitle to *Working Together*[7] (2010) (WT) is *A Guide to Inter-agency Working to Safeguard and Promote the Welfare of Children.* At the heart of the model of child protection embedded in the framework is the Local Safeguarding Children's Board (LSCB). This is defined (WT § 3.1) as 'the key statutory mechanism for agreeing how the relevant organisations in each local area will co-operate to safeguard and promote the welfare of children in that locality, and for ensuring the effectiveness of what they do.' (See S. 14 and 14A of the CA 2004).

The work of the LSCB is divided up into three broad areas of activity: first, the LSCB is concerned with identifying and preventing maltreatment (or impairment of health or development) in respect of the whole population of children in an area and ensuring that children grow up in 'circumstances consistent with safe and effective care' (WT § 3.8). This includes:

- work to increase understanding of safeguarding children issues in the professional and wider community, promoting the message that safeguarding is everybody's responsibility

- work to ensure that organizations working or in contact with children, operate recruitment and human resources practices that take account of the need to safeguard and promote the welfare of children

- ensuring children know who they can contact when they have concerns about their own or others' safety and welfare

- ensuring that adults (including those who are harming children) know who they can contact if they have a concern about a child or young person.

The second area of activity for the LSCB is 'proactive work that aims to target particular groups'. For example:

- developing/evaluating thresholds and procedures for work with children and families where a child has been identified as 'in need' under the Children Act 1989, but where the child is not suffering or likely to suffer significant harm; and

---

7   All references to *Working Together* in this Study Text are to the text of WT as published in March 2010. This version of WT applies to England only although there are some common features with practice in Wales, including the establishment of LSCBs and the provisions of the 1989 CA. However, for those working in Wales, further reference should be made to the *All Wales Child Protection Procedures* (WAG, 2008), which are under review at the time of writing (August 2010).

- work to safeguard and promote the welfare of groups of children who are potentially more vulnerable than the general population, for example children living away from home, children who have run away from home, children missing from school or child care, children in the youth justice system, including custody, disabled children and children and young people affected by gangs.

The final area of activity is that concerned with 'responsive work to protect children who are, or are likely to suffer significant harm'.

One of the core functions of LSCBs relates to establishing local thresholds, policies and procedures for responding to child abuse (see WT § 3.13–3.26). It is the LSCB that will have determined the 'child protection procedures' that operate where you work or where you are on placement (in England and Wales). The LSCB also has a critical role in monitoring and evaluating the effectiveness of local practice and in driving improvements. LSCBs have to produce an Annual Report that comments on local arrangements and their effectiveness and we strongly urge you to at least read the one for your area (most are available on-line) as these can be an invaluable source of information on local practices, the incidence and prevalence of abuse locally and on the child protection services on offer to children and families. (See France, Munro and Waring 2010 for an evaluation of the operation of LSCBs in England.)

THE INVESTIGATIVE PROCESS

Upon receipt of a referral suggesting concern about a child's welfare, the relevant social care department of the local authority should decide, within one working day, whether an initial assessment (as defined by the *Framework for the Assessment of Children in Need and their Families*, Department of Health and others 2000, and described in Unit 7) is required (WT § 5.34 and 5.38 ff.). This may be very brief if it becomes clear that there is a need for urgent action to safeguard the child concerned. The maximum time for completing an initial assessment is ten working days (WT § 5.39).

After the initial assessment, where there is 'reasonable cause to suspect' (WT § 5.56) that the child is suffering or likely to suffer significant harm, then a 'strategy meeting' is likely to be convened, involving the social services department, the police and other relevant agencies. This meeting, as well as sharing available information, will decide what further action is needed immediately to safeguard the child (if this has not been decided already using the emergency protection powers available under the CA 1989) and determine whether enquiries under s. 47 of the Act should be initiated.

The local authority has a statutory duty under s. 47 of the Act to investigate whenever it 'has reasonable cause to believe that a child who lives, or is found, in their area is suffering, or is likely to suffer significant harm' (s. 47 (1)(b)) (see Study Text 10.1 for a full definition of 'significant harm'). Section 47 of the Act requires the local authority to determine whether it should apply to the court for an order or exercise any of its powers under the Act, including the provision of services to the child and its family. In order to assist in this determination, Section 47 also requires the local authority to take 'such steps as are reasonably practical' (s. 47 (4)) to obtain access to the child, either directly or through a person authorized by the authority 'unless they are satisfied that they already have sufficient information with respect to [the child]'. If access is frustrated, the local authority must apply to the court for one of a range of orders unless it is satisfied that the child's welfare can be 'satisfactorily safeguarded without their doing so' (s. 47 (6)). In the course of its investigations under s. 47, the local authority can make reasonable requests for information from any local authority, including education and housing authorities.

In effect, the s. 47 enquiry is carried out via a 'core assessment' (as defined by the *Framework for the Assessment of Children in Need and their Families*, Department of Health and others 2000, and described in Unit 7). WT offers useful advice to social workers engaged in s. 47 enquiries to bear in mind the potential impact of such enquiries on the family and child and to conduct them in such a way:

> that allows for future constructive working relationships with families. The way in which a case is handled initially can affect the entire subsequent process. Where handled well and sensitively there can be a positive effect on the eventual outcome for the child.

THE INITIAL CHILD PROTECTION CONFERENCE

Where the agencies concerned judge that a child may continue to suffer or be likely to suffer harm, the local authority social care department should convene a child protection conference. Local procedures will determine the arrangements for the chairing of case conferences and the provision of support services, including the taking of minutes. The purpose of the case conference is to bring together the family and the professionals involved so that they can analyze the information that has been obtained, to make judgements about the likelihood of a child suffering significant harm in the future and, most important, to decide what further action is needed to safeguard the child and to form this into an outline child protection plan. The case conference will also make decisions about which workers are to form the 'core group' (WT § 5.72). These are the workers who will be 'responsible for developing the child protection plan as a detailed working tool and implementing it within the outline plan agreed at the initial child protection conference.'

If the conference decides that the child is in need of a child protection plan, the chair will decide which category of abuse that the child has suffered (or is likely to suffer).

THE CHILD PROTECTION PLAN

The aim of the child protection plan is to:

- ensure the child is safe from harm and prevent him or her from suffering further harm by supporting the strengths, addressing the vulnerabilities and risk factors and helping meet the child's unmet needs

- promote the child's health and development, i.e. his or her welfare; and

- provided it is in the best interests of the child, to support the family and wider family members to safeguard and promote the welfare of their child.

It should make clear 'who is to do what and by when' and provide a clear focus for the work of the core group (and others). It should therefore (WT § 5.123):

- describe the identified developmental needs of the child and what therapeutic services are required to meet these needs

- include specific, achievable, child-focussed outcomes intended to safeguard and promote the welfare of the child

- include realistic strategies and specific actions to bring about the changes necessary to achieve the planned outcomes

- set out when and in what situations the child will be seen by the lead social worker, both alone and with other family members or caregivers present

- clearly identify and set out roles and responsibilities of family members and professionals including those with routine contact with the child... and the nature and frequency of contact by these professionals with the child and family members

- include a contingency plan to be followed if circumstances change significantly and require prompt action (including initiating family court proceedings to safeguard and promote the child's welfare); and

- lay down points at which progress will be reviewed and the means by which progress will be judged.

THE CHILD PROTECTION REVIEW CONFERENCE

The first child protection review conference should be held within three months of the initial child protection conference and subsequent reviews should take place at no more than six-monthly intervals for as long as the child remains the subject of a child protection plan (WT § 5.136).

CONCLUSION

We would stress that the account of child protection processes and protocols that we have given in this Study Text is highly schematic. Matters do not necessarily proceed in the rather linear way that we have described, for example. Nor have we provided you with an account of those actions and formal orders that usually accompany the more urgent cases that come to the attention of children's services authorities. We are assuming that you are not at the stage in your career when you will have to take a lead role in child protection but, as we pointed out in Unit 6, you may find yourself engaged in a child protection investigation long before you think you are ready and it is essential that you are able to locate your place in the overall process.

Perhaps the most useful service we can provide to you at this stage in your professional development is to reinforce the point that you must ensure that you have access to the child protection procedures for the area in which you work, or are on placement, at the earliest possible stage of your induction period. Your agency has a professional obligation to provide such access. You have a professional responsibility to make full use of it.

COURSE TEXT: WHERE NEXT?

We are conscious that we have frequently told you how little we are telling you during the course of this Unit. We hope that we have explained the reasons for this as we have progressed. However, we know that you will want to further develop your capacity to practise long after this book has ended. There are a number of sources that you can use to develop your knowledge base. There are 'specialist' journals that report research findings (such as *Child Abuse and Neglect* and *Child Abuse Review*) and there is a growing number of research-informed text books on the subject (see suggestions for further reading at the end of this Unit.). There are other sources of information on improving your practice that are readily available too, including some policy documents (such as *Working Together*).

You should also consider reading any published report that arises from a child death or from a serious case review. A serious case review (SCR) is undertaken by a LSCB where it is considered that agencies can 'learn lessons to improve the way in which they work both individually and collectively to safeguard and promote the welfare of children' (WT § 8.1 – see WT Chapter 8 for a full discussion of the purpose and process of SCRs). Regular syntheses of SCRs have been published by the DCSF (see Brandon and others 2008, 2009; Rose and Barnes 2008) that try to distil the lessons for practice that emerge from such problematic cases. There are also the reports of public inquiries to consider (see Butler and Drakeford 2003). However, in relation to both SCRs and public inquiry reports, there are some cautions to observe. Even the authors of the synopses of SCRs are clear about the limitations of extrapolating from the kinds of cases reported. Brandon and others (2009, p.110) state that 'careful interpretation is needed since these reviews are not necessarily typical of safeguarding practice and it is important to avoid making predictions and claims'.

In the case of public inquiries, even more caution needs to be exercised. Public inquiries can easily become 'scandalized' and invested with all kinds of meanings and used for all kinds of moral and political purposes such that the original 'facts' of the case can become almost wholly obscured (see Butler and Drakeford 2011 for a detailed specific example). In such cases also, a considerable distortion can be added through being refracted through the lens of the mass media.

We are aware that in this Unit too, we have focussed very much on *what* to do and said very little about *how* to go about it. With some exceptions (e.g. the report into the death of 'Baby P', Haringey 2009), most policy documents, SCRs, public inquiry reports and much of the academic literature do not have a noticeable focus on skills. And yet, in terms of preparing yourself for practice in child protection, developing your skills is one of the surest ways of increasing your effectiveness. Disappointingly, the research on what are the necessary skills for effective work in child protection is somewhat lacking (see Keys 2009a and 2009b). However, it is possible to identify the broad headings under which you will need to monitor your progress. Keys has identified the following taxonomy of skills for which there is some research evidence of their relevance to effective practice in child protection:

- carer-focussed communication skills

- inter-professional communication skills

- managing conflict and change

- decision-making skills

- problem-solving skills

- procedural skills.

We do not have the space to discuss each of these in this Unit but, as far as communicating with children is concerned (in our view the fundamental skill) for example, the Children's Workforce Development Council (CWDC 2010) has produced a very concise account of the essentials of good practice that would easily transfer into a child protection setting. *The Common Core of Skills and Knowledge: At the Heart of What You Do* (which is a particularly good title it seems to us) describes how through 'listening and building empathy'; 'summarising and explaining'; 'consultation and negotiation' you can develop the kind of 'understanding, respectful and honest' (*ibid.* §1.4) relationship with children and families that is essential in any professional context. You should consider what you have learned about child observation in this context too (see Unit 7). You should also reflect on the skills required at each of the points that we have asked you to consider the circumstances of the Taylor family. And to make an honest assessment of your current degree of proficiency in them. That way, you can actively plan strategies to improve your skills further.

CONCLUSION

Recognition of abuse, even in apparently 'clear cut' situations, must be preceded by an *awareness* on your part of the potential for abuse. We emphatically do *not* mean by this that every child and family case in which you are involved must be considered as a potential case of child abuse. What we mean is that if you do not have a clear sense of what is meant by 'good enough parenting', the needs and rights of children and a clear sense of your personal, professional and agency thresholds, then you might not be able to recognize abuse even when confronted with an unambiguous instance of it. The same point must be made in your consideration of an appropriate response. Both remain questions of professional judgement. That judgement can be informed by specialist knowledge and improved by the use of lessons learned by research but it must be predicated on a thorough grounding in the essentials of good practice, including the development of the core skills of social work.

We do not want you to feel intimidated by work in child protection. In this Unit, you have already begun the process of making, testing and reflecting on your professional judgement in such cases, albeit only on paper. That judgement is rooted in your existing knowledge, skills and values. It is important to hold on to this thought, not just at the beginning of your career when it should give you confidence to extend your professional competence, but also later in your career when familiarity with abuse can arouse no more than a weary cynicism.

☀ NOTES AND SELF-ASSESSMENT

1. Do you want to work in child protection? Can you explain why/why not?

2. How prepared are you to work in child protection, in terms of knowledge and skills?

3. How prepared are you emotionally to work in this area?

4. What personal qualities could you bring to work in child protection?

5. Do you know what to do when you are confronted with an incident of possible abuse?

6. Where would you find the child protection procedures where you work or are on placement?

📚 RECOMMENDED READING

Munro, E. (2008) *Effective Child Protection* (Second Edition). London: Sage.

Wilson, K. and James, A. (eds) (2007) *The Child Protection Handbook* (Third Edition). London: Bailliere Tindall.

And, on neglect specifically:

Horwath, J. (2007) *Child Neglect: Identification and Assessment.* Basingstoke: Macmillan.

👥 TRAINER'S NOTES

Exercise 9.1: Safeguarding and Promoting

Tasks 1, 2 and 3 can be undertaken either in small groups or by 'quickthinking' in a larger group. Material generated can be organized according to the proto-assessment prepared as part of Exercise 7.3. It is important that Task 3 is not carried out with too much emphasis on what a local authority might do at this stage. The emphasis should be on John's needs. Ideas generated here can be reviewed in the light of participants' reading of Study Text 9.1 and compared to the range of options considered as part of Exercise 4.2.

Exercise 9.2: Signs of Neglect

This exercise is best conducted in pairs, with a plenary session to compare notes. Participants should be encouraged to let their imaginations operate freely at Task 2. The plausibility of each explanation can be tested in debate between its proponent(s) and the rest of the group. This usually demonstrates where individuals feature on the pessimistic/optimistic continuum. The kind of information (i.e. doctor's assessments, teacher's observations, etc.) that may be suggested as part of Task 3 must include reference to the participant's own 'observations', notes, records and professional knowledge, etc. as there is sometimes a tendency for workers in child protection to look for 'proof' outside of their own knowledge and expertise.

Court Craft

OBJECTIVES

In this Unit you will:

- Rehearse the process for obtaining a care order.
- Learn how to prepare a witness statement.
- Explore some fundamentals of court craft.

COURSE TEXT: GOING TO COURT

Despite international conventions, protocols and treaties in such areas as children's rights, adoption and trafficking, family law remains substantially defined by national boundaries. Court structures and the administration of family justice are also a function of specific jurisdictions. This makes it much harder to generalize about the legal and judicial frameworks that govern social work practice with children and families. This is not to say that useful international comparisons cannot be made but these are beyond the scope of this book.

Even within a specific jurisdiction however, the law, rather than being a fixed and certain body of knowledge and professional practices, is constantly changing as the socio-political context in which it is embedded also changes. New law is made and existing law evolves, not only by way of formal amendments through successive Acts of parliament and/or through the introduction of regulations but also in response to judicial decisions as they set precedent and establish 'case law'. Administrative systems and court structures also respond to legislative, socio-economic and political changes.

Notwithstanding this general point, the statutory framework provided by the 1989 Children Act has provided a remarkably stable context for social work practice with children and families in England and Wales. Despite the alterations that have been made to it, the Act has largely 'stood the test of time' (see

Doughty 2010 for a concise account of the amendments made to the Act and the forces that have impelled them). Even the several volumes of guidance and regulations that accompanied the introduction of the Act have remained largely unaltered. However, the administrative arrangements for applying for a care or supervision order under s. 31 of the Act is an area that has changed substantially since the Act was introduced and may well alter again as the family justice system becomes the focus of even greater political interest. It does seem likely that there will be further, far reaching changes to the family justice system in England and Wales (see Masson 2010a) in the short to medium term and, possibly, even to some of the core principles on which child and family law is currently based; especially as this relates to so-called 'alternative forms of dispute resolution' whereby more and more 'family matters' are dealt with outside of the formal court setting. This means that you may need to be more alert to developments in family law than many of your predecessors have needed to be over recent years.

Whatever developments take place, the purpose of going to court will still be to obtain, vary or discharge an order in respect of a child. For many social workers, even the most experienced, going to court can seem a daunting prospect. We may feel uncertain at finding ourselves on unfamiliar territory where people around us dress differently, use a strange vocabulary and engage in rituals that we do not fully understand. Our apprehension may be increased by our awareness that a great deal depends on the outcome of the court hearing, not least for us as individuals and as professionals. We may feel that our own reputation and self-esteem might be threatened if we do not play our part fully.

Families, too, can find the experience of going to court intimidating, as Douglas and others have reported (2006, p.148) in relation to their study of cases where the children were represented in court separately from their parents:

> I would have preferred it not to have been in court as such, just a place that wasn't court because just that word sounds terrible. It scared me really even though I'd done nothing wrong. [Vicky, Resident Aunt]

Other research (see, for example, Brophy 2006; Brophy and others 1999; Freeman and Hunt 1998) has also demonstrated how parents can find themselves psychologically ill-prepared, anxious about having to speak in public and also having to face a great many practical problems in simply attending the hearing. Children too may be anxious, having developed wholly inaccurate impressions of what 'going to court' involves; often basing their expectations on what they have seen on television, especially soap operas and American (criminal) court dramas. In relation to divorce proceedings, for example, the following anxieties would not appear to be unusual (Butler and others 2003, p.175):

I don't want my mum to be, or my dad to be guilty. But one of them has
to be guilty, but I don't want none of them to be guilty. I felt scared, 'cos I
thought we had to go with him and stand up in one of those boxes, if we
were older, and say who we wanted to live with and who we wanted to put
down as guilty or something. Now I'd say I don't want anyone to be guilty.
(Lucy, aged 8)

Those children who did not receive adequate support, according to Douglas
and others (2006, p.10) 'appeared "lost", withdrawn, depressed and sometimes
angered and intimidated, by their contact with the family justice system'.

Some of these deficiencies could be addressed by better information being
made available to parents and children at an early stage in the conduct of
proceedings and by a more inclusive approach being adopted by social workers.
However, our primary focus in what follows is on the social worker's role in the
court process but we do not under-estimate the importance and the impact of
the court experience on families and children and we want you to bear them in
mind as you work through this Unit.

As for the social worker, a degree of apprehension, which appropriately reflects
the seriousness of the occasion, is certainly preferable to a sense of complacency.
If that apprehension provokes us to prepare assiduously and reflect seriously on
the case before the court then it will have served a very useful purpose, for there
can be no doubt that the courtroom can be a rigorous test of what we do and
believe as social workers. We would probably agree that if our work could not
bear close scrutiny then its deficiencies should be exposed. On the other hand,
if it can withstand a thorough examination then we can proceed strengthened
by the knowledge that our work has demonstrable rigour and coherence.

Just how early in your professional career or how frequently you will find
yourself in court is very much more dependent on *where* you work than you
might imagine. The total number of looked after children (in England) as at
March 2009 was approaching 61,000, slightly up on the previous year but
relatively unchanged since 2005; i.e. approximately 0.5 per cent of all children.
The proportion of children looked after (expressed as a rate per 10,000 young
people aged under 18) has also changed very little over recent years; being 55
per 10,000 in 2005 and in 2009. However, regional rates in England differ
markedly; ranging from 42 per 10,000 in the East Midlands to 71 per 10,000
in the North West. Even more striking variations can be seen within regions; in
the North West, the differential ranges from 146 (Manchester) to 45 (Cumbria)
and in London from 159 (City of London) to 45 per 10,000 (Richmond upon
Thames) (DCSF/ONS 2009).

Geography itself is not the issue, of course, even taking into account broad economic and social differences between areas. The rate of applications to the court is in no small measure a function of 'differences in the responses of... individual social services departments in meeting the needs of the children in their area' (Department of Health 2003, § 1.13). The national context can however have a significant impact on the nature of local decision making. For example, there is some evidence of a distinctive 'Baby P' effect on the change in the rate of applications for care orders since the 'scandal' surrounding his death. Data from the Children and Family Court Advisory Service indicate a 34 per cent increase (2188 cases) in the commencement of care cases between 2009 and 2010 (CAFCASS 2010). This exceptional increase in demand, not yet fully exhausted nor fully understood (but see Hall and Guy 2009), produces its own effects and it could be that current levels of care cases are a function not so much of demand but of the capacity of the family court system to process that demand.

The degree to which the state is prepared and permitted to intervene in private and domestic life also alters over time as arrangements for the governance of the family reflect broader socio-political trends (see, for example, Munro and Ward 2008, for an interesting discussion on balancing parents' and young children's rights in the context of the Human Rights Act 1998 and Welbourne 2008, for an account of how the financial cost may also be a powerful agent of change in the family justice system and for a broader consideration of some of the more recent procedural innovations described in Study Text 10.1).

Our point is that there is no simple relationship between the number of children who are suffering or who are likely to suffer harm at any given point and the number of applications made to the court for care (or supervision) orders. As Narey (2007, p.11) has suggested, such variations as exist over time and at local, regional and national level are just as likely to mean 'children who should be in care are being left at home in potentially dangerous situations for far too long, as... that many children made the subject of care orders should have been left at home with more intensive support programmes'.

What this implies is that the kinds of decisions you make about whether or when to go to court may be as important as the actual circumstances of children and families in determining the use made of compulsory powers (see Brophy 2006 and Masson and others 2008 for an account of the characteristics of families who are the subject of care proceedings).

This Unit aims to provide you with a practical appreciation of the process of going to court. Our specific interest in this Unit is in orders under s. 31 of the 1989 Children Act and, in particular, the care order. But, before we look in detail at what is involved in applying for an order, we should catch up with events in the Taylor family.

TAYLOR FAMILY CASE FILE

Following the incident in the first week of July, Tracy attended a meeting with you, your managers and your legal advisors. Tracy was told that the local authority had begun to form the view that John needed the additional protection that a care order would bring but that you would be willing to work with Tracy to avoid court proceedings.

Tracy responded very positively and said that she and her mother would do everything they could to look after John. The trouble, according to Tracy, was that Alun kept turning up at Mrs Taylor Senior's house asking for money or somewhere to stay. He had no place of his own and he was in debt; Tracy assumed that he was involved in drugs but she didn't know what.

You agreed a programme of supervised attendance at the local family centre for Tracy and John; a series of medical examinations and weekly visits by you. The first week of the plan went well. However, on 3 August, you called at Mrs Taylor Senior's house for your next planned visit, only to be told that Tracy had moved back in with Alun who now had a house not far away although Mrs Taylor did not know exactly where. Mrs Taylor told you that she and Tracy had had a major row over her various choices of partner. You were not able to locate Alun's address nor visit Tracy in New Estate that day.

At lunchtime on 4 August, you received a telephone call from a very distraught Mrs Taylor (senior). She told you that Tracy has been to see her, with John, and that John had a very big bruise over his eye. Tracy had told her that Alun had hit John and Tracy. Mrs. Taylor had told Tracy that 'she had made her bed and so must lie in it' and to go home to Alun. She now very much regrets having said this and wants you to go and 'make sure that Tracy is all right'. She gives you the address of Alun's house.

You arrived at Alun's house at around 2.00 p.m. Upon arrival you found John playing in the front garden. He was digging a hole in the ground with a tin can. There was no gate on the garden which fronts on to the busy main road. John was only wearing a T-shirt and nappy despite the fact that it was drizzling and far from warm. There was no immediate sign of Tracy or Alun. As you picked John up you could feel how cold he was. You could also see what appeared to be bruises. There was a dark bruise over John's left eye and his right ear was red and swollen. There were also some yellow/brown marks on his neck. There were three on the left side of his neck and one on the right side. The one on the right side was bigger than the others, about the size of a 50p piece. There was a similar pattern of marks on John's left leg, above the knee. The larger mark was on the inside of his thigh. You took John into the house, the front door was open, and wrapped him in a towel that was lying in the hall at the foot of the stairs. You called out but received no answer.

On entering the front room, you found Alun. He did not respond to your call and appeared to be asleep. On the floor were several cans of Special Brew, apparently empty. Alun eventually woke when you touched his arm. He smelled strongly of drink and appeared disorientated. He seemed not to recognize you. His speech was slurred and he had difficulty in rising to his feet. He eventually told you, in reply to your questioning, that Tracy was upstairs. She also appeared to be asleep. She had a black eye and a scratch on her right cheek. You could not rouse her.

Keeping John with you, you went into the garden and called an ambulance and the police on your mobile. Upon returning to the house, you found that Alun had gone back to sleep. The ambulance arrived before the police. Alun woke and started to shout at you and the ambulance crew. John was clearly very distressed and began to cry. This seemed to make Alun even more aggressive and you were relieved when the police arrived. Alun was blocking the doorway as they approached the house, preventing your exit and that of the ambulance crew who were trying to bring Tracy down the stairs. John was very distressed by this stage and Alun tried to take him out of your arms. A policeman tried to hold on to Alun's arm but Alun hit out at him. Alun was arrested.

The police exercised their powers under the Children Act 1989 (Section 46) and escorted you to Southtown General Hospital with John. You were joined at the hospital by a colleague who stayed with John while you went to secure an emergency protection order (EPO), which you successfully did by application to a single magistrate at around 4.00 p.m.

John was admitted to the paediatric ward at Southtown General that same afternoon, shortly after your return. Upon examination, he was found, in the opinion of the paediatrician, to be severely underweight and developmentally delayed. You were told that the marks that you saw were bruises at different stages of healing and that they were consistent with a sharp blow to the side of the head and to being gripped very tightly around the back of the neck and on the leg. The paediatrician also told you that there were other marks on John's back, consistent with being hit with a strap. He told you that, in his opinion, all of the injuries were consistent with non-accidental injury and that the police should be informed. In the view of the paediatrician, John will need nursing care for at least four to six weeks on an in-patient basis as he has so much weight to gain. John has quietened down and is asleep by the time that you leave the hospital at around 7.00 p.m.

It transpires that Tracy had taken an overdose of painkillers and was admitted overnight to the same hospital as John. Alun was detained overnight in police cells but was bailed the next morning. He was re-arrested after his appearance in court and was charged with the assault on John. He appeared in court for the second time later in the day and was remanded on bail for a week, despite police objections.

On the next day (5 August) you visited Tracy in hospital. She appeared horrified to hear of the bruises to John and denied all knowledge of them. Tracy says that she intends to return to Alun as soon as she can and will take John with her. She says that she does not want to see you again and that she does not need or want any help from you or your agency. Tracy seems to believe that Alun was attacked by the police and even suggests that the bruises to John may have been caused in the scuffle at the house. The ward manager told you that Tracy is very depressed and that she ought to stay in hospital for a few days. Tracy however discharged herself later that day. John remained in hospital under the terms of the EPO. Tracy visited her mother to tell her, according to a later conversation you had with Mrs. Taylor (senior) that she no longer wanted anything to do with her mother whom she blamed for 'causing all this trouble'. Tracy returned to Alun's house.

It is decided to proceed to make application for a Care Order in respect of John.

i STUDY TEXT 10.1: THE CARE ORDER

The remainder of this Unit will focus on the application for a care order in respect of John.[8] We have chosen to do this not necessarily because we consider this the typical or inevitable outcome of such cases, nor because we believe that a care order has a particular significance above that of other orders, but principally so that we can explore in greater depth what is involved in securing one particular order rather than take a wider, but necessarily more superficial, view of the range of possible outcomes in this case.

PRIOR TO MAKING AN APPLICATION

The social work processes and procedures that are to take place before and during proceedings under s. 31 of the CA 1989 are set out in statutory guidance (SG).

---

8   As provided for in England and Wales in August 2010.

This guidance is contained in *The Children Act 1989, Guidance and Regulations: Volume 1 Court Orders* (DCSF 2008). The process for making and managing a specific application for an order under s. 31 is set out in the *Practice Direction Guide to Case Management in Public Law Proceedings* (MOJ, March 2010; effective from 6 April 2010), commonly known as the 'public law outline' (PLO). You should also be aware of the Ministry of Justice' best practice guide (BPG), *Preparing for Care and Supervision Proceedings* (MOJ/DCSF 2009). This offers a commentary on how both sets of guidance should be applied in practice and contains several useful templates for correspondence and outline agendas for key meetings.

The SG repeats the principles on which the Children Act 1989 is based and which reflect the Act's broad purpose; to strike a 'balance between the rights of children, the responsibilities of both parents to the child and the duty of the state to intervene when the child's welfare requires it' (SG, § 1.4). It emphasizes the duty under s. 17 of the Children Act 1989 and makes clear that the Act is 'based on the belief that children are generally best looked after within the family, with the parents playing a full part in their lives and with least recourse to legal proceedings'. The SG makes specific reference to several leading cases to make the point that 'Interference in family life may only be justified by the overriding necessity of the interests of the child' (SG, § 38 footnote).

Consequently, the SG makes clear that any application to a court ('provided that this does not jeopardise the child's safety and welfare', SG, § 3.7) should be preceded not only by a thorough assessment of the child's circumstances and his or her needs but also by a comprehensive exploration of possible alternative arrangements that might be made for the care of the child, including the wider family and community. The SG suggests the use of family group conferences as an 'important opportunity to engage friends and members of the wider family at an early stage of concerns about a child' and makes it clear that the 'local authority will be required to demonstrate that it has considered family members and friends as potential carers at each stage of its decision making' (SG, §3.8).

That decision making should be based on a full and detailed assessment of the child, ideally an 'initial assessment' and a subsequent 'core assessment', as defined by the *Framework for the Assessment of Children in Need and their Families* (DH and others 2000 – see Unit 7). The SG states that 'compliance with the requirement to complete the core assessment will be scrutinised by the responsible court as part of the court's first consideration of any application under s. 31' (SG, § 3.15). The SG also makes clear that the core assessment 'forms the central part of the evidence supporting any application' for an order under s. 31 and that the findings of the assessment (and any initial assessment)

should form the basis for the local authority's plans for the child(ren) (SG, §
3.17 and 3.18).

Where, following a thorough assessment and a consideration of possible
alternative arrangements for the care of the child, the local authority intends to
pursue its application for an order under s. 31, the decision to proceed should
be fully reviewed at a 'legal planning/legal gateway meeting' held between the
social worker(s) responsible and the local authority's legal advisers. This must be
followed, if the decision to proceed remains in place, by appropriate notification
to parents[9] (and relevant others) and a 'letter before proceedings' (LbP) issued.
This is an important document that will be filed with the court and which triggers
entitlement to 'Family Help' (publically funded legal advice and assistance) for
parents. Both the BPG and the SG stress the need to ensure that the contents
of the letter (and its implications) are fully and effectively communicated to
parents. How far the PLO and the BPG are being realized in practice remains at
issue of course while courts and children's services departments continue to face
unprecedented levels of demand.

Where the circumstances permit, the LbP should include an invitation to a
'Pre-Proceedings Meeting' (PPM). Both the LbP and the PPM are intended,
not only to inform the parents of the intentions of the local authority, but also
to provide a further opportunity to engage with the family so that proceedings
might be avoided and alternative, voluntary arrangements put in place. The
PPM is, according to the BPG, 'a social work led meeting' (BPG, § 2.5.2) and
should not be 'adversarial' in nature. While legal representatives may be present,
the PPM is not intended as a multi-disciplinary meeting and, according to the
BPG (§ 2.5.3) it would not be appropriate for other agencies to attend. Should
it still not prove possible to put in place a plan that will avoid proceedings,
the PPM should at least try to narrow down the focus of the local authority's
continuing concerns.

EMERGENCY ORDERS

Sometimes, as in the Taylor case, the application for a care order will be
preceded by court intervention to provide short term protection via an
emergency protection order (EPO) under s. 44 of The Children Act 1989. As
in the Taylor case, it is possible for an order to be made by a single justice,
however in most cases the application will be made to the family proceedings
court and the parents will be present at the hearing. The practice of applying

---

9   The term 'parents' is used here and throughout this Study Text to include all of those with
    parental responsibility for the child, as defined by Part 1 of the 1989 CA.

for EPOs without giving notice to the parents (sometimes referred to as *ex parte* applications) is permissible where to give notice would place the child at risk. Recent caselaw however has considered the impact of the Human Rights Act 1998 on emergency protection orders and warns against making applications without notice (*ex parte*) other than in 'wholly exceptional cases'. In X Council v B (Emergency Protection Orders) [2004] EWHC 2015 (Fam) Munby J Described the EPO as 'a "draconian" and "extremely harsh" measure, requiring 'exceptional justification' and 'extraordinarily compelling reasons'. He also noted that, 'an order should not be made unless the court is satisfied that it is both necessary and proportionate and that no other less radical form of order will achieve the essential end of promoting the welfare of the child'. The judgement contains key guidance on when it is appropriate to apply for an EPO with particular emphasis on the need for proportionate responses in child protection.

In the artificial circumstances of the Taylor case we are not able to judge entirely satisfactorily that the decision to apply for a care order is the only or best alternative. For the purposes of the remainder of this Unit, we will ask you to assume that it is, although you will have an opportunity to reflect further on this in Exercise 10.1.

But what precisely is a care order? The remainder of this Study Text offers an abbreviated account.

EFFECT AND DURATION

When a care order is made with respect to a child it becomes the duty of the local authority named in the order to receive that child into its care (s. 33 (1))[10] and to accommodate him and maintain him during the currency of the order and to safeguard and promote his welfare (s. 22 (3)) (See Study Text 5.2). The local authority will assume parental responsibility for the child and acquire the power to determine how far others shall be allowed to exercise their parental responsibility in respect of the child (see s. 33 (4) and (6) for further details on the limitations that apply to the local authority's exercise of parental responsibility). Any residence order in force before the care order is extinguished (see s. 91 for a full account of the effect of a care order on other orders). Proceedings for a care order cannot be brought before the birth of a child or after the age of 17 (16 if married) and no care order can last beyond the child's 18th birthday (s. 31 (3)).

---

10 All references to legislation in the remainder in this Study Text are to the CA 1989, unless otherwise stated.

THE COURT'S DECISION

The decision of the court to make a care order or not is taken in two stages: first, the court must decide whether the statutory 'threshold' criteria have been satisfied and, second, that the principles contained in Part I of the Act have been applied. The 'threshold' criteria relate to whether the child has suffered, or is likely to suffer, 'significant harm' (see below). The relevant Part I principles are that the child's welfare must be the court's paramount consideration (s. 1 (1)), understood in the light of the 'welfare check-list' (s. 1 (3)). This 'check-list' requires the court to consider, for example, the wishes and feelings of the child and the child's physical, emotional and educational needs, and to have regard to the range of powers at its disposal. The court must also determine that making an order will be 'better for the child than making no order at all' (s. 1 (5)). It is not possible for the court to make a care order until it has considered the local authority care plan (s. 31A).

THE THRESHOLD CRITERIA

Section 31 (2) of the Act establishes that:

A court may only make a care order or supervision order if it is satisfied

(a) that the child concerned is suffering, or is likely to suffer, significant harm; and

(b) that the harm, or likelihood of harm is attributable to –

(i) the care given to the child, or likely to be given to him if the order were not made, not being what it would be reasonable to expect a parent to give to him; or

(ii) the child's being beyond parental control.

By 'is suffering' it means at the point of the hearing or the point at which the local authority initiated the procedure to protect the child, provided that whatever arrangements were put in place then have remained in place (Re M [1994] 3 WLR 558). In this way, the fact that the child has been removed from immediate danger does not mean that a finding of significant harm cannot be made. In the case of John Taylor, assuming that the EPO is still in force and/or an interim care order was made, the time at issue would include the day of your visit to his home.

'Harm' is defined (s. 31 (9) CA 1989, as amended by s. 120 of the Adoption and Children Act 2002) as meaning 'ill-treatment or the impairment of health or development' including, for example, impairment suffered from seeing or hearing the ill-treatment of another: development means 'physical, intellectual, emotional, social or behavioural development': health means 'physical or mental health' and ill-treatment includes 'sexual abuse and forms of abuse which are not physical'. You should note that ill-treatment without consequent impairment might still constitute harm.

The harm caused to the child must be attributable to the care given to the child or to its being beyond parental control. The test of what would 'be reasonable to expect a parent to give him' is an objective one and does not depend on the motives or capacity of the carer. A parent may be trying very hard but still not be able to provide an adequate standard of care to meet the needs of the particular child.

In some cases, it is not possible to directly attribute the harm caused. For example, in *Lancashire County Council* v *B* [2000] 1 FLR 583 a seven-month-old baby had suffered at least two episodes of shaking but it was not clear whether this was at the hands of the mother, father or childminder. The House of Lords ruled that it was sufficient for the court to be satisfied that the harm was caused by one of the child's primary carers. Where a child suffers harm, as well as care proceedings, action may of course be taken to prosecute the perpetrator and it will usually be necessary in such circumstances to exactly identify the perpetrator. However the Domestic Violence Crime and Victims Act 2004 introduced the new offence of 'causing or allowing the death of a child' whereby it may be possible to prosecute more than one person where the exact perpetrator cannot be identified. This in fact was the offence under which the parents of Peter Connelly (see Unit 6) were convicted (see Drakeford and Butler 2009).

A series of cases have established a positive duty on local authorities to take action where there are child protection concerns. These cases have arisen from claims of negligence by local authorities and breach of Article 3 of the Human Rights Act (HRA) 1998 for failure to protect children. Article 3 states that, 'no-one shall be subjected to torture or to inhuman or degrading treatment or punishment'. In *E* v *United Kingdom* (2002) *The Times*, 4 December, ECHR, the court followed the line established by *X* v *Bedfordshire* [1995] AC 633. The local authority had failed in its duty to protect E and her brothers and sisters and to monitor the behaviour of a known offender who lived with the children and their mother. In the view of the court, damage caused to the children by the offender could have been minimized or avoided had the authority acted properly. As a result of the breach, the children were entitled to an award in damages.

The Act does not offer a gloss on 'significant'. However, in *Humberside CC v B (1993) 1 FLR 257*, the High Court has accepted the dictionary definition of 'considerable, noteworthy or important'. Note that it is the harm that has to be significant, not whatever act caused it. Hence, a sustained series of privations, not individually harmful, as in the case of neglect, could amount to significant harm as far as the child's development was concerned. Not all harm will be significant nor will significant harm in one context necessarily be significant in another. Ultimately, it is a matter for the court to determine whether the harm is significant for the particular child in question. In those circumstances where the harm is said to be to the child's health or development, the court must compare it with what could be reasonably expected of a similar child (s. 31 (10)). A 'similar child' is one with the same attributes, needs and potential of the child in question, taking into account, for example, any particular learning or physical disability.

You should note that in the case of *MA v Swansea (2009) EWCA Civ 853* some doubt has been cast on previous understanding of what is implied by the term 'significant', especially where past harm to one child may be held as indicative of harm to another. This was a particularly complex and unusual case and it is not clear how far the judgement will be held to be 'fact specific'. For this reason, we will not elaborate on it here (but see Masson 2010b for full account of the case and its possible implications and also Harwin and Madge 2010 for a wider discussion of the interpretation of 'significant harm' in case law). We note it simply as an example of how the law is constantly developing and as a reminder of the importance of you being in receipt of expert legal advice throughout the process of decision making in care proceedings.

Working Together (2010, § 1.28 – see Unit 9) recognizes that 'there are no absolute criteria on which to rely when judging what constitutes significant harm'. As Harwin and Madge (2010, p.80) concluded in their review of the 'concept of significant harm in law and practice':

> The complexity of significant harm, and its lack of a clear operational definition, provides the opportunity for subjective decision making. The strength of the concept of significant harm is at once its weakness.

Such a view is reinforced by research that suggests that certain forms of harm (and therefore certain types of cases) are more likely than others to lead to formal care proceedings. For example, Harwin and others (2009) detected the differential effect on the speed with which proceedings were instigated when alcohol abuse alone was a key issue as opposed to when alcohol abuse was associated with the use of illegal drugs (see also Forrester and Harwin 2008) although it should be noted that Masson and others (2008) in their study of 386 s. 31 cases found that there was no evidence to suggest that local authorities brought care proceedings without good reason. The fact remains however, that the determination of significant harm remains an interpretive process, as the Act permits, and one in which your professional judgement is key.

PROCESS

The *Practice Direction Guide to Case Management in Public Law Proceedings* (MOJ 2010, commonly known as the Public Law Outline and abbreviated here to 'PLO') sets out the arrangements for making an application for an order under s. 31 of the 1989 CA. It is a staged process but one that is intended to be flexible in order to meet the specifics of each case (PLO, § 18.1). What follows is necessarily an abbreviated and schematic account.

Proceedings formally commence once an application is lodged with the court. The application is made on a prescribed form (C110). The application should be accompanied by:

- a social work chronology
- an initial social work statement
- initial and core assessments
- copies of any letters before proceedings (LbP)
- a schedule of proposed findings
- a care plan.

Where these documents cannot be supplied at the time that the application is made, reasons must be given (on the C110 form) and the date on which they will be made available to the court specified. The PLO also specifies other documents that will need to be provided to the court in due course, including 'other relevant reports and records; records of discussions with the family, key local authority minutes and records for the child'. What is included will vary case to case and will be the subject of discussion between you and your legal advisors and, possibly the direction of the court.

Care and supervision proceedings are 'family proceedings' (see s. 8(3) 1989 CA) and may be heard at any level of the family courts although most cases will begin in the family proceedings court, a magistrates court.

Upon receipt of the application, the case will be managed according to the requirements of the PLO, the overriding objective of which is to enable 'the court to deal with cases justly' (PLO, § 2.1). This means ensuring that the case is dealt with 'expeditiously and fairly'; in such a way as is 'proportionate to the nature, importance and complexity of the issues'; ensuring that the parties 'are on an equal footing' and 'saving expense' while apportioning the resources of the court taking into account the 'need to allot resources to other cases' (PLO, § 2.1). Central to achieving this overriding objective is the 'timetable for the child'. In order to fulfil its duties under s. 1 of the Act (to have the welfare of the child as its 'paramount consideration') and under s. 32 (to avoid delay in dealing with cases), the court will establish and actively manage a timetable for proceedings that takes into account 'dates of the significant steps in the life of the child' and which is 'appropriate for [the] child' (PLO, § 3.2). This is in order to 'ensure that the court remains child-focussed throughout' (PLO, § 3.5).

The first formal stage in proceedings is the 'First Appointment'. This should take place by the sixth day after proceedings have been commenced. The First Appointment confirms the allocation of the case to the relevant court and gives initial case management directions covering such matters as the service of documents, what other documents are to be filed with the court and initial witness statements. Directions may also be given relating to the 'identification of family and friends as proposed carers' (PLO, § 13.3 (d)).

The second formal stage is the 'Case Management Conference' (CMC), which should take place no later than 45 days after the application was lodged with the court. As the name suggests, the purpose of the CMC is to identify the key issues in the case and to give full case management directions. Crucially for the social worker, the CMC will also 'scrutinise the care plan' for the child (PLO, § 15.3 (3)). Subsequently, the court will issue a Case Management Order that will give effect to the decisions of the CMC and that will confirm the timetable for the next stages in the process.

The case may proceed at this point to an 'Early Final Hearing' or move onto an 'Issues Resolution Hearing' which is intended to 'resolve and narrow issues' outstanding and/or to 'identify key remaining issues requiring resolution' (PLO, § 16.1). The final stage for such cases would be the 'Final Hearing' where the case is decided.

The PLO is clear that 'throughout proceedings the parties and their representatives should co-operate wherever reasonably practicable to help towards securing the welfare of the child as the paramount consideration' (PLO, § 20.1).

INTERIM CARE ORDERS

Interim orders may be made during the course of proceedings if the court is satisfied that there are 'reasonable grounds for believing' (s. 38 (2)) that the circumstances of the child would fulfil the criteria for the making of a 'full' care order (i.e. that the child is suffering or likely to suffer significant harm, etc.). The effect of an interim order is substantially the same as if the 'full' order were made except that an interim order is time limited (the duration being set by the court) and that an interim order may contain directions to the local authority as to what specialist or additional assessments are to be carried out.

An interim order (and an EPO) may also include an 'exclusion requirement' (s. 38A(1), inserted by the Family Law Act 1996). The requirement may require a particular person to leave the child's home, forbid them from entering it or exclude them from a defined area around the child's home. The order is designed to allow the child to remain in the home, so long as another person living in the house is willing and able to care for the child and agrees to the exclusion requirement.

THE ROLE OF CAFCASS

In care proceedings, the child is automatically a party and is represented by a children's guardian appointed by the Children and Family Court Advisory and Support Service (CAFCASS) usually at or even before the First Appointment stage. CAFCASS (in England) is an 'arms length public body', sponsored by the Department of Education and CAFCASS Cymru (in Wales) is part of the Welsh Assembly Government. CAFCASS has other duties besides those related to proceedings under s. 31 of the 1989 CA, including in respect of certain private law proceedings, such as divorce. Further details of the wider role and organization of CAFCASS can be obtained via their website, which incidentally provides one of the most useful, user-friendly and most easily understood sources of information to parents, children and teenagers that we know of!

The SG (§ 1.29) sets out the functions of CAFCASS as being to:

- safeguard and promote the welfare of the children
- give advice to any court about any application made to it in such proceedings
- make provision for the children to be represented in such proceedings; and
- provide information, advice and other support for the children and their families.

In effect, this means, in care proceedings, that the children's guardian will appoint a solicitor for the child (unless the child is of sufficient age and understanding to appoint their own or the court so directs). Hence the child's interests will normally be represented by two professionals (the guardian and the solicitor) and for this reason, this arrangement is sometimes referred to as the 'tandem system'. The guardian will offer independent advice to the court during the course of proceedings on case management (including in respect of the timetable for the child) as well as providing written reports to the court making recommendations about how the case should be decided. The PLO defines the 'case analysis and recommendations' required of the children's guardian (PLO, § 26(10)) as one prepared 'from the child's perspective' and covering such issues as the child's own views, the work of the local authority and its proposed care plan as well as 'recommendations for outcomes, in order to safeguard and promote the best interests of the child in the proceedings' (PLO, § 26(10) (b)). In order to fulfil this expectation, children's guardians have access to the records of the local authority, may consult with others and will liaise with family members.

The question has been raised (see James, James and Macnamee 2004) as to how far the professional opinions and perspectives of the guardian either further or frustrate the expression of the child's own views to the court and the comparison has been drawn (Williams 2008, p.175) to the circumstances in which a child's medical care is an issue before the court. In these circumstances, the child would expect to be asked for his or her views directly, as per the 'Gillick' principles (*Gillick v West Norfolk and Wisbech Area Health Authority and the DHSS [1986]*).

POWERS OF THE COURT

Upon hearing an application for a care order, the court has access to the full range of orders available under the Act. Accordingly, the court may make any of the following orders in addition to a care order:

- parental responsibility order (if applied for)
- appointment (termination) of guardianship order
- care contact order (s. 34).

The court may also, on refusing a care order, make a supervision order or any of the orders listed above or any s. 8 order, with or without an application having been made. The influence of the HRA 1998 means that the order which the court ultimately makes must be proportionate in all the circumstances, adopting a preference for the least interventionist stance. In *Re O (Supervision Order; Future Harm)* [2001] 1 FCR 289, the court held that, in the circumstances, a supervision order was more appropriate than a care order in the light of Article 8 of the HRA 1998, the right to respect for private and family life.

OTHER CONSIDERATIONS

The plans that the local authority intends to make for the child in order to meet his or her needs will be subject to scrutiny by the court (and the children's guardian) throughout proceedings. You will recall that a copy of the care plan, based on a 'core assessment' wherever possible, is to be attached to the C110 form at the commencement of proceedings or very shortly thereafter. At the end of proceedings, the children's guardian will ensure that the care plan, as agreed by the court, is made available to an Independent Reviewing Officer (IRO). The appointment of an IRO is a statutory requirement under s. 118 of the Adoption and Children Act 2002. The duties of the IRO are set out in the *IRO Handbook* (DCSF 2010c; § 2.9 and 2.10) as being to:

- monitor the performance by the local authority of their functions in relation to the child's case

- participate in any review of the child's case

- ensure that any ascertained wishes and feelings of the child concerning the case are given due consideration by the appropriate authority; and perform any other function which is prescribed in regulations.

In essence, the primary task of the IRO is to ensure that the care plan for the child continues to fully reflect the child's current needs and that the actions set out in the plan are consistent with the local authority's legal responsibilities towards the child.

The CA 1989 makes a presumption in favour of 'reasonable contact' (s. 34 (1) CA 1989) between the child and his/her parents and others who are important in their lives, including brothers and sisters. Consequently, the court is obliged (s. 34 (11)) to consider the arrangements for contact with parents that are proposed by the local authority before it makes an order. Wherever possible, arrangements for contact should be agreed between all of the parties prior to the Final Hearing with the court having a role only where no agreement can be reached.

THE DECISION OF THE COURT

The court will reach its conclusions on matters of fact 'on the balance of probabilities', which means, in Lord Denning's famous dictum (*Miller* v *Ministry of Pensions* [1947] 2 All ER 372), that the court must be satisfied that it is 'more likely than not' that the particular events took place.

Some doubt had arisen since the passing of the 1989 Act as to whether the standard of proof required rose in proportion to the seriousness of the allegations of harm made in care proceedings. *Re B (Children) (FC) UKHL 35* would appear to have resolved any such doubts: 'the time has come to say, once and for all, that there is only one standard of proof and that is proof that the fact in issue more probably occurred than not'. (See also *Re S-B (Children) [2009] UKSC 17.*)

The burden of proof is on the local authority to satisfy the court that the s. 31 threshold criteria have been met. It is not for a parent to exculpate him- or herself (*Re O 7 N [2002] EWCA Civ 1271*). The court must record the reasons for its decision and any findings of fact. This is essential where there is any prospect of an appeal.

You may find the arrangement of material in this Study Text a useful template for your study of other orders under the Children Act 1989.

✎ EXERCISE 10.1: ESTABLISHING THE GROUNDS

This exercise is designed to give you an opportunity to familiarize yourself with the grounds on which a care order is made.

TASKS

1. Examine recent entries in the Taylor Case File and determine whether a reasonable case can be made for the making of a care order in respect of John. You should structure your response as follows:

   - Is he suffering harm?

   - Is he likely to suffer harm?

   - What is the precise nature of the harm he is, or is likely to, suffer?

   - Is it ill-treatment?
     - physical
     - sexual
     - mental

   - Is it impairment of health?
     - physical
     - mental

- Is it impairment of development?
  - physical
  - emotional
  - behavioural
  - intellectual
  - social

- Is it impairment suffered from seeing or hearing the ill-treatment of another?

- Is that harm significant?

- Is it attributable to the standard of care given to him?

- Is it attributable to the standard of care likely to be given to him?

- Is it attributable to his being beyond parental control?

2. Consider whether the use of compulsory powers is justified in this case. In particular, you might consider:

- How can John's immediate and medium-term needs best be met, such that his welfare is properly safeguarded and protected?

- What potential for change exists in John's carers' circumstances or capacity to provide for his needs?

- What services would need to be provided in order to enable John to continue in the care of his parents?

- What is the likely level of co-operation from Tracy, Alun and Mrs Taylor?

POINTS TO CONSIDER

1. How does the Children Act 1989 concept of 'significant harm' correspond with your definition of abuse? Is it a broader or a narrower definition?

2. Look back at the answers you gave in Exercise 6.2. Would an understanding of 'significant harm' have helped you to make your decisions more easily? Might it have led you to make different decisions?

3. Would your understanding of 'significant harm' have helped you to determine more easily whether John was subject to abuse before this recent series of incidents?

4. Do you think that the flexibility inherent in determining the 'threshold criteria' adequately 'safeguards and promotes' a child's welfare?

5. What does the fact that you have access to compulsory powers in this way tell you about the nature of your role at the boundaries of the family, the state and the law?

COURSE TEXT: PREPARING FOR THE HEARING

Once the decision is made to apply for a care order and the procedural timetable is set, you will have to devote a considerable amount of your time as the responsible social worker to the preparation of the statement of evidence that you will provide to the court in support of your application. The following Study Text and exercise will familiarize you with what is required in the preparation of your evidence.

i STUDY TEXT 10.2: EVIDENCE

THE WITNESS STATEMENT

You may have noted that one of the considerations to be made at the First Appointment concerned the submission of evidence. The *Family Proceedings Courts* (Children Act 1989) Rules 1991 (r. 17) explains that parties to the proceedings (i.e. applicants and respondents) must file with the court, and serve on the remaining parties, 'written statements of the substance of the oral evidence which the party intends to adduce at a hearing...[and]...copies of any documents, including ...experts' reports, upon which the party intends to rely...' That is to say that you will have to prepare, in advance of the hearing and in accordance with the timetable for the child established by the court, a comprehensive account of the evidence you intend to give at the hearing and co-ordinate the submission of any other reports that it is intended to use in pursuit of the application. Paragraph 3 of Rule 17 establishes that you will need the permission of the court to adduce additional evidence or seek to rely on a document that you have not filed with the court and served on the remaining parties. You may not be able to rely on your case notes, for example, unless you have previously filed them with the court or are prepared to have them scrutinized by the other parties' representatives, nor will you be allowed to call a mystery expert at the last dramatic moment. The principle of 'advance disclosure' is an important one in family proceedings.

It should be clear just how important your witness statement will be. It will form the basis of the 'evidence in chief' that you will present to the court and on which you will be cross-examined; it will be closely read by the magistrates before the case and by the lawyers representing the respondents, as well as by family members. This Study Text will provide some guidance on the preparation of your witness statement, but it will be necessary first to make some general points about evidence in civil proceedings.

THE RULES OF EVIDENCE

Rules of evidence differ between civil and criminal cases. The focus here is on evidence relating to care proceedings, which are civil proceedings. It should be borne in mind, however, that the same facts might lead to both civil and criminal proceedings. For example, an alleged case of sexual abuse could give rise to care proceedings in order to protect the child, and to a criminal charge to prosecute the perpetrator.

In order to be taken into account by a court making a decision in any matter before it, evidence must be relevant and admissible. In order to be relevant, the evidence must logically bear on proving or disproving the point at issue. Unless a particular exclusion applies, all relevant evidence is admissible. The general exclusions are hearsay evidence, evidence concerned with opinion and evidence concerned with character. However, in the case of proceedings under the Act, certain qualifications apply to these general exclusions (the rules of evidence relating to character apply largely to criminal proceedings and are not considered here).

HEARSAY EVIDENCE

The general rule is that witnesses should give evidence of that which they have actually observed. Hearsay evidence is 'evidence of a statement made to a witness by a person who is not himself a witness' and is generally inadmissible. However, in order, particularly, to bring the evidence of children before the court in such a way that the child need not be present, The Children (Admissibility of Hearsay Evidence) Order 1993 does allow such evidence where it relates to the upbringing, maintenance or welfare of the child to be admitted. (It remains the case that in exceptional circumstances, a child may still be called to give evidence in care proceedings.) This provision does not apply only to statements made by the child concerned. It can also extend to the information passed to you from other professionals. However, the court, which will always have a preference for the best and most direct evidence, will have to assess what weight to attach to hearsay evidence. Cross-examination of hearsay is likely to focus on the source and reliability of the evidence.

OPINION EVIDENCE

The general rule that witnesses should confine themselves to matters of fact and not offer an opinion does not apply when the opinion offered is that of an expert (in the view of the court) and that the opinion will be of use to the court in determining the matter in question. As has been said (in Re R (A minor) (Expert evidence) [1991] 1FLR 291): 'outside the legal field the court itself has no expertise and for that reason frequently has to rely on the evidence of experts.'

Expert witnesses, including social workers, will usually give evidence on matters of fact observed by them or interpretations of those or other facts adduced in evidence and offer an opinion on the significance of the facts or interpretation. All expert witnesses, including social workers, must only offer opinions that they genuinely hold and not just those that favour one or other party to the proceedings. Detailed guidance on the role of the expert witness is contained in a Practice Direction from the President of the Family Division, *Experts in Family Proceedings Relating to Children* (MOJ 2008).

As Davis has noted (2010, p.52), a 'common feature of social workers as professionals is a remarkable lack of confidence in their own expertise'. If you have no claim to expertise then you should probably stick to giving factual evidence but of course you *do* have expertise although you should be prepared to justify and defend your opinions when your evidence is tested in court.

PREPARING YOUR STATEMENT

Perhaps the most important point of all to bear in mind when preparing your witness statement is that you cannot make it better than the assessment that informs it or the work that has already gone into the case. You should not now be at the point of reading the case file for the first time or of imposing a structure on your knowledge of the family! You will need to re-read the file and refresh your memory as you compile your statement, of course. As part of this process, you may identify material that you wish to rely on in your evidence, such as a piece of correspondence or a working agreement, which could then be appended to your statement. But, the real preparation for drawing up your statement began when you were first allocated this case and committed yourself to working to the highest professional standards that both families and the court have a right to expect of you.

If it is the case that you cannot make a witness statement better than the thinking and the work that has preceded it, the converse certainly does not hold. It is perfectly possible to prepare a witness statement that makes well thought out and skilfully delivered work seem confused and poorly planned. Remember that your witness statement will precede you in the sense that it will have been read by the magistrate, the parties to proceedings and their lawyers before you arrive in person before the court. You will want to make the best 'first impression' that you can; not only to help the court do its work but also to ensure that you establish your credibility as a professional in the eyes of your fellow professionals. Witness statements need time to prepare and you will need to rid yourself of as many distractions as you can in order to concentrate on researching, thinking and writing the statement. You should try to 'block out' at least two or three days for the purpose. It is important to seek the advice and support of your lawyer at this stage too.

GENERAL ADVICE

- *Stick to the point.* It is a more demanding task to select relevant material that you wish to present to the court than to include everything you ever knew about the family and the practice of social work. In the Taylor case, it is not relevant to anything that Ron is a mechanic and that so was his brother-in-law! Extraneous material obscures more than it reveals.

- *Differentiate between fact and opinion.* Consider the following sentence: 'When I arrived at the house, John was in danger from the traffic on the main road as he was playing, unattended, in an un-gated garden.' It is a matter of fact that John was playing in the garden with easy access to the main road but it is a matter of opinion as to whether that was potentially dangerous.

- *Make sure that any opinion you offer is within your competence* (i.e. within your observations and professional expertise). Consider this sentence: 'When I entered the living room, Mr Evans, who was drunk, lay asleep on the sofa.' You are not competent to judge Alun Evans' state of intoxication (certainly not when he is asleep!). You are not a doctor nor do you have any knowledge or training that would enable you to determine his state of mental or physical alertness.

- *Wherever possible, let the facts speak for themselves.* Compare the following statement with the one above and decide which is the most helpful to the court in understanding what you saw and what subsequently happened: 'I observed Mr Evans lying on the sofa. There were a number of empty beer cans on the floor around him. Upon my waking him, he appeared disorientated and his speech was slurred.'

- *Clearly distinguish between hearsay and direct evidence.* Compare the following statements:

  a. 'Ms Taylor later denied that Mr Evans had hit John, although previously she had said that Mr Evans was responsible for the bruises to John.'

  b. 'I was informed by Mrs Taylor (senior) that her daughter had told her that Mr Evans had hit Ms Taylor and John. Mrs Taylor reported this conversation to me on 4 August during the course of a telephone call requesting that I visit her grandson. Mrs Taylor seemed very agitated during the course of the telephone conversation and expressed her concern for the well-being of both Ms Taylor and John. During the course of an interview with Ms Taylor, conducted by me on 6 August while Ms Taylor was still a patient in Southtown General Hospital, Ms Taylor said that she did not know anything about the bruises to John and suggested to me that they may have been caused during the incident which led to the arrest of Mr Evans.'

It is important that the court is fully aware of the circumstances in which hearsay evidence was gathered in order to determine what weight to attach to it.

- *Present a balanced account.* You have a duty to tell the whole truth to the court and not simply to select those 'facts' that fit your case. Consider these versions of the same event:

  a. 'I first became involved with the Taylor family when arrangements for the care of her two older children had reached the point of breakdown.'

  b. 'Ms Taylor referred herself to the social services department, seeking help to manage difficulties that had arisen concerning the upbringing of her two older children.'

- *Avoid jargon.* What does the following actually mean? 'The dysfunctional relationship between the two older siblings and Ms Taylor's former spouse had expressed itself in acting-out behaviour on Michael's part.'

- *Use language that is respectful, authoritative, that you understand and with which you feel comfortable.* You will need to ensure that the importance of your statement is reflected in the tone that you adopt, but resist the temptation to write in your 'telephone voice'. Use family names and polite forms of address and make sure that your grammar and spelling are of the highest order. What might the following tell the court about the author of the statements?

a. 'I implied from what Tracy said to her mum that John had got his bruises from Alun who hit him the previous day when she spoke to me on the phone.'

b. 'I had facilitated access for Tracy and John to the local family treatment resource. This she had not availed herself of.'

Neither of these statements would tell the court very much about the facts of the case.

The structure of your witness statement will be determined to a great extent by the nature of the evidence that you wish to present (but see Davis 2010 for an account of what might be contained in most statements).

EXERCISE 10.2: WRITING A WITNESS STATEMENT

Using the material included in Units 7–10, and the advice provided in the previous Study Text, write a full witness statement to support an application for a care order in respect of John Taylor.

POINTS TO CONSIDER

1. Is your conclusion a convincing argument that the making of a care order is necessary to adequately safeguard and promote John's welfare?

2. Do your plans for John reflect the need to exercise compulsory powers?

3. Do you feel confident in the opinions that you offer?

4. Are these opinions based on, and justified by, the facts of the case?

5. Can you ground your opinions in an established body of social work (or other) knowledge?

6. Does your statement represent your honest belief that the course of action proposed will allow the court fairly to discharge its burden to have John's welfare as its paramount consideration?

📖 COURSE TEXT: GIVING EVIDENCE

The process of compiling a witness statement is a complex and daunting one. Once you have finished it, however, provided that it is based on competent practice and a well-considered analysis, your confidence in the course of action you are about to undertake should begin to rise. If you are not confident that what you are asking the court to sanction is, in all the circumstances, the best course of action open to you in order to safeguard and promote the welfare of the child concerned, then you must seek professional advice immediately. In any well-considered case there will be some residual uncertainty, of course; but if you are not convinced that what you propose will enable the court to make the order with the child's welfare as its paramount consideration then you should not be asking the court for such a decision.

Your confidence in your plans for the child and its family may not, however, equate to confidence in your own ability as a witness during the course of the hearing. The following Study Text offers some guidance on giving oral evidence. It begins with a brief account of the procedures likely to be encountered in the courtroom and a description of who else may be present.

i STUDY TEXT 10.3: IN THE BOX

COURTROOM LAYOUT AND KEY PERSONNEL

Almost invariably, proceedings such as the one we are simulating will commence in the Family Proceedings Court. The physical layout of such courts varies considerably, not least with the age of the court building, but, generally speaking, the 'bench' of magistrates (usually three) will sit together facing the 'well' of the court. It is the magistrates alone who determine matters of fact in proceedings and who decide what order(s), if any, to make. The court clerk, who will be legally qualified, will usually sit in front of the bench but sufficiently close to be able to speak to the bench easily. The court clerk is there to advise the bench on points of law and procedure and quite often will act as 'ringmaster' in the court. S/he is assisted by one or more ushers who will call witnesses, direct them to the witness box and administer the oath or affirmation.

Usually facing the bench will sit the lawyers representing the various parties to the proceedings. Sometimes the party from whom they are 'receiving instructions' will sit behind them but it is not uncommon for parties to be excluded at various points in the proceedings. The general public will not be allowed into the courtroom although, subject to certain safeguards in relation to preserving the anonymity of children, the press may be present. Provision has been made in Part 2 of the Children, Schools and Families Act 2010 to allow the publication of 'court orders and judgements' but, at the time of writing (August 2010), it is not clear how these provisions of the Act will work in practice. Usually present throughout will be the Children's Guardian.

PROCEDURE IN THE COURTROOM

The evidence is usually 'adduced' in the following order, although the court can direct otherwise:

- the applicant
- any party with parental responsibility
- other respondents (e.g. unmarried father)
- the Guardian
- the child (if not a party and there is no Guardian).

Closing speeches are usually in the following order:

- other respondents
- any party with parental responsibility
- the applicant
- the Children's Guardian
- the child (if not a party and there is no Guardian).

Once called to give evidence, you will be asked to take an oath or make an affirmation that the evidence you are about to give will be truthful. Your legal representative will then question you on the basis of the written statement you have filed with the court and which will form the basis of your 'evidence in chief'. Even though almost everyone in the room will have read your statement, the evidence it contains will be brought out in the course of this 'examination'. You will then be 'cross-examined' on the evidence you have given by the legal representatives of the other parties to the proceedings. The express purpose of this process is to test your evidence and, where it is weak or open to other interpretations, to make that clear to the court. Your legal representative may then re-examine you. This re-examination is not to adduce fresh evidence but to clarify any possible confusion or misunderstandings that may have arisen as a result of your cross-examination.

GIVING EVIDENCE

One important way in which courts evaluate the credibility and reliability of a piece of evidence is by the reliability and credibility of the witness. In other words, how you are perceived will strongly influence how much weight can be attached to what you have to say. Managing your 'performance' in the witness box is a skill that develops with experience. For present purposes, bearing in mind all of the points made in relation to the presentation of written submissions, we offer the following 'do's' and 'don'ts':

- *Do* read your written statement again and then re-read it on the day before the hearing. It might be several weeks since you finished writing it and you must ensure that you are entirely familiar with what you have included in your evidence to the court. Everyone else will know what is in your statement. Make sure that you do too.

- *Do* think hard about what impression your clothing and demeanour will make on the court. If you arrive breathless, bedraggled and spilling papers on the floor (it has been known!), you will look as disorganized and ill-prepared as you probably are. Courtrooms are probably less formal than they used to be but everyone else will be dressed soberly, recognizing the seriousness of the business in hand. If you turn up in clothes more suited for the beach, you will attract the same kind of opinion as if you turned up for the beach in a dark suit. Remember, the court will only have what they hear and see before them to help them make up their minds about you and what you have to say.

- *Do* address your evidence to the bench. All of your answers are for the benefit of the whole court, not just the questioner. There are a number of things you can do to remind yourself to address the bench. Position your feet facing towards the bench when you enter the witness box and keep them pointing in the same direction once you are seated. Then, as you begin to respond to questions, even if you have turned to hear what the questioner is asking, your body will naturally return to face in the direction of your feet. Alternatively, you can begin your answers with the words 'Your Worships, I…' This, again, will have the effect of making you turn towards the bench.

- *Don't* engage the lawyer asking you questions in conversation. Although it is 'natural' to wish to respond directly to the person asking you questions, an experienced advocate will be looking for visual clues from you in order to know when to interrupt. If you have not finished your answer, it is much easier to continue if it is your 'conversation' with the bench that the advocate has interrupted. It is the lawyer who will be disadvantaged if s/ he appears to be rude. Engaging the bench, rather than your inquisitor, helps to avoid confrontation too.

- *Do* make sure that you can be heard. You can use the taking of the oath to 'warm up' your voice. Remember also that a great deal of additional information can be imparted through the tone of voice used. An expressive voice will secure greater attention than a flat monotone.

- *Don't* allow yourself to be flustered. Sort your papers out well in advance. If you need to, ask permission to consult your papers, then do so carefully. If the questioner is pushing you along at too fast a pace or not allowing you to say what you want, try to impose a structure on your answers. One tried and tested technique is to reply: 'Your Worships, there are four points I would like to make in reply to that question…' If you run out of 'points', either say so or say that you have substantially dealt with them in what you have already said.

- *Do* tell the truth! If you don't know the answer to a question, or cannot remember, say so. If you find yourself saying something that is misleading, untrue or incomplete, or if your questioner creates the impression that you believe something that you do not, then you must say so.

- *Don't* be taken by surprise. You should be able to predict, with a reasonable degree of accuracy, what the difficult questions are likely to be. Why did you not make more frequent visits to the Taylor family after the two older children had left? Why did you not do more to ensure Tracy attended the health centre? What happened to the place at the family centre that you had promised but not delivered?

- *Do* be ready to deal with alternative explanations of events. As an expert witness, you will be allowed to give your opinion on certain matters. This means that you should predict what other inferences could be drawn from the facts and be ready with an account of why your opinion contains the correct interpretation.

There are not many situations in life when the express purpose of the person asking you questions is to cast doubt on everything you say. Of course it is uncomfortable. Quite often, it is meant to be. Remember, however, that you and your evidence are vital to the court's decision making. However uncomfortable you may feel, you have an important job to do and a perfect right to have your evidence, your professional expertise and personal integrity respected by the court. In one sense, giving evidence is no more than a continuation of professional practice by other means:

> The witness who is regarded as serious, caring, undogmatic, well-informed, fair and reasonable, and who shows respect for the family concerned, will be effective in helping the court to establish what is in the child's best interests... It is not suggested that [these qualities] can be acquired for the limited purpose of giving evidence. (Biggs and Robson 1992, p.13)

CONCLUSION

The decision to proceed to court in furtherance of your duty to safeguard and promote the welfare of children with whom you are working should never be taken lightly or alone. In reaching your decision, you will need to seek and consider the advice of senior colleagues and of specialists in other fields than your own. This can be a testing process whereby your judgement and your expertise may be questioned. We hope that you would not wish it any other way.

Similarly, when invoking the powers of the court is the best and most appropriate route to securing the welfare of a child we would not wish you to shy away from your responsibilities. Going to court is an integral part of social work with children and families. Good social workers are good social workers in the witness box just as much as they are in case conferences, team meetings or in direct work with families. It is only the other kind that need have any concerns.

⌐ঁ⌐ NOTES AND SELF-ASSESSMENT

1. What might the court process do to your future relationship with the child or family concerned? What can you do to maintain an effective relationship?

2. Who is most/least powerful or influential in the court process, do you think? Who should be?

3. Do you think that a courtroom is the most appropriate place in which to resolve complex family problems?

4. What does 'justice' mean in the context of family proceedings?

5. What impression do you want to make in court?

6. How close is that impression to the reality?

 **RECOMMENDED READING**

Davis, L. (2010) *See You in Court: A Social Worker's Guide to Presenting Evidence in Care Proceedings*. London: Jessica Kingsley Publishers.

Brammer, A. (2009) *Social Work Law*. Harlow: Longman.

TRAINER'S NOTES

Exercise 10.1: Establishing the Grounds

This exercise can best be undertaken by a group, either as a debate or in the form of a simulated case conference, strategy meeting or professional supervision session. The trainer will need to be able to offer expert advice and allocate roles accordingly. In a simulated case conference, it is sometimes difficult for participants to role play family members or the child concerned. If this is the case, John's interests can be represented by a Children's Guardian (adjusting the fiction a little so that the meeting takes place after the First Appointment). Other members of the group should observe the interactions and imaginatively re-create what this might signify for Tracy and Alun, without becoming actively involved in the drama. This arrangement is closer to what might usually happen in reality.

Exercise 10.2: Writing a Witness Statement

This is a difficult exercise to manage with a large group. However, the most effective way of testing the witness statement, and the court skills described in Study Text 10.3, is to simulate the hearing itself. If at all possible, such an exercise should take place in a real courtroom. These can be hired (and can be quite expensive!) through your court clerk's office or through the administrator for the county court in your area. It is possible to re-arrange the furniture and simulate a courtroom elsewhere but something of the sense of atmosphere and occasion is lost in the process. The trainer should try to secure the services of an experienced local solicitor specializing in family matters to appear on behalf of Tracy. The trainer can act as the solicitor representing the local authority. It is not necessary to rehearse the whole hearing. The most important element is to provide participants with the opportunity to have their evidence adduced and to be cross-examined by someone with the necessary skills and with whom they have no previous acquaintance. The greater the verisimilitude (including insistence on the appropriate dress code), the more useful participants will find the exercise. Trainers may be surprised by the degree of anxiety demonstrated by participants.

References

ACTS/CASW (Association canadienne des travailleuses et travailleurs sociaux/ Canadian Association of Social Workers) (2005) *Code of Ethics*. Ottawa: ACTS/CASW.

Aldgate, J. and Statham, D. (2001) *The Children Act Now: Messages from Research*. London: The Stationery Office.

Aldgate, J. and Tunstill, J. (1995) *Making Sense of Section 17: Implementing Services for Children in Need within the 1989 Children Act*. London: HMSO.

Aldridge, J. (2008) 'All work and no play? Understanding the needs of children with caring responsibilities.' *Children and Society 22*, 4, 253–264.

Aldridge, J. and Becker, S. (1993) *Children who Care: Inside the World of Young Carers*. Loughborough: Young Carers Research Group, Loughborough University.

Aldridge, J. and Becker, S. (2003) *Children Caring for Parents with Mental Illness: Perspectives of Young Carers, Parents and Professionals*. Bristol: The Policy Press.

AlEissa, M.A., Fluke, J.D., Gerbaka, B., Goldbeck, L., Gray, J., Hunter, N., Madrid, B., Van Puyenbroeck, B., Richards, I. and Tonmyr, L. (2009) 'A commentary on national maltreatment surveillance systems: Examples of progress.' *Child Abuse and Neglect 33*, 11, 809–814.

Alison, L. (2000) 'What are the risks to children of parental substance misuse?' In F. Harbin and M. Murphy (eds) *Substance Misuse and Child Care: How to Understand, Assist and Intervene when Drugs Affect Parenting*. Lyme Regis: Russell House Publishing.

Anderson, S. (1984) 'Goal setting in social work practice.' In B.R. Compton and B. Galaway (eds) *Social Work Processes*. Chicago: Dorsey Press.

Archard, D. (1993) *Children – Rights and Childhood*. London: Routledge.

Archard, D. (2001) 'Philosophical perspectives on childhood.' In J. Fionda (ed.) *Legal Concepts of Childhood*. Oxford: Hart Publishing.

Aries, P. (1960) *L'Enfant et la vie familiale sous l'Ancien Regime*. Paris: Librairie Plon. Translated by R. Baldick as *Centuries of Childhood* (1962). London: Jonathan Cape.

ASSR (The Association of Graduates in Social Science, Personnel and Public Administration, Economics and Social Work) (2006) *Ethics for Social Work*. Stockholm: ASSR.

Atherton, C. and Dowling, P. (1989) 'Using written agreements: The family's point of view.' In J. Aldgate (ed.) *Using Written Agreements with Children and Families*. London: FRG.

Audit Commission (2008) *Are We There Yet? Improving Governance and Resource Management in Children's Trusts*. London: Audit Commission.

Aunola, K. and Nurmi, J-K. (2005) 'The role of parenting styles in children's problem behaviour.' *Child Development 76*, 6, 1144–1159.

Australian Association of Social Workers (2002) (Second Edition) *Code of Ethics*. Barton (Canberra, ACT): AASW.

Baistow, K., Cooper, A., Hetherington, R., Pitts, J. and Spriggs A. (1995) *Positive Child Protection*. Dorset: Russell House Publishing.

Bandura, A. (1997) *Self-efficacy: The Exercise of Control*. New York: Freeman.

Bar-Yam, Y. (2003) *Dynamics of Complex Systems*. Boulder, CO.: Westview Press.

BASW (British Association of Social Workers) (2002) *The Code of Ethics for Social Work*. Birmingham: BASW.

Baumrind, D. (1967) 'Child-care practices anteceding three patterns of preschool behavior.' *Genetic Psychology Monographs 75*, 43–88.

Baumrind, D. (1991) 'The influence of parenting style on adolescent competence and substance use.' *Journal of Early Adolescence 11*, 1, 56–95.

Becker, S. (2000) 'Young carers' in M. Davies (ed.) *The Blackwell Encyclopaedia of Social Work*. Oxford: Blackwell.

Beckett, C. and McKeigue, B. (2010) 'Objects of concern: Caring for children during care proceedings.' *British Journal of Social Work 40*, 7, 2086–2101.

Beek, M. and Schofield, G. (2004) *Providing a Secure Base in Long-term Foster Care*. London: British Agencies for Adoption and Fostering.

Belsky, J and Rovine, M. (1987) 'Temperament and attachment security in the strange situation: an empirical rapprochement.' *Child Development 58*, 3, 787–795.

Beresford, P. (1994) *Positively Parents: Caring for a Severely Disabled Child*. York: Social Policy Research Unit.

Berne, E. (1964) *Games People Play: The Psychology of Human Relationships*. Penguin New Impression Edition (1973). London: Penguin Books.

Beunerman, J. (2010) *People Make Play: The Impact of Staffed Play Provision on Children, Families and Communities. A Research Report Written by Demos for Play England*. London: Play England/ National Children's Bureau (NCB).

Biggs, V. and Robson, J. (1992) *Developing Your Court Skills*. London: BAAF.

Blakemore, S. J., and Choudhury, S. (2006) 'Development of the adolescent brain: Implications for executive function and social cognition.' *Journal of Child Psychology and Psychiatry 47*, 3–4, 296–312.

Bloom, M. (1993) *Single System Designs in the Social Services: Issues and Options for the 1990s*. New York: Haworth.

BMRB Social Research and The Futures Company (2008) *National Survey of Parents and Children: Family Life, Aspirations and Engagement with Learning 2008*. Research Report DCSFRR059. London: DCSF.

Bowlby, J. (1970) *Attachment*. New York: Basic Books.

Bowlby, J. (1973) *Attachment and Loss, Vol. II: Separation, Anxiety and Anger*. London: Hogarth Press.

Bowlby, J. (1980) *Attachment and Loss, Vol. III: Loss, Sadness and Depression*. London: Hogarth Press.

Bradshaw, J. and Holmes, J. (2010) 'Child poverty in the first 5 years of life'. In K. Hansen, H. Joshi and S. Dex (eds) *Children of the 21st century (Vol. 2): The first five years*. Bristol: The Policy Press.

Brammer, A. (2009) *Social Work Law*. Harlow: Longman.

Brandon, M. and Thoburn, J. (2008) 'Safeguarding children in the UK: a longitudinal study of services to children suffering or likely to suffer significant harm.' *Child and Family Social Work 13*, 4, 365–377.

Brandon, M., Bailey, S., Belderson, P., Gardner, R., Sidebotham, P., Dodsworth, J., Warren, C. and Black, J. (2009) *Understanding Serious Case Reviews and their Impact: A Biennial Analysis of Serious Case Reviews 2005–07*. Research Report DCSF-RR129. Norwich: University of East Anglia.

Brandon, M., Belderson, P., Warren, C., Howe, D., Gardner, R., Dodsworth, J. and Black, J. (2008) *Analysing Child Deaths and Serious Injury through Abuse and Neglect: What Can We Learn? A Biennial Analysis of Sserious Case Reviews 2003–2005*. Research Report DCSF-RR023. London: DCSF.

Brandon, M., Howe, A., Dagley, V., Salter, C., Warren, C. and Black, J. (2006) *Evaluating the Common Assessment Framework*. Research Report RR740. London: Department for Education and Skills (DfES).

Brewer, M., Browne, J., Joyce, R. and Sutherland, H. (2009) *Micro-simulating Child Poverty in 2010 and 2020*. London: Institute for Fiscal Studies.

Broadhurst, K., Wastell, D., White, S., Peckover, S., Thompson, K., Pithouse, A. and Davey, D. (2010) 'Performing 'Initial Assessment': Identifying the latent conditions for error at the front-door of local authority children's services.' *British Journal of Social Work 40, 2*, 352–370.

Brophy, J. (2006) *ResearchRreview: Child Care Proceedings under the Children Act 1989*. DCA Research Series. London: Department for Constitutional Affairs.

Brophy, J. with Bates, P., Brown, L., Cohen, S., Radcliffe, P. and Wale, C.J. (1999) *Safeguarding Children with the Children Act 1989*. London: The Stationery Office.

Brown, G. W. and Harris, T. (1978) *Social Origins of Depression: A Study of Psychiatric Disorder in Women*. New York: Free Press.

Bullock, R., Courtney, M.E., Parker, R., Sinclair, I. and Thoburn, J. (2006) 'Can the corporate state parent?' *Adoption and Fostering 30, 2*, 6–19.

Bullock, R., Little, M. and Milham, S. (1993) *Residential Care for Children – A Review of the Research*. London: HMSO.

Burden, D.S. and Gottlieb, N. (eds) (1987) *The Woman Client*. London: Tavistock.

Burghardt, G. M. (2005) *The Genesis of Animal Play. Testing the Limits*. Cambridge, MA: MIT Press.

Buss, A.H. and Plomin, R.A. (1984) *Temperament Theory of Personality Development*. New York: Wiley–Interscience.

Butler, I. (2000) 'Child abuse.' In M. Davies (ed.) *The Blackwell Encyclopaedia of Social Work*. Oxford: Blackwell Publishers.

Butler, I. and Drakeford, M. (2003) *Social Policy, Social Welfare and Scandal: How British Public Policy is Made*. London: Palgrave/Macmillan.

Butler, I. and Drakeford, M. (2010) 'Children and young people's policy in Wales' in P. Ayre and M. Preston-Shoot (eds) *Children's Services at the Crossroads: A Critical Evaluation of Contemporary Policy for Practice*. Lyme Regis: Russell House Publishing.

Butler, I. and Drakeford, M. (2011) *Social Work on Trial: The Case of Maria Colwell and the State of Welfare*. Bristol: Policy Press.

Butler, I. and Pugh, R. (2004) 'The politics of social work research' in R. Lovelock and J. Powell (eds) *Reflecting on Social Work – Discipline and Profession*. Aldershot/ Dartmouth: Ashgate.

Butler, I. and Williamson, H. (1994) *Children Speak: Children, Trauma and Social Work*. London: Longman.

Butler, I., Robinson, M. and Scanlan, L. (2005) *Children and Decision Making*. London: National Children's Bureau for the Joseph Rowntree Foundation.

Butler, I., Robinson, M., Scanlan, L., Douglas, G. and Murch, M. (2003) *Divorcing Children: Children's Experience of their Parents' Divorce*. London: Jessica Kingsley Publishers.

CAFCASS (Children and Family Court Advisory and Support Service) (2010) *CAFCASS Care Demand Statistics Quarter 4: 2009–10*. London: CAFCASS.

Calderwood, L., Kiernan, K., Joshi, H., Smith, K. and Ward, K. (2005) 'Parenthood and parenting'. In S. Dex and H. Joshi (eds) *Children of the 21st Century: From Birth to Nine Months*. Bristol: The Policy Press.

Chartier, M.J., Walker, J.R. and Naimark, B. (2010) 'Separate and cumulative effects of adverse childhood experiences in predicting adult health and health care utilization.' *Child Abuse and Neglect 34, 6*, 454–464.

Children's Workforce Development Council (CWDC) (2010a) *Early Identification, Assessment of Needs and Intervention. The Common Assessment Framework for Children and Young People: A guide for practitioners*. Leeds: CWDC.

Children's Workforce Development Council (CWDC) (2010b) *The Common Core of Skills and Knowledge: At the Heart of What You Do*. London: CWDC.

Clement Brown, S. (1947) 'Foreword.' In D.M. Dyson *The Foster Home and the Boarded Out Child*. London: George, Allen and Unwin.

Cleveland Report (1988) *Report of the Inquiry into Child Abuse in Cleveland.* London: HMSO.

Colwell Inquiry Report (1974). London: HMSO.

Community Care, Services for Carers and Children's Services (Direct Payments) (England) Regulations 2009 (SI 2009/1887). Available at www.legislation.gov.uk/uksi/2009/1887/contents/made, accessed 10.03.11.

Community Care, Services for Carers and Children's Services (Direct Payments) (Wales) Regulations 2004 (SI 2004/1748). Available at www.legislation.gov.uk/wsi/2004/1748/contents/made, accessed 10.03.11.

Cook, D.T. (2009) 'When a child is not a child, and other conceptual hazards of childhood studies' (Editorial) *Childhood 16,* 1, 5–10.

Cook, K. S., and Rice, E.W. (2003) 'Social exchange theory.' In J. DeLamater (ed.) *The Handbook of Social Psychology.* New York: Kluwer Academic/Plenum Publishers.

Corbett, V. (2005) '"I just knew to keep it quiet…" Living with parental problematic substance use.' *Adoption and Fostering 29,* 1, 98–100.

Corby, B. (2005) *Child Abuse: Towards a Knowledge Base.* (Third Edition). Milton Keynes: Open University Press.

Corby, B. (2006) 'The role of child care social work in supporting families with children in need and providing protective services – past, present and future.' *Child Abuse Review 15,* 3, 159–177.

Cournoyer, B. (1991) *The Social Work Skills Workbook.* Belmont, CA: Wadsworth.

Daniel, B., Wassell, S. and Gilligan, R. (1999) *Child Development for Child Care and Protection Workers.* London: Jessica Kingsley Publishers.

Davis, L. (2010) *See you in Court: A Social Worker's Guide to Presenting Evidence in Care Proceedings.* London: Jessica Kingsley Publishers.

Dawson, A. and Butler, I. (2003) 'The morally active manager'. In J. Henderson and D. Atkinson (eds) *Managing Care in Context* London: Routledge in association with the Open University.

DCP (Department of Child Protection – Western Australia) (2008) *Adoption of Signs of Safety as the Department for Child Protection Practice Framework – Background Paper.* Perth: DCP.

DCSF (Department for Children, Schools and Families) (2004) *Every Child Matters: Change for Children.* London: DCSF.

DCSF (Department for Children, Schools and Families) (2008) *The Children Act 1989, Guidance and Regulations: Volume 1 Court Orders.* London: DCSF.

DCSF (Department for Children, Schools and Families) (2009a) *Care Matters: Ministerial Stocktake Report.* London: DCSF.

DCSF (Department for Children, Schools and Families) (2009b) *Children Assessed to be in Need by Children's Services, England, 6 months ending 31 March 2009: Experimental Statistical Release 19th November 2009.* London: DCSF.

DCSF (Department for Children, Schools and Families) (2010a) *Children's Homes: National Minimum Standards. Formal Consultation Draft.* London: DCSF.

DCSF (Department for Children, Schools and Families) (2010b) *Children's Trusts: Statutory Guidance on Co-operation Arrangements, including the Children's Trust Board and the Children and Young People's Plan.* Nottingham: DCSF Publications.

DCSF (Department for Children, Schools and Families) (2010c) *IRO Handbook: Statutory Guidance for Independent Reviewing Officers and Local Authorities on their Functions in Relation to Case Management and Review for Looked After Children.* London: DCSF.

DCSF (Department for Children, Schools and Families) (2010d) *Promoting the Educational Acheivement of Looked After Children. Statutory Guidance for Local Authorities* London: DCSF.

DCSF (Department for Children, Schools and Families) (2010e) *The Children Act 1989 Guidance and Regulations Volume 2: Care Planning, Placement and Case Review.* London: DCSF.

DCSF (Department for Children, Schools and Families) (2010f) *Working Together to Safeguard Children: A Guide to Inter-agency Working to Safeguard and Promote the Welfare of Children*. London: DCSF/ HM Government.

DCSF and DoH (Department for Children, Schools and Families and Department of Health) (2009) *Statutory Guidance on Promoting the Health and Well-being of Looked After Children*. London: DCSF.

DCSF/ ONS (Department for Children, Schools and Families/ Office of National Statistics) (2009) *Children Looked After in England (including adoption and care leavers) year ending 31 March 2009*. SFR 25/2009 London: DCSF.

Dearden, C. and Aldridge, J. (2010) 'Young carers: Needs, rights and assessment' In Horwath, J. (ed.) *The Child's World, The Comprehensive Guide to Assessing Children in Need*. London: Jessica Kingsley Publishers.

Dearden, C. and Becker, S. (2000) *Growing Up Caring: Vulnerability and Transitions to Adulthood – Young Carers' Experiences*. Leicester: Youth Work Press.

Dearden, C. and Becker, S. (2004) *Young Carers in the UK: The 2004 Report*. London: Carers UK and The Children's Society.

de Mause, L. (1976) *The History of Childhood*. London: Souvenir Press.

Department for Communities and Local Government (2007) *The New Performance Framework for Local Authorities & Local Authority Partnerships: Single Set of National Indicators*. London: Department for Communities and Local Government.

Department for Education (DfE) (2010) *Referrals, Assessments and Children who were the Subject of a Child Protection Plan (Children in Need Census – Provisional) Year Ending 31 March 2010*. OSR24/2010. London: DfE.

Department for Education and Skills (DfES) (2006a) *Care Matters: Transforming the Lives of Children and Young people in Care*. London: DfES.

Department for Education and Skills (DfES) (2006b) *What to do if You're Worried a Child is Being Abused*. London: DFES.

Department for Education and Skills (DfES) (2007) *Care Matters: Time for Change*. London: DfES.

Department of Health (1990) *The Care of Children – Principles and Practice in Regulations and Guidance*. London: HMSO.

Department of Health (1991a) *The Children Act 1989 Guidance and Regulations Volume 2 Family Support, Day Care and Educational Provision for Young Children*. London: HMSO.

Department of Health (1991b) *Patterns and Outcomes in Child Placement – Messages from Current Research and their Implications*. London: HMSO.

Department of Health (1995) *Child Protection – Messages from Research*. London: HMSO.

Department of Health (1998) *Modernising Social Services*. Cm 4169. London: The Stationery Office.

Department of Health (2000) *Excellence Not Excuses: Inspection of Services for Ethnic Minority Children and Families*. London: The Stationery Office.

Department of Health (2001) *Transforming Social Services: An Evaluation of Local Responses to the Quality Protects Programme, Year 3*. London: Department of Health.

Department of Health (2002) 'LAC 2202 (19)' (Unpublished Local Authority Circular). London: Department of Health).

Department of Health (2003) *Children Looked After by Local Authorities. Year Ending 31 March 2002. England. Volume 1: Commentary and National Tables*. London: Department of Health.

Department of Health and Social Security (1985) *Social Work Decisions in Child Care – Recent Research Findings and their Implications*. London: HMSO.

Department of Health, Department for Education and Employment and Home Office (2000) *Framework for the Assessment of Children in Need and their Families*. London: The Stationery Office.

Department of Health, Office for National Statistics (2000) *Children in Need in England: First Results of a Survey of Activity and Expenditure as Reported by Local Authority Social Services' Children and Family Teams for a Survey Week in February 2000.* London: The Stationery Office.

DfE (2010) *Review of Child Protection: Better Fronline Services to Protect Children.* Press Notice, available at www.education.gov.uk/inthenews/inthenews/a0061426/review-of-child-protections-better-frontline-services-to-protect-children

Dingwall, R. (1989) 'Some problems about predicting child abuse and neglect.' In O. Stevenson (ed.) *Child Abuse: Public Policy and Professional Practice.* Hemel Hempstead: Harvester Wheatsheaf.

Dominelli, L. (2007) *Cross-Cultural Child Development for Social Workers. An Introduction.* London: Palgrave Macmillan.

Doughty, J. (2010) 'Amendments to the legislation: 1989-2009.' *Journal of Children's Services 5,* 2, 7–16.

Douglas, G., Murch, M., Miles, C. and Scanlan, L. (2006) *Research into the Operation of Rule 9.5 of the Family Proceedings Rules 1991.* London: Department of Constitutional Affairs.

Dozier, M. (2005) 'Challenges of foster care.' *Attachment and Human Development 7,* 1, 27–30.

Drakeford, M. and Butler, I. (2009) 'Familial homicide and social work.' *British Journal of Social Work 40,* 5, 1419–1433.

DWP (Department for Work and Pensions) (2010) *Households Below Average Income Statistics: First Release: 20th May 2010: IFD200510-HBAI.* London: DWP.

Easton, C., Morris, M. and Gee, G. (2010) *LARC2: Integrated Children's Services and the CAF Process.* Slough: National Foundation for Educational Research (NFER).

Elias, N. (1939) *Über den Prozes der Zivilisation* ('The Civilising Process'). Basel: Falken.

English, D. (1996) 'The promise and reality of risk assessment.' *Protecting Children 12,* 2, 14–19.

Fahlberg, V. (1985) 'Checklists on attachment.' In M. Adcock and R. White (eds) *Good Enough Parenting: A Framework for Assessment.* London: BAAF.

Fahlberg, V. (1988) *Fitting the Pieces Together.* London: BAAF.

Fahlberg, V. (1994) *A Child's Journey through Placement.* London: BAAF.

Farmer, E., Sturgess, W. and O'Neill, T. (2008) *Reunification of Looked After Children with their Parents: Patterns, Interventions and Outcomes.* Research Brief DCSF-RBX-14-08. London: DCSF.

Fawcett, M. (2009) *Learning Through Child Observation* (Second Edition). London: Jessica Kingsley Publishers.

Featherstone, B. (2003) 'Taking fathers seriously'. *British Journal of Social Work 33,* 2, 239–254.

Featherstone, B., Hooper, C., Scourfield, J. and Taylor, K. (eds) (2010) *Gender and Child Welfare in Society.* Chichester: Wiley-Blackwell.

Fischer, J. (1993) 'Empirically based practice: The end of ideology?' In M. Bloom (ed.) *Single System Designs in the Social Services: Issues and Options for the 1990s.* New York: Haworth.

Forester, D. (2007) 'Describing the needs of children presenting to children's services: Issues to reliability and validity.' *Journal of Children's Services 2,* August 2007, 2, 48–59.

Forrester, D. (2008) 'Is the care system failing children.' *The Political Quarterly 79,* 2, 206–211.

Forrester, D. and Harwin, J. (2008) 'Parental substance misuse and child welfare: outcomes for children two years after referral.' *British Journal of Social Work 38,* 8, 1518–1534.

Fortin, J. (1998) *Children's Rights and the Developing Law.* London: Butterworths.

Foucault, M. (1980) (ed. C. Gordon) *Power/Knowledge: Selected Interviews and Other Writings 1972–1977.* Brighton: Harvester.

France, A., Munro, E. R. and Waring, A. (2010) 'The Evaluation of arrangements for effective operation of the new Local Safeguarding Boards in England'. Research Brief DCSFRBX- 10-03. London: DCSF.

Frank, J. (2002) *Making it Work. Good Practice with Young Carers and their Families.* London: The Children's Society and the Princess Royal Trust for Carers.

Frank, J. (1995) *Couldn't Care More: A Study of Young Carers and their Needs.* London: The Children's Society.

Frankenburg, S. (1946) *Common Sense in the Nursery.* London: Penguin.

Franklin, B. (ed.) (1995) *The Handbook of Children's Rights – Comparative Policy and Practice.* London: Routledge.

Freeman, P. and Hunt, J. (1998) *Parental Perspectives on Care Proceedings.* London: The Stationery Office.

Fry, S. (1993) 'The family curse.' In *Paperweight.* London: Mandarin.

Gambe, D., Gomes, J., Kapur, V., Rangel, M. and Stubbs, P. (1992) *Improving Practice with Children and Families.* Leeds: CCETSW.

Garrett, P.M. (1999) 'Mapping child-care social work in the final years of the twentieth century: A critical response to the "looking after children" system.' *British Journal of Social Work 29,* 1, 27–47.

Garrett, P.M. (2002) 'Yes Minister: Reviewing the 'Looking After Children' experience and identifying the messages for social work research.' *British Journal of Social Work 32,* 7, 831–846.

Garrett, P.M. (2003) 'Swimming with dolphins: The assessment framework, New Labour and new tools for social work with children and families.' *British Journal of Social Work 33,* 3, 441–463.

Garrett, P.M. (2008) 'How to be modern: New Labour's neoliberal modernity and the *Change for Children* programme.' *British Journal of Social Work 38,* 2, 270–289.

Gaskell, C. (2010) ''If the social worker had called at least it would show they cared' Young care leavers' perspectives on the importance of care.' *Children and Society 24,* 1, 136–147.

Gelles, R. (1975) 'The Social Construction of Child Abuse.' *American Journal of Orthopsychiatry 45,* 3, 363–371.

Gerhardt, S. (2004) *Why Love Matters: How Affection Shapes a Baby's Brain.* Hove, UK: Brunner/ Routledge.

Gibbs, L. and Gambrill, E. (2002) 'Evidence-based practice: Counterarguments to objections.' *Research on Social Work Practice 12,* 3, 452–476.

Giddens, A. (1992) *The Transformation of Intimacy – Sexuality, Love and Eroticism in Modern Societies.* Oxford: Polity.

Giedd, J.N. (2004) 'Structural magnetic resonance imaging of the adolescent brain.' In R. E. Dahl and L. P. Spear (eds) *Adolescent Brain Development: Vulnerabilities and opportunities.* New York: New York Academy of Sciences.

Gilbert, T. (2009) 'Ethics in social work: A comparison of the international statement of principles in social work with the Code of Ethics for British social workers.' *Journal of Social Work Values and Ethics 6,* 2. Available at www.socialworker.com/jswve.

Gilby, N., Hamlyn, B., Hanson, T., Romanou, E. and Mackey, T. / BRMB Research (2008) *National Survey of Parents and Children: Family Life, Aspirations and Engagement with Learning.* DCSF Research Report RR059. London: DCSF.

Gilligan, R. and Manby, M. (2008) 'The Common Assessment Framework: does the reality match the rhetoric?' *Child and Family Social Work 13,* 2, 177–187.

Goldman, L. (1994) *Life and Loss: A Guide to Helping Grieving Children.* Brighton: Brunner/ Routledge.

Gould, N. (2010) 'Integrating qualitative evidence in practice guideline development: Meeting the challenge of evidence-based practice for social work.' *Qualitative Social Work 9,* 1, 93–110.

Greenfield, E.A. and Marks, N.F. (2010) 'Identifying experiences of physical and psychological violence in childhood that jeopardize mental health in adulthood.' *Child Abuse and Neglect 34,* 3, 161–171.

Grimshaw, R. and Sinclair, I. (1997) *Planning to Care: Procedure and practice under the Children Act 1989.* London: National Children's Bureau.

GSCC (General Social Care Council) (undated) *Code of Practice for Social Care Workers.* London: GSCC.

Hakim, C. (2004) *Key Issues in Women's Work: Female Diversity and the Polarisation of Women's Employment.* London: Routledge-Cavendish.

Hall, E. and Guy, J. (2009) *The Baby Peter effect and the Increase in Section 31 Care Order Applications.* London: CAFCASS.

Hanks, H. and Stratton, P. (2007) 'Common forms and consequences of abuse'. In K. Wilson and A. James (eds) (Third Edition) *The Child Protection Handbook.* London: Bailliere Tindall.

Häring, B. (1972) *Medical Ethics.* Slough: St Paul.

Haringey Local Children's Safeguarding Board (2009) *Serious Case Review: Baby Peter.* London: Haringey LSCB.

Harris, C.C. (1984) *The Family and Industrial Society.* London: Allen and Unwin.

Hart, D. and Williams, A. (2008) *Putting Corporate Parenting into Practice: Developing an Effective Approach.* London: National Children's Bureau.

Harwin, J. and Madge, N. (2010) 'The concept of significant harm in law and practice.' *Journal of Children's Services 5,* 2, 73–83.

Harwin, J., Matias, C., Pokhrel, S., Ryan, M., Schneider, M.S., Tunnard, J. and Alrouh, B. (2009) *The Family Drug and Alcohol Court (FDAC) Evaluation Project: Interim Report to the Nuffield Foundation and Home Office.* London: Brunel University.

Hayden, C., Goddard, J., Gorin, S. and Van Der Spek, N. (1999) *State Child Care: Looking After Children.* London: Jessica Kingsley Publishers.

Helm, D. (2010) *Making Sense of Child and Family Assessment: How to Interpret Children's Needs.* London: Jessica Kingsley Publishers.

Hendrick, H. (1994) *Child Welfare England 1872–1989.* London: Routledge.

Heptinstall, E., Bhopal, K. and Brannen, J. (2001) 'Adjusting to a foster family: Children's perspectives.' *Adoption and Fostering 25,* 4, 6–16.

Hepworth, D.H. and Larsen, J.A. (1982) *Direct Social Work Practice: Theory and Skills.* Chicago, IL: Dorsey Press.

HM Government (1998) *The Human Rights Act 1998.* London: The Stationery Office.

HM Government (2003) *Every Child Matters* Cm. 5860 London: The Stationery Office.

Hockey, J. and James, A. (2003) *Social Identities Across the Life Course.* Basingstoke: Macmillan.

Holland, S. (2004) *Child and Family Assessment in Social Work Practice.* London: Sage.

Holman, R. (1975) 'The place of fostering in social work.' *British Journal of Social Work 5,* 1, 3–29.

Holman, R. (1988) *Putting Families First.* Basingstoke: Macmillan.

Homan, R. (1991) *The Ethics of Social Research.* London: Longman.

Horwath, J. (ed.) (2001) *The Child's World: Assessing Children in Need.* London: Jessica Kingsley Publishers.

Horwath, J. (2005) 'Is this child neglect? The influence of differences in perceptions of child neglect on social work practice'. In J. Taylor and B. Daniel (eds) *Child Neglect: Practice Issues for Health and Social Care.* London: Jessica Kingsley Publishers.

Horwath, J. (2007) *Child Neglect: Identification and Assessment.* Basingstoke: Macmillan.

House of Commons, Children, Schools and Families Committee (2009) *Looked-after Children. Third Report of Session 2008–2009, Volume 1.* London: The Stationery Office.

Houston, S. (2003) 'A method from the 'Lifeworld': some possibilities for person centred planning for children in care.' *Children and Society 17,* 1, 57–70.

Howe, D. (1987) *An Introduction to Social Work Theory.* Aldershot: Wildwood House.

Howe, D. (1994) 'Modernity, postmodernity and social work.' *British Journal of Social Work 24,* 5, 513–532.

Howe, D. (1997) 'Psychosocial and relationship based theories for child and family social work: Politics, philosophy, psychology and welfare practice.' *Child and Family Social Work, 2,* 3, 162–169.

Howe, D. (2001) 'Attachment.' In J. Horwath (ed.) *The Child's World: Assessing Children in Need.* London: Jessica Kingsley Publishers.

Howe, D. (2005) *Child Abuse and Neglect: Attachment, Development and Intervention.* Basingstoke: Palgrave Macmillan.

Hudson, C. (2009) 'Decision making in evidence-based practice: Science and art.' *Smith College Studies in Social Work 79,* 2, 155–174.

Humphrey, J.C. (2002) 'Joint reviews: Retracing the trajectory, defining the terms.' *British Journal of Social Work 32,* 4, 463–476.

Humphrey, J.C. (2003) 'Joint reviews: The methodology in action.' *British Journal of Social Work 33,* 2, 177–190.

Hunt, J., Macleod, A. and Thomas, C. (1999) *The Last Resort: Child Protection, the Courts and the 1989 Children Act.* London: The Stationery Office.

Husband, C. (1995) 'The morally active practitioner and the ethics of anti racist social work'. In Hugman, R. and Smith, D. (eds) *Ethical Issues in Social Work.* London: Routledge.

International Federation of Social Workers (IFSW) (2004) *Ethics in Social Work: Statement of Principles.* Geneva: IFSW.

International Labour Office (ILO) (2004) *Child Labour: A Textbook for University Students.* Geneva: ILO.

Isen, A. and Labroo, A. (2003) 'Some ways in which positive affect facilitates decision making and judgement'. In S. Schneider and J. Shanteau (eds) *Emerging Perspectives on Judgement and Decision Research.* Cambridge: Cambridge University Press.

James, A. and James, A. (2003) *Childhood: Theory, Policy and Practice.* Basingstoke: Palgrave Macmillan.

James, A. and James, A.L. (2004) *Constructing Childhood: Theory, Policy and Practice.* Basingstoke: Macmillan.

James, A. and Prout, A. (1997) 'A new paradigm for the sociology of childhood? Provenance, promise and problems.' In A. James and A. Prout (eds) *Constructing and Reconstructing Childhood: Contemporary Issues in the Sociological Study of Childhood.* London: The Falmer Press.

James, A., James, A. and Macnamee, S. (2004) 'Turn down the volume? – Not hearing the children in family proceedings.' *Child and Family Law Quarterly 16,* 2, 189–202.

James, A.N. (1998) 'Supporting families of origin: An exploration of the influence of the Children Act 1948.' *Child and Family Social Work 3,* 3, 173–181.

Jensen, A.M. and McKee, L. (2003) *Children and the Changing Family: Between Transformation and Negotiation.* London: Routledge/Falmer.

Jewett, C. (1984) *Helping Children Cope with Separation and Loss.* London: BAAF.

Jones, D. (2001) 'The assessment of parental capacity.' In J. Horwath (ed.) *The Child's World: Assessing Children in Need.* London: Jessica Kingsley Publishers.

Jones, R.L. (1991) *Black Psychology* (Second Edition). Berkeley, CA: Cobb and Henry.

Jordan, B. (1981) 'Prevention.' *Adoption and Fostering 5,* 3, 20–22.

Kates, V. (1985) 'Success, strain and surprise.' *Issues in Science and Technology 2,* 1, 46–58.

Kearney, P., Levin, E. and Rosen, G. (2000) *Working with Families: Alcohol, Drugs and Mental Health Problems.* London: National Institute of Social Work.

Kenney, M. (2007) *Hidden Heads of Households: Child Labour in Northeast Brazil.* Peterborough, Ontario: Broadview.

Keys, M. (2009a) 'Determining the skills for child protection practice: Emerging from the Quagmire!' *Child Abuse Review 18,* 5, 316–332.

Keys, M. (2009b) 'Determining the skills for child protection practice: From quandary to quagmire?' *Child Abuse Review 18,* 5, 297–315.

Koprowska J. (2007) 'Communication skills in social work'. In M. Lymbery and K. Postle (eds) *Social Work: A Companion for Learning.* London: Sage.

Kroll, B. (2004) 'Living with an elephant: Growing up with parental substance misuse.' *Child and Family Social Work 9,* 2, 129–140.

Kroll, B. and Taylor, A. (2003) *Parental Substance Misuse and Child Welfare.* London: Jessica Kingsley Publishers.

Lansdown, G. (2002) 'The participation of children'. In H. Montgomery, R. Burr and M. Woodhead (eds) (2003) *Changing Childhoods: local and global.* Chichester: Wiley (with the Open University).

Little, M. (2010) 'Looked after children: Can existing services ever succeed?' *Adoption and Fostering 34,* 2, 3–7.

Lloyd, M. and Taylor, C. (1995) 'From Hollis to the Orange Book: Developing a holistic model of social work assessment in the 1990s. ' *British Journal of Social Work 25,* 6, 691–710.

Long, A.F., Grayson, L. and Boaz, A. (2006) 'Assessing the quality of knowledge in social care: Exploring the potential of a set of generic standards.' *British Journal of Social Work 36,* 2, 207–226.

Lorde, A. (1984) *Sister Outsider.* New York: Crossing Press.

Lorek, A., Ehntholt, K., Nesbitt, A., Wey, E., Githinji, C., Rosser, E. and Wickramasinghe (2009) 'The mental and physical health difficulties of children held within a British immigration detention center: A pilot study.' *Child Abuse and Neglect 33,* 9, 573–585.

Luborsky, L. (1994) 'Therapeutic alliances as predictors of psychotherapy outcomes: Factors explaining the predictive success.' In A.O. Horvath and L.S. Greenberg (eds) *The Working Alliance: Theory, Research and Practice.* New York: John Wiley & Sons, Inc.

Maccoby, E.E. (1992) 'The role of parents in the socialization of children: An historical overview.' *Developmental Psychology 28,* 1006–1017.

Maccoby, E. E., and Martin, J. A. (1983) 'Socialization in the context of the family: Parent–child interaction.' In P. H. Mussen and E. M. Hetherington *Handbook of Child Psychology: Vol. 4. Socialization, personality, and social development* (Fourth Edition). New York: Wiley.

MacDonald, G. (1994) 'Developing empirically-based practice in probation.' *British Journal of Social Work 24,* 4, 405–427.

MacDonald, G. (1998) 'Promoting evidence-based practice in child protection.' *Clinical Child Psychiatry and Psychology 3,* 1, 71–85.

MacDonald, G. and Sheldon, B. (1992) 'Contemporary studies in the effectiveness of social work.' *British Journal of Social Work 22,* 5, 615–643.

MacFarlane, A. (1986) *Marriage and Love in England: Modes of Reproduction.* Oxford: Blackwell.

MacInnes, T., Kenway, P. and Parekh, A. (2009) *Monitoring Poverty and Social Exclusion 2009.* York: JRF/ New Policy Institute.

Madge, N. (2001) *Understanding Difference: The Meaning of Ethnicity for Young Lives.* London: National Children's Bureau.

Masson, J. (2010a) 'Judging the Children Act 1989: Courts and the administration of justice.' *Journal of Children's Services 5,* 2, 52–59.

Masson, J. (2010b) '(Mis)understandings of significant harm.' *Child Abuse Review 19,* 4, 291–298.

Masson, J., Pearce, J. and Bader, K. with Joyner, O., Marsden, J and Westlake, D. (2008) *Care Profiling Study.* Ministry of Justice Research Series 4/08. London: Ministry of Justice.

Masten, A.S. (2001) 'Ordinary magic: Resilience processes in development.' *American Psychologist 56,* 3, 227–238.

McGuire, J. (1995) *What Works? – Reducing Reoffending.* Chichester: Wiley.

Meyer, D.J. (ed.) (1995) *Uncommon Fathers: Reflections on Raising a Child with a Disability.* Bethesda, MD: Woodbine House.

Minty, B. (2005) 'The nature of emotional neglect and abuse'. In J. Taylor and B. Daniel (eds) *Child Neglect: Practice Issues for Health and Social Care.* London: Jessica Kingsley Publishers.

Minty, B. and Patterson, G. (1994) 'The nature of child neglect.' *British Journal of Social Work 24,* 6, 734–747.

MOJ (Ministry of Justice) (2008) *Practice Direction Experts in Family Proceedings Relating to Children.* London: MOJ.

MOJ (Ministry of Justice) (2010) *Practice Direction Guide to Case Management in Public Law Proceedings.* London: MOJ.

MOJ (Ministry of Justice) and DCSF (Department for Children, Schools and Families) (2009) *Preparing for Care and Supervision Proceedings: A Best Practice Guide for use by All Professionals Involved with Children and Families Pre-proceedings and in Preparation for Applications Made under Section 31 of the Children Act 1989.* London: MOJ/ DCSF.

Montgomery, H., Burr, R. and Woodhead, M. (eds) (2003) *Changing Childhoods: Local and Global.* Chichester: Wiley (with the Open University).

Moran, P., Ghate, D. and v.d. Merwe, A. (2004) *What Works in Parenting Support? A Review of the International Evidence* London: DfES/ Policy Research Bureau.

Morgan, R. (2006) *Being a Young Carer: Views from a Young Carers' Workshop.* Newcastle: Office of the Children's Rights Director/ Commission for Social Care Inspection (CSCI).

Mullender, A. (2004) *Tackling Domestic Violence: Providing Support for Children who have Witnessed Domestic Violence.* Home Office Development and Practice Report. London: Home Office.

Mullender, A., Kelly, L., Hague, G., Malos, E., and Iman, U. (2002) *Children's Perspectives on Domestic Violence.* London: Routledge.

Munro, E. (1996) 'Avoidable and unavoidable mistakes in child protection work.' *British Journal of Social Work 26,* 6, 795–810.

Munro, E. (1998) 'Improving social workers' knowledge base in child protection work.' *British Journal of Social Work 28,* 1, 89–105.

Munro, E. (2002) *Effective Child Protection.* London: Sage.

Munro, E. (2008) *Effective Child Protection* (Second Edition). London: Sage.

Munro, E. (2010) *The Munro review of Child Protection Part One: A Systems Analysis.* London: Department for Education.

Munro, E.R. and Ward, H. (2008) 'Balancing parents' and very young children's rights in care proceedings: decision-making in the context of the Human Rights Act 1998.' *Child and Family Social Work 13,* 2, 227–234.

Narey, M. (2007) *Beyond Care Matters: Future of the Care Population Working Group.* London: DfES.

Newell, P. (1993) *The UN Convention and Children's Rights in the UK.* London: NCB.

NICE (National Institute for Health and Clinical Excellence) (2009) *When to Suspect Child Maltreatment: NICE Clinical Guideline 89.* London: NICE.

NICE (National Institute for Health and Clinical Excellence) and SCIE (Social Care Institute for Excellence) (2010) *Promoting the Quality of Life of Looked-after Children and Young People. NICE Public Health Guidance 28.* London: NICE.

Nieuwenhuys, O. (2009) 'Is there an Indian childhood?' (Editorial) *Childhood 16,* 2, 147–153.

Office of the Deputy Prime Minister/ Social Exclusion Unit (2003) *A Better Education for Children in Care.* London: Social Exclusion Unit.

Ofsted (The Office for Standards in Education, Children's Services and Skills) (2009) *Life in Children's Homes: A Report of Children's Experience by the Children's Rights Director for England.* London: Ofsted.

Ofsted (The Office for Standards in Education, Children's Services and Skills) (2010) *Inspection of Children's Homes: Consultation Document.* London: Ofsted.

ONS (Office for National Statistics) (2001) *The Census Survey.* London: The Stationery Office.

ONS (Office for National Statistics) (2009) *Social Trends: 39.* Basingstoke: Palgrave Macmillan.

ONS (Office for National Statistics) (2010(a)) *Social Trends: 40.* Basingstoke: Palgrave Macmillan.

ONS (Office for National Statistics) (2010(b)) 'Marriages in England and Wales 2008.' *Statistical Bulletin 11th February 2010.* London: ONS.

ONS (Office for National Statistics) (2010(c)) 'Divorces in England and Wales 2008.' *Statistical Bulletin 28th January 2010.* London: ONS.

ONS (Office of National Statistics) and DCSF (Department for Children, Schools and Families) (2009) *Children Looked After in England (Including Adoption and Care Leavers) Year ending 31 March 2009.* London: ONS/ DCSF.

ONS/ DfES (2006) *Children in Need in England: Results of a Survey of Activity and Expenditure as Reported by Local Authority Social Services' Children and Family Teams for a Survey Week in February 2005.* London: ONS/DfES.

Osmond, J. (2005) 'The Knowledge Spectrum: A framework for teaching knowledge and its use in social work practice.' *British Journal of Social Work 35,* 6, 881–900.

Packman, J. and Jordan, B. (1991) 'The Children Act: Looking forward, looking back.' *British Journal of Social Work 21,* 2, 315–327.

Parker, R., Ward, H., Jackson, S., Aldgate, J. and Wedge, P. (1991) *Assessing Outcomes in Child Care.* London: HMSO.

Parton, N. (1985) *The Politics of Child Abuse.* Basingstoke: Macmillan.

Parton, N. (1997) *Child Protection and Family Support: Tensions, Contradictions and Possibilities.* London: Routledge.

Parton, N. (2009) 'From Seebohm to *Think Family*: reflections on 40 years of policy change of statutory children's social work in England.' *Child and Family Social Work, 14,* 1, 68–78.

Pearson, G. (1992) (Reprint Edition) *Hooligan: A History of Respectable Fears.* Basingstoke: Macmillan.

Pellis, S. and Pellis, V. (2009) *The Playful Brain: Venturing to the Limits of Neuroscience.* London: Oneworld Publishers.

Phillipson, J. (1992) *Practising Equality: Women, Men and Social Work.* London: Central Council for Education and Training in Social Work (CCETSW).

PIU (2000) *Prime Minister's Review of Adoption: A Performance and Innovation Unit Report.* London: The Stationery Office.

Pollock, L.H. (1983) *Forgotten Children: Parent–Child Relations from 1500 to 1900.* Cambridge: Cambridge University Press.

Quinton, D. (1994) 'Cultural and community influences.' In M. Rutter and D.F. Hay (eds) *Development Through Life: A Handbook for Clinicians.* Oxford: Blackwell Scientific Publications.

Rashid, S.P. (1996) 'Attachment reviewed through a cultural lens.' In D. Howe (ed.) *Attachment and Loss in Child and Family Social Work.* Aldershot: Avebury.

Reder, P., Duncan, S. and Gray, M. (1993) *Beyond Blame – Child Abuse Tragedies Revisited.* London: Routledge.

Reid, W. (1994) 'Reframing the epistemological debate.' In E. Sherman and W. Reid (eds) *Qualitative Research in Social Work.* New York: Catholic University Press.

Reijntjes, A., Kamphuis. J.H., Prinzie, P. and Telch, M.J. (2010) 'Peer victimization and internalizing problems in children: A meta-analysis of longitudinal studies.' *Child Abuse and Neglect 34,* 4, 244–252.

Reynaert, D., Bouverne-de-Bie, M. and Vandevelde, S. (2009) 'A review of children's rights literature since the adoption of the United Nation's Convention on the Rights of the Child' *Childhood 16,* 4, 518–534.

Ritchie, C. (2005) 'Looked after children: Time for change?' *British Journal of Social Work* 35, 5, 761–767.

Roach, G. and Sanders, R. (2008) 'The best laid plans? Obstacles to the implementation of plans for children.' *Adoption and Fostering 32,* 4, 31–41.

Robinson, L. (2007) *Cross-Cultural Child Development for Social Workers: An Introduction.* London: Palgrave Macmillan.

Rogers, C.M. and Wrightsman, L.S. (1978) 'Attitudes towards children's rights: Nurturance or self determination.' *Journal of Social Issues 34,* 2, 59–68.

Rogers, C.R. (1957) 'The necessary and sufficient conditions of therapeutic personality change.' *Journal of Counselling Psychology 21,* 2, 95–103.

Rose, W. (2001) 'Assessing children in need and their families: An overview of the framework.' In J. Horwath (ed.) *The Child's World: Assessing Children in Need.* London: Jessica Kingsley Publishers.

Rose, W. and Barnes, J. (2008) *Improving Safeguarding Practice: Study of serious case reviews 2001–2003.* Research report DCSF-RR022. London: DCSF.

Ruch, G., Turney, D. and Ward, A. (eds) (2010) *Relationship-based Social Work: Getting to the Heart of Practice.* London: Jessica Kingsley Publishers.

Sackett, D.L., Richardson, W.S., Rosenberg, W.S. and Haynes, R.B. (1997) *Evidence-based Medicine: How to Practice and Teach EBP.* New York: Churchill Livingstone.

Schofield, G. (2002) 'The significance of a secure base: A psychosocial model of long-term foster care.' *Child and Family Social Work 7,* 4, 259–272.

Schofield, G., Moldestad, B., Höjer, I., Ward, E., Skilbred, D., Young, J . and Havik, T. (2010) 'Managing loss and a threatened identity: Experiences of parents of children growing up in foster care, the perspectives of their social workers and implications for practice.' *British Journal of Social Work 41,* 1, 74–92.

Schraufnagel, T.J., Davies, K.C., George, W.H. and Norris, J. (2010) 'Childhood sexual abuse in males and subsequent risky sexual behaviour: A potential alcohol-use pathway.' *Chid Abuse and Neglect 34,* 5, 369–378.

Schore, A. (2003) *Affect Dysregulation and Disorders of the Self.* New York: Norton.

Schön, D.A. (1991) *The Reflective Practitioner.* Aldershot: Arena.

Scott, J., Dex, S. and Joshi, H. (eds) (2009) *Women and Employment: Changing Lives and New Challenges.* Cheltenham: Edward Elgar.

Secretary of State for Health, Home Secretary (2003) *The Victoria Climbié Inquiry: Report of an Inquiry by Lord Laming.* CM 5730. Norwich: The Stationery Office.

Seden, J. (2001) 'Assessment of children in need and their families: A literature review.' In Department of Health *Studies Informing the Framework for the Assessment of Children in Need and their Families.* London: The Stationery Office.

Shaw, I. (2008) 'Ways of knowing in social work,'. In S. Webb and M. Gray (eds) *Theory and Social Work.* London/ Thousand Oaks: Sage.

Shaw, M. (1989) 'Social work and children's rights.' Paper presented at a conference at the University of Leicester School of Medical Sciences, 19 April.

Sheppard, M. with Kelly, N. (2001) *Social Work Practice with Depressed Mothers in Child and Family Care.* London: The Stationery Office.

Shorter, E. (1976) *The Making of the Modern Family.* London: Collins.

Sinclair, I. (2010) 'Looked after children: Can existing services ever succeed? A different view.' *Adoption and Fostering 34,* 2, 8–13.

Sinclair, I., Baker, C., Lee, J. and Gibbs, I. (2007) *The Pursuit of Permanence: A Study of English Child Care Systems.* London: Jessica Kingsley Publishers.

Skarsater, I. (2006) 'Parents with first time major depression: Perceptions of social support for themselves and their children.' *Journal of Caring Science 2006,* 20, 308–314.

Smale, G., Tuson, G. and Statham, D. (2000) *Social Work and Social Problems: Working towards Social Inclusion and Social Change.* Basingstoke: Macmillan.

Social Services Improvement Agency (SSIA) (2007) *What Works in Promoting Good Outcomes for Children in Need in the Community.* Cardiff: SSIA.

Somers, V. (2007) 'Schizophrenia: The impact of parental illness on children.' *British Journal of Social Work 37,* 8, 1319–3134.

Spencer, N. (2005) 'Economic, cultural and social contexts of neglect'.In J. Taylor and B. Daniel (eds) *Child Neglect: Practice Issues for Health and Social Care.* London: Jessica Kingsley Publishers.

Spinka, M., Newberry, R.C. and Bekoff, M. (2001) 'Mammalian play : Training for the unexpected. *Quarterly Review of Biology 76,* 2, 141–169.

Stainton Rogers, R. (1989) 'The social construction of childhood'. In W.S. Rogers, D. Hevey and E. Ash (eds) *Child Abuse and Neglect: Facing the Challenge.* Milton Keynes: OUP.

Stalford, H., Baker, H. and Beveridge, F. (2003) *Children and Domestic Violence in Rural Areas.* London: Save the Children.

Stanley, N., Miller, P., Richardson Foster, H. and Thomson, G. (2009) *Children Experiencing Domestic Violence: Police and Children's Social Services' Responses.* London: NSPCC.

Stassen Berger, K. (2007) 'Update on bullying at school: A science forgotten?' *Developmental Review 27,* 1, 90–126.

Stone, L. (1977) *The Family, Sex and Marriage in England 1500–1800.* London: Weidenfeld and Nicholson.

Stoppard, M. (1983) *The Baby Care Book.* London: Dorling Kindersley.

Sudbury, J. (2002) 'Key features of therapeutic social work: The use of relationship. *Journal of Social Work Practice 16,* 2, 149–162.

Taylor, C. (2004) 'Underpinning knowledge for child care practice: Reconsidering child development theory.' *Child and Family Social Work 9,* 3, 225–235.

Teater, B. (2010) *An Introduction to Applying Social Work Theories and Methods.* Milton Keynes: OUP.

Thoburn, J. (1999) 'Trends in foster care and adoption.' In O. Stevenson (ed.) *Child Welfare in the UK.* Oxford: Blackwell Science.

Thoburn, J. (2007) 'Out-of-home care for the abused or neglected child: a review of the knowledge base for planning and practice'. In K. Wilson and A. James (eds) *The Child Protection Handbook.* London: Bailliere Tindall.

Thoburn, J. (2010) 'Towards knowledge-based practice in complex child protection cases: a research-based experts' briefing.' *Journal of Children's Services 5,* 1, 9–24.

Thomas, N. and O'Kane, C. (1999) 'Children's participation in reviews and planning meetings when they are looked after in middle childhood.' *Child and Family Social Work 4,* 3, 221–230.

Timms, J. and Thoburn, J. (2006) 'Your shout! Looked after children's perspectives on the Children Act 1989.' *Journal of Social Welfare and Family Law 28,* 2, 153–170.

TNS-BMRB (2009) *Parental Opinion Survey 2009.* Research Report DCSF-RR194. London: DCSF.

Tunstill, J. (1996) 'Family support.' *Child and Family Social Work 3,* 3, 151–158.

Tunstill, J. and Aldgate, J. (2000) *Services for Children in Need: From Policy to Practice.* London: The Stationery Office.

UNCRCC (2008) *Consideration Of Reports Submitted By States Parties Under Article 44 of The Convention: Concluding Observations: United Kingdom of Great Britain and Northern Ireland.* CRC/C/GBR/CO/4. Geneva: UN.

Ungar, M., Tutty, L.M., McConnell, S., Barter, K. and Fairholm, J. (2009) 'What Canadian youth tell us about disclosing abuse.' *Child Abuse and Neglect 33,* 10, 699–708.

UNICEF (United Nations Children's Fund) (2007) *The State of the World's Children.* New York: UNICEF.

Utting, W., Department of Health, Welsh Office (1997) *People Like Us – A Report of the Review of Safeguards for Children Living Away from Home.* London: The Stationery Office.

Van Bueren, G. (1995) *The International Law on the Rights of the Child.* Dordrecht and London: Martinus Nijhoff Publishers.

WAG (Welsh Assembly Government) (2004) *Children and Young People: Rights to Action.* Cardiff: WAG.

WAG (Welsh Assembly Government) (2008) *All Wales Child Protection Procedures.* Cardiff: WAG.

Walby, S. and Allen, J. (2004) *Domestic Violence, Sexual Assault and Stalking: Findings from the British Crime Survey.* (Home Office Research Study 276). London: Home Office Research, Development and Statistics Directorate.

Walker, J. (2008) 'The use of attachment theory in adoption and fostering.' *Adoption and Fostering 32,* 1, 49–57.

Walker, J., Barrett, H., Wilson, G. and Chang, Yan-Shing (2010) *Understanding the Needs of Adults (Particularly Parents) Regarding Relationship Support.* (DCSF Research Brief 10-01). London: DCSF.

Warren, J. (2008) *Service User and Carer Participation in Social Work.* Exeter: Learning Matters.

Waterhouse, Sir R. (2000) *Lost in Care: The Report of the Tribunal of Inquiry into the Abuse of Children in Care in the Former County Council Areas of Gwynedd and Clwyd since 1974.* HC 201. London: The Stationery Office.

Wates, M. (2002) *Supporting Disabled Adults in their Parenting Role.* York: Joseph Rowntree Foundation.

Webb, S.A. (2001) 'Some considerations on the validity of evidence-based practice in social work.' *British Journal of Social Work 31,* 1, 57–80.

Welbourne, P. (2008) 'Safeguarding children on the edge of care: Policy for keeping children safe after the Review of Child Care Proceedings System, Care Matters and the Carter Review of Legal Aid.' *Child and Family Law Quarterly 20,* 3, 335–358.

White, S., Wastell, D., Broadhurst, K. and Hall, D. (2010) 'When policy o'erlaps itself: The "tragic tale" of the integrated children's system.' *Critical Social Policy 30,* 3, 405–429.

Williams, J. (2008) *Child Law for Social Work.* London: Sage.

Wilson, K. and James, A. (eds) (2007) (Third Edition) *The Child Protection Handbook.* London: Bailliere Tindall.

Wilson, K., Ruch, G., Lymbery, M. and Cooper, A. (2008) *Social Work: An Introduction to Contemporary Practice.* London: Pearson Longman.

Winnicott, D.W. (1965) *The Maturational Processes and the Facilitating Environment: Studies in the Theory of Emotional Development.* London: Hogarth.

Woodhead, M. (1999) 'Reconstructing developmental psychology – some first steps.' *Children and Society 13,* 1, 3–19.

Worrall, A., Boylan, J., and Roberts, D. (2008) *Children's and Young People's Experiences of Domestic Violence Involving Adults in a Parenting Role.* SCIE Research Briefing 25. London: Social Care Institute for Excellence.

Yeh, C. J. and Huang, K. (1996) 'The collectivist nature of ethnic identity development among Asian-American college students.' *Journal of Adolescence, Fall 1996, 31,* 123, 645–663.

Zielinski, D.S. (2009) 'Child maltreatment and socioeconomic well-being.' *Child Abuse and Neglect 33,* 10, 666–678.

Zimmerman, B.J. (2001) 'Theories of self-regulated learning and academic achievement: An overview and analysis.' In B.J. Zimmerman and D.H. Schunk (eds), *Self-Regulated Learning and Academic Achievement: Theoretical Perspectives.* Mahwah, NJ: Lawrence Erlbaum Associates, Publishers.

Subject Index

Author Index